The Best American Short Plays

2008–2009

The Best American Short Plays

2008–2009

edited with an introduction by
Barbara Parisi

APPLAUSE THEATRE & CINEMA BOOKS
An Imprint of Hal Leonard Corporation

The Best American Short Plays 2008–2009
Edited with an introduction by Barbara Parisi

Published in 2010 by Applause Theatre & Cinema Books
An Imprint of Hal Leonard Corporation
7777 West Bluemound Road
Milwaukee, WI 53213

Trade Book Division Editorial Offices
33 Plymouth St., Montclair, NJ 07042

Printed in the United States of America
Book composition by UB Communications

ISBN 978-1-55783-761-5 [cloth]
ISBN 978-1-55783-760-8 [paper]
ISSN 0067-6284

www.applausepub.com

To William and Gloria Parisi,
Rochelle Martinsen,
and my husband—
Michael Ronald Pasternack

contents

Foreword
A Simple, Brilliant Idea
by David Ives

The great Murray Schisgal (one of whose very best plays is contained in the volume in your hand) has said, "Dialogue cannot be spoken. It is always an outburst." He has also said, "A play cannot succeed unless it takes place during a storm."

These are sentiments I especially subscribe to about the one-act play. A short play's effect should be that of someone suddenly screaming—or laughing, perhaps—in your face. During a thunderstorm, of course, though the storm needn't be literal. And then, just as suddenly, the commotion is over. Let me quote myself:

> What the best one-acts compress superbly is *all of human life*. What they deal with by their very nature is Time. They partake of mortality by the implicit brevity of their form. *Life is short and so is this play*. With its reduced cast and isolating focus, the one-act often seems in love with loneliness. With its necessarily meager production elements, the one-act is naturally at home with themes of deprivation and loss. With its concision, it instantly attains the lapidary urgency of a death-bed wish. A full-length play, you might say, carpet-bombs its subject; a one-act play is an exploding rose in the hand of a lone assassin. [From "The Exploding Rose: On the One-Act Play," in the March/April 2006 issue of *The Dramatist*]

There's a brief poem by Keats, which for me perfectly encapsulates the effect of a good one-act:

> This living hand, now warm and capable
> Of earnest grasping, would, if it were cold
> And in the icy silence of the tomb,
> So haunt thy days and chill thy dreaming nights
> That thou wouldst wish thine own heart dry of blood
> So in my veins red life might stream again,
> And thou be conscience-calmed—see here it is—
> I hold it toward you.

The first time I read that poem, I startled backward upon hitting the final line. I recall the physical jolt. It was as if Keats, nearly two hundred years dead, had thrust his dead hand out of the pages of my book just as the poem submits. In similar fashion a good one-act makes us feel the playwright has abruptly gripped us by the throat and rattled us—or stroked our cheek. In the hands of a one-act we should be like that character in Chekhov's great short story "The Kiss," who enters a dark room only to find himself kissed by a woman whose identity he does not know. The woman, realizing her mistake, flees. The man's life is changed.

The essence and meaning of a short play are so often to be found in the chosen setting. In this volume, Carey Lovelace set *The Stormy Waters, the Long Way Home* on a beach in a tempest (a fine example of the metaphoric power of the Schisgal doctrine). Neil LaBute has located *A Second of Pleasure* in Grand Central, "near the clock"—literally putting a clock on the action, as they say. I love it. Adam Kraar, Maria Filimon, and Tasnim Mansur in *Sisters* use a rushing subway car, adding breathlessness and a different kind of clock as the stations in a sororal relationship are announced.

A good one-act—unlike full-length plays—often produces its particular thrills by taking place in the great theatrical void that is nowhere and everywhere, nothing and everything. The result: visionary drama, poetic drama of a sort that's out of the question in longer form, like the plays here by Meg Miroshnik, Emily Conbere, and Polly Frost and Ray Sawhill. Sometimes someplace becomes everyplace, as in Marla Del Collins's *The Lovers and Others of Eugene O'Neill*, whose set "vaguely resembles a Victorian sitting room, a funeral parlor and an opium den." Eric Lane's police station in *Early Morning* is not only instantly dramatic (*what's going to happen, what crime is being investigated here?*) but a sort of classic Greek arena for elemental human drama. For in *The True Author*...James Armstrong sets his extraordinary little mad scene in "an auditorium," nothing more, with a telling sign. To place an actress in such a space is to set Wallace Stevens's jar "in Tennessee." The world rises up to surround such a play. Billy Aronson in *Little Duck* specifies no set and doesn't need to, as he paints his world with character.

A whole patch of history and biography may be compressed in the one-act, as Joe Salvatore does in *III*, or a whole patch of gay experience, as Rick Pulos does in *Decades Apart*. We also have the more homely and familiar, which it is the playwright's job to make less homely and less familiar, like the bar in Lewis Gardner's *Pete and Joe at the Dew Drop Inn*, or the apartment in Amy Herzog's *508*.

One of the marvels of the short play is how little it can be made out of—or rather, how much can be made out of what is apparently nothing. (*Like life*, oddly enough.)

So here you have them. Sixteen miniature worlds.

Plunge in.

Introduction
by Barbara Parisi

This is my fifth edition as editor of the Best American Short Plays series and the experience of reading many plays has afforded me the opportunity to share with you the newest one-act plays written by established and seasoned playwrights.

In the past, my introductions have explored definitions of the one-act play and defined themes, plots, and characters. A playwright's voice through spoken language can help develop the titles playwrights use for their plays. The title of a one-act play is the first message you get about the meaning of the play.

In the *Playwriting Seminars*, Richard Toscan says: "The best titles come as flashes of insight as you're writing the play.... When titles really catch fire, they're often intuitive responses to the play you're creating." Toscan describes titles in two categories, metaphoric and descriptive.

Toscan uses *Bedroom Farce* as an example of a descriptive title for a play. In the *Playwriting Seminars*, playwright Alan Ayckbourn states: "Some people were quite shocked by the fact that there was no nudity, no swearing, no sex in *Bedroom Farce*. The joke I wanted was: Let's write a play about three bedrooms, and the first thing you expect to happen in that bedroom never happens." Metaphoric titles can have double meanings or be symbolic of the play's thematic content. Playwright David Henry

Hwang told a story about his wife, Ophelia, who thought *Monsieur Butterfly* too obvious a title and suggested that he abbreviate it in the French fashion. "Hence, *M. Butterfly*, far more mysterious and ambiguous, was the result."

A playwright's voice is always felt through their writing. In the *Playwriting Seminars*, playwright Michael Weller states: "I don't write, I listen, and I take dictation. I was trained as a musician. I'm a terrible speller, and I don't have a sense of prose as a discipline. I only hear people talking, and I put down what they say." This process can be used to create titles of one-act plays.

Richard Toscan believes: "Playwrights build a physical construction onstage—with spoken words." These words are the language of the story of the play. The spoken language in life is recorded by playwrights to create titles, characters, plots, and the themes of one-act plays.

As an experiment, take a look at the titles of these one-act plays as you read thought this edition. What will you discover? Are the titles metaphoric or descriptive? As you read the play, can you see how the spoken language helped generate the title of the one-act play, as well as the theme, plot, and characters?

Titles are important to the reader. They are the first window into the mind of the playwright. As in the past, I have asked the playwrights to express the theme, plot, and inspiration for their one-act plays.

A Second of Pleasure
by Neil LaBute

"Regret" is probably the strongest theme in the piece and the one that runs most thoroughly through the text. A woman regrets the decision to go off for the weekend with her lover, and through that confession she comes to realize that perhaps the entire affair has been a mistake.

The "plot" of the play is extremely simple: a man and a woman stand at the train station waiting to leave for the weekend. Suddenly the woman decides that she'd rather not go and it leads to the unraveling of their illicit relationship.

"Breakups" are one of the most interesting things to write in literature, I think. To find a couple at that place in their collective lives—and to do it in public, no less!—allows us to examine lives at a difficult juncture, which helps to create drama. The pain of leaving someone is fertile ground for the dramatist.

St. Francis Preaches to the Birds
by David Ives

St. Francis wakes in a desert to find himself the prospective dinner of a couple of hungry vultures with whom he engages in theological banter concerning his imminent demise. My inspiration was all the holy cards I used to pack my Sunday missal with when I was a young and wide-eyed Catholic many, many centuries ago. What I'd like to the viewer to take away from this play: Its faults.

The Stormy Waters, the Long Way Home
by Carey Lovelace

A woman on a chilly, fog-wrapped beach in early morning waits for others. Gradually, we realize that things are not what they seem. *The Stormy Waters, the Long Way Home* was inspired by a crest of sandy dunes on the Sagaponack beach and a group of friends, artists, who meet there on summer days. One of them, the video-artist wife of a well-known architect, with her relaxed melancholy beauty, was kind of the group's gravity center. Against the natural order of things, she fell ill at a relatively young age; she fought a valiant battle to the death. The piece is about the enduring tug of friendship, about profound love—of the ocean, of one another, of partners even when they are selfish and unfair. Like the tides, they bring us back again and again. It is also dedicated to the late, great Curt Dempster. With him, I had a contentious apprenticeship; from him I learned much. He was very supportive of this particular piece.

Early Morning
by Eric Lane

So many things inspire me to write a play. It may be a person, emotion, moment, song, story, or image. Once I saw a father walking in the snow, and sticking out underneath the hem of his coat were another pair of legs. It was his son trying to keep warm. Out of that image a play appeared.

This play started with Doris. I had written a one-act play, *The Nearness of You*, about a young woman working in a dance hall during World War II. It takes place on the night Doris meets a young soldier heading off to combat. The two begin to fall in love against the backdrop of the war.

A few months later, I started thinking about Doris again. I wondered what had happened to her during the next twenty-five years—how had she transformed from a young, vibrant woman to someone isolated and fearful? That led to a second one-act, *How to Boil a Frog*.

A few years later, Doris started to appear again in my thoughts. We had seen her against the backdrop of WWII and the Vietnam War. Thinking twenty-five years forward, I felt the war we were battling in the mid-1990s was AIDS.

I originally told Doris's story in *Early Morning* in monologue form. Yet I felt that something was missing. It was the wrong form for the piece; the play lacked conflict. Doris's grandson dies under mysterious circumstances. In telling her story, Doris needed someone to butt up against—someone who would challenge her account of what happened and who had his own need for finding out the truth.

One thing I often think about when writing a play is, if you could have any characters in the scene, why these particular ones? What is it that each character brings out in each other and in the situation that makes him the right one for this story? What unique history or needs make him the one person that must be in the scene over anyone else?

Enter Detective Diamantini. I once had a friend with the last name Diamantini, meaning "little diamonds." I thought it was a great name for a character, especially if his appearance and manner were in contrast to his name. Detective Diamantini questions Doris to arrive at the truth of what actually happened. His single-mindedness and gentleness beneath the surface really intrigued me. He wants to convict Doris, yet at the same time feels compassion for her.

Doris is a character who keeps returning to me. We performed the first three one-acts at the Adirondack Theatre Festival, directed by Martha Banta under the title *Times of War*. One of the challenges with all of these plays was how to set the piece against the backdrop of war and tell the story in a way that was original and new. How to use the period in American history to inform the characters, story, themes, and shape of the piece without it becoming the sole point of the play.

Since then, Doris has reappeared in a fourth one-act, *Now Comes the Night*. I think it's the final Doris story. Of course, there are always prequels....

Sisters
by Adam Kraar, Maria Filimon, and Tasnim Mansur

Rani and Mallika, sisters, are South Asian immigrants living together in New York City. Rani has just bailed Mallika out of jail for shoplifting. Mallika tries to deny the seriousness of her situation, but when Rani threatens to cut her out of her life, Mallika is forced to face the ways she's not fitting in, in America. This leads the sisters to a deeper appreciation of what they mean to each other.

This play was developed collaboratively in an acting class at the NY Institute of Technology. I gave two of the students, Maria Filimon and Tasnim Mansur, a basic scenario, around which they improvised a long scene. This scene was filmed, and based on what we saw, adjustments were made. Then—over a period of several weeks—Maria and Tasnim worked further on their own and brought the scene back to me. I then cut and shaped the scene into a script that became the play that they performed in our school production.

The inspiration for this play was the students at NY Institute of Technology, many of whom are immigrants. As Tasnim writes in her bio: "It's safe to say that I am the generation that is in between two very different cultures. However, I have tried to go along with both to the best of my abilities."

The play explores the ways that the pull of one's original "home" is inescapable—yet it's still possible to make a new home.

Little Duck
by Billy Aronson

The main theme of *Little Duck* is collaboration. It's about people at a children's television company struggling to work together. Another theme is sadomasochism. As the people try to work together, they impose their various weird sexual energies on one another. I was inspired to write the play because I wanted to see a bunch of people onstage trying to work together while imposing their weird sexual energies on one another.

A Portrait of the Woman as a Young Artist
by Meg Miroshnik

In *A Portrait of the Woman as a Young Artist*, Mr. Joyce, a fictionalized literary icon in spectacles, and Mr. James, a paranoid, inpatient person, inhabit parallel dreamscapes with Leda, a muse who has recently developed creative ambitions all her own. As the men struggle to maintain control—and sanity—in the fantastical, imploding universe of the play, Leda begins work on her masterpiece: A feathery transformation of mythic proportions.

Portrait began in response to a challenge put forth by playwright Paula Vogel: In forty-eight hours, write a play inspired by W. B. Yeats's poem "Leda and the Swan" and Elizabeth Egloff's play *The Swan*. In addition to these avian-themed ingredients, I added two of my own: *Swan Lake* and an extract from Joyce's semi-autobiographical novel, *A Portrait of the Artist as a Young Man*. In the passage in question, Joyce's literary alter ego realizes his artistic destiny when he mentally transfigures a silent woman standing on the beach into a "strange and beautiful seabird." The convention of male artists re-imagining female muses as birds is well established (the bird-women of John William Waterhouse's nineteenth-century painting

Ulysses and the Sirens, for one). But what, I wondered, would be the inverse of this image? How might a female artist announce her status as creator and destroyer of imaginative worlds? With this question in mind, I began to look at arguably the most famous portrayal of swans onstage, Tchaikovsky's *Swan Lake*. In that tale, a prince falls in love with a white swan maiden, Odette, and is determined to take her as his bride, but the evil sorcerer Von Rothbart replaces her with his black swan daughter, the seductress Odile, and the prince unwittingly marries the imposter. Again, I thought, who is the silent bird-woman of the story: How would the black swan Odile represent herself if she were not trapped in the prince's narrative?

Slapped Actress
by Emily Conbere

I would like any audience who sees this play to feel completely, physically and emotionally, inspired to be part of this temporary theater company. This play ideally ends in a riot that scares some, captures some, and embraces some. This riot never leaves the room. It exists only in the theater.

A little girl interrupts the money-grubbing Evangelical Theater Creep with the truth about theater. Her insistence on the truth brings back to the theater the Woman in the Window, otherwise known as the Goddess of the Great White Way, despite her fear of getting slapped in the face. This return inspires the audience one by one to join the theater company and turn against those who simply "accept."

Slapped Actress was written as part of Youngblood's Asking for Trouble series at Ensemble Studio Theater in New York.

The Last Artist in New York City
by Polly Frost and Ray Sawhill

We take a lot of our inspiration from the amazing performers and theater people we work with and hang out with in NYC. With *The Last Artist in New York City*, we wanted to create a fabulous role for one of our favorite performers, Karen Grenke; a juicy theater piece for the brilliant Jason

Jacobs of Theatre Askew to direct...and we wanted to make audiences laugh.

The Last Artist is a one-handed comedy. Set only slightly in the future, it concerns a woman artist who finds herself increasingly alone in New York City. She finally gets her dream e-mail from the *New York Times* saying they want to profile her. Have her struggles and sacrifices finally paid off? Or has the real arts action perhaps gone elsewhere, leaving her behind?

The play is both a satire of the current crazy conditions artists in New York City endure and a tribute to the enduring spirit and tenacity of creative people everywhere. We're hoping audiences will be amused and touched by our somewhat (but only somewhat) absurd portrayal of the struggles that all artists have between their dreams of recognition, the sacrifices they make for their art, and the clash between artists and American conventional life.

The True Author of the Plays Formerly Attributed to Mister William Shakespeare Revealed to the World for the First Time by Miss Delia Bacon

by James Armstrong

This play is inspired by the life of nineteenth-century scholar, author, and complete basket case Delia Bacon.

Delia was brilliant—there's no doubt about that—but wrong, wrong, wrong, both in her scholarship and in her personal life. After traveling across the United States and England, winning the support of a number of influential people, including author Nathaniel Hawthorne, poor Delia met her end spouting gibberish in an insane asylum.

The play imagines Delia's breakdown, not over the course of years, as it really occurred, but over the course of a single lecture at the American consulate in Liverpool, where she delivered a message she was sure would shock and amaze her audience. It probably did, just not in the way she intended.

There is a bit of Delia, a hint of madness, in all of us. Perhaps that is why audiences sympathized with her so much in the New York production, where she was portrayed flawlessly by the brilliant Katherine Harte-DeCoux. Staring out into the void, she realizes the idol of her life, her salvation, her god, isn't even out there, and he probably never was. Perhaps we fear the same thing.

The Lovers and Others of Eugene O'Neill
by Marla Del Collins

Who was that masked man, Eugene O'Neill? Eugene O'Neill once said, "What do I care what they say—the further from the truth they have it, the more privacy I have. It's like a mask" (Sheaffer, *Playwright 215*). My quest to "unmask" America's most extraordinary playwright began with a conversation about the origins of his "masked identity." My colleague had prototyped O'Neill as the quintessential "brooding artist," dwelling on his "cursed and tormented soul." He suggested O'Neill was a man who hid behind a "mask of pain and suffering" as if to say his discontent was triggered by some inexplicable inner force.

I suggested that more likely when socialization is set aside, Eugene O'Neill was a visionary Everyman—a complicated figure tormented not so much by his artistic nature per se, but by social norms rooted in dualistic thinking—the illusionary duality of logic versus emotion and the masculine mystique that denied him his humanity and his natural proclivity toward circular trains of thought. In this regard, the characters and themes in his plays reflect his varying states of rebellion against dualistic thinking (a belief in opposites) and the dualism doctrine (everything in the universe is divided into opposites, one being "good" and the other "evil"). I set out to know the themes of his plays by knowing the playwright himself—and I discovered him through the voices of the women who knew him.

The Lovers and Others of Eugene O'Neill (profiling the life and times of Eugene O'Neill from the perspective of the predominant women in his life) was highlighted in *O'Neill's People* (1995); produced at the international conference on *O'Neill's People*, sponsored by the Eugene O'Neill Society, Suffolk University, Boston (May 1995); at the Arts and Letters Festival, East Stroudsburg University (1994); and at The Blackbox Theatre, New York City.

The play served to educate audiences about O'Neill and his innovative style with a somewhat "tongue-in-cheek" tribute to O'Neill's thematic and theatrical innovations. Based on historical research, the play presents a more complicated perspective on O'Neill's personality and temperament in relationship to the women in his life and the female characters in his plays.

Agnes Boulton, his second wife; Sarah Sandy, his nanny; Ella O'Neill, his mother; and Carlotta Monteray, his third wife, reveal Eugene O'Neill's complex nature through their monologues. The "Narrator-guide" (speaking through O'Neill's poetry represents O'Neill himself) provides a transitional interlude from one monologue to the next.

There is another Celtic/pagan "character" in the play, an ensemble of Irish musicians (harp, violin, bodhran (Irish drum), flute, and tin whistle). Their music serves to punctuate transitions or reflect the moods or inner monologues of the characters. At certain moments, the characters transcend normalcy by inhabiting the bodies of one another or speaking out at inopportune times. For example, Carlotta, in a fit of frustration, speaks through Ella in order to hurry her scene along and finally overpowers her, becoming metaphorically, if not literally, his mother in the end. The female characters evolve from two-dimensional "masked" prototypes (the characters in O'Neill's plays), to "unmasked" multi-dimensional human beings by the time they directly address the audience. And in the end, Carlotta has the final word.

The entire play is generative/circular in structure, punctuated with the lighting of candles, burning incense, music, and bell ringing (not unlike the Catholic Mass). Lasting an hour and thirty minutes without intermission, it builds quickly toward an emotional climax.

If the play were to be broken down into phases and periods of transition, it would appear to unfold like a generative form of order or perhaps pictorially, like a mandala in motion.

III

by Joe Salvatore

I first became interested in the fifteen-year relationship (1927–1943) that *III* addresses while researching the life of George Platt Lynes. In my exploration of Lynes's life, I discovered this ménage that he formed with one of the great artistic couples of the twentieth century: the writer Glenway Wescott and the Museum of Modern Art curator Monroe Wheeler.

I believe that the relationship between Wescott, Wheeler, and Lynes has strong cultural implications for an early-twenty-first-century society wrestling with gay marriage, monogamy, and relationship construction. Glenway Wescott and Monroe Wheeler met in 1919 at the University of Chicago, and they continued to be lifelong companions until Wescott's death in 1987. Wheeler died in 1988. Throughout this long relationship, lovers entered and exited for both Wescott and Wheeler, but they had agreed that this was permissible.

In writing this play, I wanted to explore the construction of this relationship. Based on the letters and journals of these men, it seems that family members and friends embraced the relationship with open arms. Given the current debate over gay marriage in the United States, I was curious to explore the differences and similarities between the past and the present. This partnership provided a specific snapshot of a certain segment of society and its cultural attitudes in a time that I would have assumed to be more conservative in regard to sexuality and relationships. Through a theatrical exploration of this relationship, I wanted to provide a space for dialogue around the history of relationship construction and societal acceptance of what might be considered an "alternative lifestyle."

Pete and Joe at the Dew Drop Inn

by Lewis Gardner

A few years ago, I put together a one-woman show for actress Kimberly Kay. I used already-written material of mine—mainly comic—that I assumed was accurate in portraying female speech and action; the test was whether women in a cast or audience would say I'd got it wrong.

Since I had far more material about men, the success of the one-woman show led to my compiling a one-*man* show. I gave the script to two actors, asking if either would be interested in performing it. When they both said yes, I decided the show could be for two men, and after further compilation, we began rehearsing a two-man show called *Guy Stuff*.

While we worked, I wrote a number of short scenes for two men in a bar. The men discuss some of the things men might discuss in a bar— relations with women, how the world is changing, issues with self-image. They never say much about their feelings, of course, or about their relationship with each other, but I think those areas were implied within the material.

As an experiment, I combined the Pete and Joe scenes, with revision, into a one-act play. A workshop reading worked well and a local theater included it in a festival of one-acts in 2008—asking me first if I minded their breaking the play into separate scenes to be performed between the other one-acts.

Either way, I think Pete and Joe are specific enough, and yet typical enough, to represent what I have to say right now about the male condition. It's comedy, though, and not a treatise, and until someone says I've got it wrong, I'll stand by it.

Decades Apart: Reflections of Three Gay Men
by Rick Pulos

Decades Apart was inspired by personal experience, people (characters) I met while living in Los Angeles, San Francisco, and New York City, and media reports that, to this day, detail the continued oppression of gay men and women in the United States. There is still so much for us to do.

The play asks us all to be more compassionate and to pay attention to the trial and tribulations of our fellow citizens. *Decades Apart: Reflections of Three Gay Men* was selected from many entries to open the first ever Long

Island Fringe Festival in September of 2009. Although the piece is not necessarily made to incite shock or disgust, it does tell intimate details of the stories of three gay men. The audience reaction to the show was, well, it was incredibly wild. Multiple people heckled me viciously, and their outbursts were clearly homophobic at a level so powerful you could see it spilling out into the aisles. I was in a sensitive state while performing, and it took every ounce of strength in me to make it through the sixty-minute show. My immediate response when I analyzed the hectic experience was disgust, disappointment, and resentment. After analyzing the performance experience, I was able to see the importance of challenging people through art, and I reminded myself that this show was about educating others while sending a message of compassion. This is happening now, this has happened.

Decades Apart examines the attitudes and mores of three gay men living in different places and times in the United States. The first character lives in 1970s San Francisco and is a relatively carefree soul. The second man lives in 1980s New York City and is conservative to the core. The final character lives in 1990s Los Angeles and represents a return to a more carefree and possibly careless existence. Upon a closer look, *Decades Apart* asks: Has anything changed for gay men and women in the United States? Have you changed?

508

by Amy Herzog

In *508*, two ex-lovers meet in the apartment they once shared on what would be their fifth anniversary for a settling of accounts. What could be a simple, five-minute exchange quickly devolves into barbs and recriminations. Bridget and Leo know how to get at each other, and they can't resist the pleasure and pain that comes from one last reckoning.

In the year since they've broken up, Leo has hastily gotten married while Bridget has stayed in this apartment, nursing her loneliness. They scorn one another's ways of dealing with the breakup. While writing the play, I was wrestling with the question of what is the correct and authentic way to cope with heartbreak.

A note to actors: play the lighter side as long a possible. These are people who enjoy the getting and being gotten to.

Naked Old Man
by Murray Schisgal

An eighty-two-year-old man invites three of his closest friends, all recently deceased, all specters conceived in the matrix of his imagination, to spend the evening with him.

I confess to being the eighty-two-year-old man (hence the protagonist's name) and the three specters that come to share the evening with me are, even today, among my closest friends. Clearly what I've written is a memoir and yet it is dramatized, which is to say it's a work of fiction.

What inspired me to write the play? A deep, emotional need, the only reason to write anything.

The Best American Short Plays

2008–2009

A Second of Pleasure

Neil LaBute

Neil LaBute

Neil LaBute received his Master of Fine Arts degree in dramatic writing from New York University. He was the recipient of a literary fellowship to study at the Royal Court Theatre, London, and also attended the Sundance Institute's Playwrights Lab. His films include *In the Company of Men* (New York Critics' Circle Award for Best First Feature and the Filmmakers' Trophy at the Sundance Film Festival), *Your Friends and Neighbors*, *Nurse Betty*, *Possession*, *The Shape of Things* (a film adaptation of his play by the same title), *The Wicker Man*, *Lakeview Terrace*, and *Death at a Funeral*.

LaBute's plays include *bash: latter-day plays*, *The Shape of Things*, *The Mercy Seat*, *The Distance from Here*, *Autobahn* (a collection of five of his one-act plays), *Fat Pig*, *Some Girls*, *This Is How It Goes*, *In a Dark Dark House*, and *Reasons to Be Pretty* (nominated for a Tony Award for Best Play). LaBute is also the author of several fictional pieces that have been published in the *New York Times*, the *New York Times Magazine*, *Harper's Bazaar*, and *Playboy*, among others. *Seconds of Pleasure*, a collection of his short stories, was published by Grove Atlantic.

• • •

[*Silence. Darkness.*]

[*Two people standing at Grand Central. Near the clock. Let's call them "KURT" and "JESS." He is studying the train ticket in his hand. She waits patiently for him. Looks at her watch. Each of them carries a travel bag.*]

[*After a moment, she stops. Looks at him. Speaks.*]

JESS   . . . alright, here's the thing.

KURT   What?

JESS   The thing of it is, I don't really want to go. I don't. I guess that would be the actual "thing" of it.

KURT   Oh.

JESS   Yeah.

KURT   I see.

JESS   I know I'm standing here and I've got my bag in my hand and all that, but if you were to ask me right now, "Hey, you sure you wanna do this, go up to the country this weekend?" I'd say, "No, not really." I would, I'd say that. "No thank you, I don't."

[KURT *nods at this, looking around the place. Busy people moving past the two of them. Checks his watch.*]

KURT   But . . . you already said "yes" before.

JESS   I know I did.

KURT   I mean before now. Today. This minute. You said "yes" earlier this week.

JESS   You're right. I did do that.

KURT   And that was, like, Tuesday or something.

JESS   Late Tuesday, I think, but yeah. Yes, it was.

KURT   So, I mean . . . you had all week to say something.
   [*Beat.*]
   Train boards in, like, ten minutes . . .

JESS I realize this is sudden. Unexpected.

KURT Very. It's very much that...

JESS I know. I didn't want to do this. I mean, I did, I did want to tell you earlier...call you or something, an e-mail—but then today I had this...a thing happen. Something happened and it gave me this idea that I should say something.

KURT So...you gave it a lot of thought, then?

JESS Huh?

KURT I mean, it didn't just pop into your head this minute, when we were buying tickets or whatever. You mulled it over.

JESS Well, I didn't...you know, I wasn't up at *night* because of it, but yeah. I tried to find the right approach to...but then I'm suddenly standing there buying snacks and thinking to myself, "Gosh, I *really* need to say something! I do, and right now."

KURT Oh.

[*Silence as* KURT *tries to think of something to say—a proper comeback or the like.* JESS *jumps in to help.*]

JESS That's what I was doing when you touched my shoulder and said, "You okay?" That's what I was doing at that very moment.

KURT I see.

JESS I was coming to a decision about it.

KURT Without me.

JESS No! I mean, yes, alright—it's not like I was purposefully trying to leave you out, it's just that, you know, it's sort of a one-sided deal, that's all. Right?

KURT I wouldn't know.

JESS Come on...

KURT Seriously. I'm big on sharing. On being open about stuff, whether it's painful stuff or not.

JESS   Oh, please.

KURT   I am. I'm *completely* that way.

JESS   Fine, I understand.

KURT   No, I don't think you do—you don't or you wouldn't approach my feelings in so cavalier a manner.

JESS   I'm not being...that's a little dramatic, isn't it?

KURT   I think it's a pretty suitable metaphor.

[*She smiles and shakes her head; he holds up his hands as if to say, "What do you mean?" Rolls his eyes.*]

JESS   Well, it's a bit much, I think. Plus, you couldn't really...I mean, I'm a woman. It doesn't even work, your analogy.

KURT   I know that, I do, but you get my point.

JESS   I do, yes, but it's...it just seems kind of grand, that's all. I mean, "Cavalier?" Really?

KURT   Women can be "cavalier," too, you know. It's not just a, a, a male thing...

JESS   No, I know, but I mean "traditionally." Traditionally it was for men. Doing...that. Being all that way. With *swords*.

KURT   True, no, you're probably right.
         [*Beat.*]
         I was hurt, so I lashed out. Sorry...

[*People are having to walk around them now, so* KURT *signals for* JESS *to move aside. Near the newspaper machines.*]

JESS   I understand, I'm just saying—isn't it better that I bring this up now than in the middle of dinner tonight or tomorrow during a second set of tennis? I'm trying to be fair to both of us...

KURT   I see. This is you being "fair."

JESS   Well, in a way, yes. Trying to be.

KURT   Great.

JESS   I really am . . .

KURT   Terrific.

JESS   See, now you're just angry. Getting all huffy and everything . . .

KURT   No, I'm not. I'm really not.

JESS   Sounds like it to me.

KURT   I'm not. I'm just taking it all in. Dealing with it—as our train's leaving.

JESS   It's not going yet, we've still got a few minutes.

KURT   Whatever. Doesn't really matter now, does it? It's moot.

JESS   Is it?

KURT   I think so. I think it was *invented* for a moment like this, that word. "Moot." Just like this moment right here . . .

JESS   I don't know. What I'm saying is there's still time, whether we both go or just you—there's still time to get on board.

KURT   That's comforting . . .

JESS   God . . .

　　[*Beat.*]

　　Lemme walk you down. Okay?

[KURT *doesn't say anything, just turns and begins to move off. He stops, though, and looks back at her.*]

KURT   This is unbelievable.

JESS   . . . I can't help it. I needed to say what I was feeling.

KURT   And you did.

JESS   Yes I did, I did do that and I'm glad. I'm sorry if it feels . . . but I am glad. So . . .

　　[*Beat.*]

　　The rest is up to you . . .

KURT   Wow, you've got an answer for everything today! That's great . . .

[*He checks his watch. She stands still and follows him with her eyes.*]

JESS I'm just being practical. No reason that you shouldn't enjoy this—I'm just letting you know up front that I can't do it this time.

KURT Well, not exactly "up front." No, that would've been Tuesday night, up front. Wednesday morning at the latest...

JESS Right, yes, that's true...

KURT No, I think you'd have to go ahead and call this "last-minute," what you're doing here—besides thoughtless and shitty and maybe even mean-spirited. I think this would go down as "last-minute."

JESS I deserve that, so go ahead...

KURT I don't know if you deserve it or not. It's just how it makes me feel...

[*He looks off into the crowd. Waits. Turns back to her.*]

...you haven't said "why" you're...you know...nothing about that. Yet.

JESS Because. I feel bad for him.

KURT Oh.

JESS That's why. Okay?

KURT You feel "bad."

JESS Yes, I do.

KURT For him? You mean "him" him?

JESS Yes. My husband.

KURT Got it.

JESS I was packing when it started. Going up and down stairs and throwing a suitcase together, having already laid the groundwork—heading off to the Cape with some friends, getaway with the girls, blah-blah-blah—and I see him, sitting in the kitchen in his suit, still in his suit jacket and having cereal for dinner...

[*Beat.*]

It was a kid's cereal and I was watching him, leaning forward with his tie hanging in the bowl, almost touching the milk, and it hit me. It did. Right then it kind of hit me like a shock or something, a little bolt of lightning. I sat down on the stairs and, and I . . . I couldn't breathe for a minute, watching him.

[*Beat.*]

And I realized that I was feeling something that I hadn't felt in a long time. For him. My husband . . .

KURT My. My oh my.

JESS Yeah, I know . . .

KURT This is a surprise . . .

JESS Believe me, for me, too.

KURT I'm sure.

JESS I mean, we've done this before. You know? Done it and I didn't think twice about it or what it meant or how he might feel. No, I just did it. But not today.

[JESS *doesn't have anything more to offer up to* KURT *than this. He just nods his head and keeps quiet for now.*]

[*Finally he turns back to her. Trying to be nice.*]

KURT . . . so you can't go. That's what you're saying. Don't want to now.

JESS No, I can't. Not this week, anyway.

KURT Not ever, maybe, from what I'm hearing.

JESS I'm not sure. Honestly, I don't really . . . I'm confused by it myself.

KURT Right.

JESS I am—I hope you believe me, but this is the best I can do. Try and identify my feelings . . . put my finger on it.

KURT And I appreciate that. Would've been nice if you could've put your finger on it, like, say, *Thursday* or something, but . . .

[*Beat.*]

Hotel's booked now and everything.

JESS I know! I can pay you half of it, if that helps at all, or . . .

KURT No, come on, you know it's not just about that. The cost. *Please.*

JESS I know.

[*Beat.*]

It was just that image of him, sitting there in the breakfast nook with that carton of Count Chocula. I saw him with a puddle of brown milk in his . . . there in his bowl and it all made sense to me, what I'd been doing to him. The hurt that was piling up because of this. Us.

KURT "Us." You mean "us" us?

JESS Yes. You and me.

[*Beat.*]

But as I sat and watched him eat, trying to scoop up those little marshmallow pieces with his spoon, I felt a kind of pleasure. Only a second, really, but it was so deep and so honest that I remembered everything about why we had come together and married and had our children and lasted this long.

KURT Jesus, that's . . .

JESS Through sickness and money troubles and recessions and a war and even you and me. We had weathered all of that and we were still together—that man in there and me. Because of a kind of pleasure we brought to each other, something that—if I'm at all honest about it—we'll probably never have a chance of finding. Us two.

[KURT *nods at her and lets out a deep breath of air. Sound of trains in the distance.*]

Just being honest.

KURT Yes. *Brutally* honest.

JESS I'm sorry.

KURT   You could've... I mean, you could just say, "I can't make it this time." Don't have to be all Bram Stoker about it—drive a *stake* through my heart.

JESS   I don't know. Maybe I do.

KURT   God, that's... shit. Wow.

[KURT *takes all this in*—JESS *has done nothing but tell the truth. He starts to say something but stops himself.*]

[*She waits. Listening. Finally* KURT *speaks. Quietly.*]

...listen, if that's the case, then okay. I understand. Hell, I feel the same way... every time I look at one of my kids and I say how bad I feel about missing a soccer game, that kind of thing—I don't, can't stand that crap. I hate soccer, actually—but I detest lying to them.

JESS   No, I agree. I've always hated that part of this...

KURT   Not so much with my wife because, well, I dunno, I'm not sure. She's an adult and can fend for herself, I suppose, or maybe I'm just so used to it, after doing it so often over so many years that it's really become not just natural but kind of, umm, comforting... in a way. It warms me a bit, to look into her eyes and deceive her.

JESS   Oh. Well, I hope that's not true...

[JESS *studies him but can't read the guy. Good luck. After that she turns and looks over at the tracks across the way.*]

[*Finally she looks back over at* KURT—*he stares at her.*]

KURT   That sounds bad. I don't mean that I'm looking for opportunities to do it, of course not. It's just that it's become a kind of ritual between us, even if she's not really in on it. It's some form of... closeness, actually. I mean, I wouldn't lie to just anybody! I guess that's what I'm saying.

JESS   I think I understand.

KURT   [*Nodding in agreement.*] ...good.

[*Beat.*]

Well, I should probably get over there, then.

JESS   Alright.
[*Beat.*]
So you're still... I mean, you're gonna go ahead and...?

KURT   Yeah. I mean, I already did all the legwork here, might as well try to enjoy it. I can probably get a little work done... maybe a round of golf or something...
[*Beat.*]
Or maybe even come back early, take the kids to a movie. Who knows?

JESS   That'd be nice. Weather's supposed to hold through Wednesday.

KURT   That's good.

JESS   I hope the hotel's nice. It sounds nice.

KURT   Yeah, should be. I'll cancel all of your treatments—at the spa there.

JESS   You sure? I can call if you...

KURT   No, no problem. I'll take care of it.

JESS   Fine, then. So, I guess I'll see you...

[KURT *nods as he shoulders his bag again. Speaks again.*]

KURT   When?

JESS   Ohh... I don't know, actually. I just said that. It's one of those things you say if you're not sure what else to say. *Filler.*

KURT   Right.

JESS   I don't know if we will. Or should, even. Not for a while.

KURT   I figured as much.

JESS   Yes. I mean, with the way I'm feeling now... it's...

KURT   Uh-huh.

JESS   We should probably—

[*An overhead announcement from the ticket desk. They both look over to see passengers starting to form lines.*]

I think they just called for . . . they're . . .

KURT   Yeah, I better get over there.

JESS   [*Pointing.*] Track 23.

KURT   Yep, that's it. Okay, so . . .

JESS   Take care.

KURT   . . . you too, I guess.

[*They hug and then hesitate—both suddenly nervous about their surroundings rather than connected and passionate. Peck on the cheek just about does it. KURT nods and looks at her, kindly but concerned. Touches her on the shoulder.*]

. . . hey, listen . . . I was just . . . lemme ask you something, quick, and be honest . . . it seems like it's time for that. Right now. *Honesty.*

JESS   Alright. If I can.

KURT   Did you . . . in all these months together, did you ever feel that type of thing for me?

[*Beat.*]

What you described about the cereal and your husband with his tie in the milk there? Did you?

[*He stands there, still one hand on her shoulder. Waiting for something more from her. A sign.*]

JESS   Well . . .

KURT   I'm not saying that exact same kind of "pleasure," but something. Anything. Did you? From what I ever did, or, or . . .

JESS   . . . ummmmm . . .

KURT   . . . from us together?

[*Beat.*]

You can tell me. It's okay, I'm curious, that's all.

JESS   It's not really a fair . . .

KURT   Even once. Just one time.
[*Beat.*]
Once?

JESS   No. I didn't. No. Not ever.

KURT   Oh. Okay. Alright, I was just wondering ...

JESS   I'm sorry.

KURT   No problem. It's ... so, I'll see you, then.

JESS   Yeah, fine. Sometime.

[*He nods and walks away. Only gets a few steps and turns.*]

KURT   Sometime soon?

JESS   Maybe. Hope so.

KURT   Be nice if it was soon.

JESS   I know.

KURT   I'm just saying, my opinion—that'd be nice. "Soon."

JESS   We'll see.
[*Smiles.*]
Say "hello" to Big Ben for me!

KURT   Will do.
[*Beat.*]
Okay, see what happens ...

JESS   Sounds good.
[*Beat.*]
I just can't promise—listen, we bump into each other all the time. Not just *us* but people, all of us, back and forth across the world and sometimes it's all life-and-death and other days we barely even notice. That's what we do. We pass each other and maybe next time I'll *cling* to you, never let you go or, or, or maybe we'll act like we never even met. Why don't we just wait and see, okay? Life's funny that way ... you know?

[KURT *reacts to this—he nods as he lets this sink in.*]

KURT   Yep. So, I'll call ya when I get...or...

JESS   No, don't do that. Don't call.

KURT   You're right. Fine. I'll just, ummm...

JESS   Okay, then.

KURT   Okay.

JESS   Good-bye.

[*This time she is the first to go—she nods and then turns away. Moving off toward an exit without looking back.*]

KURT   [*To himself.*] ...bye.

[KURT *remains where he is. Watching her slowly disappear into the crowd. He doesn't move.*]

[*Silence. Darkness.*]

• • •

St. Francis Preaches to the Birds

David Ives

David Ives

David Ives is probably best known for his evenings of one-act plays called *All in the Timing* and *Time Flies*. Recent shows include *New Jerusalem: The Interrogation of Baruch Spinoza*; Irving Berlin's *White Christmas; Is He Dead?* (adapted from Mark Twain); *Venus in Fur*; and his translation/adaptation of Pierre Corneille's *The Liar*. He is the author of three young adult novels: *Monsieur Eek*, *Scrib*, and *Voss*. He is a graduate of Yale School of Drama and a former Guggenheim fellow in playwriting.

• • •

[A desert, defined by: a rock, a cow skull, and a human-size, two-armed cactus. Hunkered down center are two vultures, named MIKE and ANGELA. They have sharp talons and long, curving beaks, baldheads, and a ruffle of feathers around their necks.]

[At lights-up, the birds are feasting on the body of ST. FRANCIS, which lies between them, its stomach gaping open. The body is dressed in a rough brown robe bound at the waist with rope. FRANCIS also wears sandals and a golden halo on a wire.]

[The birds eat for a while, digging into the cavity with their beaks and talons, and vocally appreciating the meal.]

MIKE   *[Appreciating the food vocally.]* Mmmmmmm. Mmmmmmm. Mmmmmmm.

    [Takes some bloody pieces of meat out of the cavity.]

    Giblets. I love giblets!

    [Gulps, loudly, with a slurping sound.]

    Gimme more. Gimme more. What is that?

    [Stretches a long rubber band out of the cavity.]

    Intestine? Aaah. Too stringy.

    [Lets it snap back.]

    Where's the good stuff? Where's the liver? Angela, did you take all the good stuff?

ANGELA   I'm not talkin' to you, and I'm eatin' my dinna, do you mind?

MIKE   *[Takes some vegetables out of the body.]* The hell is this? A carrot? Eggplant? Zucchini? I think this creature was a vegetarian! Disgusting!

    [Tosses away the vegetables, takes out a rack of ribs.]

    Okay, here's some good stuff. Ribs! I love ribs! Mmmmmmmm. Mmmm-hmmmm. Mmmm-hmmmm . . .

ANGELA   Michael, could you please not eat wit' your beak open?

MIKE   Angela, va fungoo. Do not interfere wit' how I eat. Okay?

ANGELA   You are so uncouth. I ain't flyin' noplace witchoo no more.

MIKE   Aw, please, Angela.

[*Takes a heart out of the body and holds it up.*]
　　　Have a heart!

[*He squawk-laugh.*]

ANGELA   [*Deadpan.*] That's real funny, Mikey. Real, real funny.

MIKE   Yeah, well, I have a "talon" to amuse.

ANGELA   Very humoriferous.

MIKE   Angela, do you wanna tour the bottom of the Mediterranean? The hard way?

ANGELA   Yeah, yeah . . . You don't say that on a Friday night when you want a piece of tail feather. Do I have spleen in my teeth?

MIKE   You don't have teeth, Angela. You're a vulture.

ANGELA   So this is the desert all your relatives been squawkin' about, huh?

[*She squawks, raucously.*]

MIKE   Okay, so I was misinformed.

ANGELA   Lookit this décor. It's a friggin' wasteland out here!

MIKE   I did not create this desert, Angela.

ANGELA   I'm sorry, but I say overrated.

MIKE   Okay, okay, I gotta say definitely overrated.

ANGELA   And two claws down on the food. This corpus is not as *delicti* as that Chinese we had last week.

MIKE   Aw, now that was a body of work. Nice and putrid.

[*They slurp their tongues loudly, remembering the taste.*]

ANGELA   This carcass is not nearly as lyrical. It's not as light. The blood is bland. And altogether it does not have a warm and welcoming aroma of decay.

MIKE   Personally, I think this repast is gonna repeat on me.

ANGELA That's because it's O-F-F-A-L awful. This is a dish that usually turns my stomach anyways.

MIKE Homo sapiens? Eugh.

ANGELA Filthy scavengers.

MIKE And they're stupid. Wandering around in the middle o' nowhere. For what? "Let's go to the desert! Let's go to the desert!" Yeah. And *DIE*.
[*Squawks.*]
I'll tell you what I think about this species.

ANGELA It's overrated.

MIKE I would say definitely overrated.

[FRANCIS *lifts his head and looks at them.*]

FRANCIS [*Cheerily.*] Hello, Mr. and Mrs. Bird!

MIKE and **ANGELA** IT'S ALIIIIIIIIIIIVE!
[*They squawk around the stage, waddling in a panic, fluttering their "wings."*]
Brrwaaak! Brrwaaak! Brrwaaak!

MIKE and **ANGELA** It's alive!   **FRANCIS** Excuse me. Excuse me.
It's alive! It's alive!   Hello? Mr. and Mrs. Bird?
It's alive! It's alive . . . !   Hello?

[*They stop squawking around the stage.* FRANCIS *rests himself against the rock.*]

MIKE Did I not say he shoulda baked longer?

ANGELA Oh, I see, I see, this is all my fault.

MIKE Keep 'em bakin' in the sun an extra ten-twelve minutes! But no, you gotta have it medium-rare. 'Cuz that's how you always ate it back in the *nest*. With *Mom*.

FRANCIS Excuse me . . .

ANGELA Why do I stay witchoo, huh? Why, why, why?

MIKE Did I not say we shoulda stopped at that dumpster and had the smorgasbord?

ANGELA   I did not want smorgasbord. I wanted a squat-down dinner.

MIKE   Yaak, yaak, yaak...

FRANCIS   I think you're both being rather harsh to each other, Mr. and Mrs. Buzzard.

ANGELA   Hey, hey, hey! We are not *buzzards*.

FRANCIS   I'm sorry.

ANGELA   We are *vultures*. You got it?

FRANCIS   I'm sorry. I'm sorry. I'm sorry. I'm sorry.

MIKE   Didn't I tell you he was gonna repeat on me? Anyway, *signore*, we apologize for this little snafu.

FRANCIS   Snafu?

ANGELA   Yeah, please forgive us for digging in slightly premature. Now DIE, YOU BASTARD! *DIE! DIE! DIE!*
[*Stops.*]
Hey, wait a minute... We understand what you're saying!

FRANCIS   Of course you do. I'm St. Francis. I speak to birds and animals. It's sort of a special skill of mine. I also speak to quite a few of the insect species and many fish, justifying the ways of God to minnows.

MIKE   Oh. A novelty act.

FRANCIS   Lately, I've been talking to plants as well. Hello, Mr. Cactus! Hello! Hello, Mr. Cactus! Hello! Hello, Mr. Cactus!
[*No response from the cactus.*]
Have a nice day, Mr. Cactus!

MIKE   Mr. Cactus ain't too talkative.

FRANCIS   Yes, I haven't quite gotten the hang of plant language yet.

MIKE   Yeah, me neither.

FRANCIS   Oh, have you tried, too?

MIKE   Aw, I'm chattering with the dandelions all the time. Ain't that right, Angela?

ANGELA   Can't shut him up.

FRANCIS   I'd love to learn to talk to dandelions.

MIKE   You better learn how. You're gonna be pushin' em up soon enough!

[*They find that funny.*]

ANGELA   *Questionay, signore:* who the hell are you?

FRANCIS   [*Digging around.*] I think I have a holy card here somewhere...

MIKE   A "holy card"?

FRANCIS   Yes, it's sort of a Catholic headshot.

ANGELA   He's prob'ly sellin' something.

FRANCIS   [*Takes out holy card.*] There you go.

MIKE   [*Looking at it.*] Whoo, that's gaudy. Kinda 3-D, huh.

FRANCIS   The bright colors are sort of traditional.

MIKE   So lemme see, what we got here is a picture of you covered in pigeons.

FRANCIS   It sure was hard getting them to keep still.

ANGELA   Musta crapped all over you, too.

FRANCIS   Oh, I'm used to that.

MIKE   They don't show that here.

FRANCIS   They airbrushed it out. My bio's on the back.

MIKE   [*Turns the card over.*] What. I can't read this. It's written in buzzard!

ANGELA   Didn't I tell you, we are not *buzzards*!

FRANCIS   I'm sorry. I'm so sorry.
[*Flips through his other holy cards.*]
Japanese...Polish...Esperanto...Yes, here's a card in vulture.

MIKE   I can't read that. I'm *illiterate*. I'm a friggin' *vulture*.

FRANCIS   I can read it to you, if you'll forgive my pronunciation.

[*Reads.*]
"Brrwaak, brrwaak, brrwaak..."

ANGELA   [*Translating.*] "St. Francis was born to a wealthy family..."

FRANCIS   "Brrwaak, brrwaak, brrwaak..."

ANGELA   "In the town of A-sissy..."

MIKE   Rich kid, huh. No wonder he's wandering around. Prob'ly on spring break.

ANGELA   Hey, Mike, ain't A-sissy where we had that sheepdog?

MIKE   Ooh, that dog was bad.

ANGELA   Bad.

MIKE   Bad. Bad. Bad.

ANGELA   Very bad.

MIKE   Very bad. Very bad.

FRANCIS   Actually, you know, it's not "A-sissy." It's "A-*see*-see."

MIKE   Oh, pardonay mwah. Not "A-sissy." *Aseesee.*

FRANCIS   A-*see*-see.

MIKE   Can I tell you my frank assessment of A-*see*-see?

ANGELA   I say overrated.

MIKE   I would say *highly* overrated.

ANGELA   You remember the fur on that sheepdog?

MIKE   I still get hairballs from it. *Bad.*

ANGELA   Very bad.

MIKE   Very bad. Very bad.

FRANCIS   Now that I think of it, there was a sheepdog around there I used to converse with...

MIKE   In Aseesee?

FRANCIS   In Aseesee. Was he very cuddly, with a cute brown spot behind the ear?

MIKE   That was him. Tasted kinda like...

ANGELA   Chicken.

MIKE   Like chicken. But bad.

ANGELA   Very bad.

MIKE   Bad dog. Bad dog.

[FRANCIS *clears his throat to get their attention.*]

MIKE   Oh, I'm sorry. Did we interrupt you?

FRANCIS   Do you mind if I continue with the bio on my holy card?
[*Reads from holy card.*]
"Brrwaaaak, brrrrwaaaaa, brrrrwwwakkk..."

ANGELA   "St. Francis gave away all his riches..."

FRANCIS   "Brrwaaaak, brrrrwaaaaa, brrrrwwwakkk..."

ANGELA   "And left home to help the poor..."

FRANCIS   "Brwaaaak, brrwaaak..."

ANGELA   "Taking a vow of..."

FRANCIS   [*Honk.*]

ANGELA   "Chastity." What was that again?

FRANCIS   "Brwaaaak, brrwaaak." [*Honk.*]

ANGELA   Yeah, "taking a vow of chastity." What is that, "chastity"?

FRANCIS   Well, chastity means I'm not allowed to, ahh...How shall I put this? I'm not allowed to, ahh...utilize my, umm, more private areas...

MIKE   Not allowed to use utilize...

ANGELA   His more private areas...

MIKE   Hey, wait a minute. This vow of "chastity." Are you telling me...?

FRANCIS   Yes.

MIKE   Are you saying...?

FRANCIS Yes.

MIKE Are you telling me you can't [*Pumps his fist back and forth horizontally, making a suction sound.*]—?

FRANCIS Exactly. I'm sorry?

MIKE You never [*Pumps fist and makes suction sound.*]—?

[*He keeps that up while* FRANCIS *tries to figure out what that means.*]

FRANCIS I never...polish the silver? Never...pump a kerosene lantern...? Oh, that.

MIKE Yeah, *that.* You tellin' me you gave it *up?*

FRANCIS That's right. But anyway, is [*Pumps fist and makes suction sound.*] really important in the great scheme of things?

MIKE Well, it sure is fun on a Saturday night!

ANGELA Okay, so you don't [*Pumps fist and makes suction sound.*]. What else don't you do?

FRANCIS Well, I don't lie, or cheat, or steal, or use dirty language, or cause harm, or covet anything. I don't bear false witness. I don't commit adultery, whatever that is.

MIKE Dj'ever put somebody's feet in cement and drop 'em in a river?

FRANCIS Um, no.

MIKE So, like, what does that leave?

FRANCIS Well, I preach. I wander the desert. I do miracles. I'm a saint. You see?

[*Back to holy card.*]

"Brwak, brwak..."

ANGELA "Because he was a saint..."

FRANCIS "Brwak, brwak, brwak..."

ANGELA "Francis had a remarkable gift for talking to animals..."

FRANCIS [*Cheep!*]

ANGELA   "...though some say this is merely a colorful legend."

FRANCIS   Wait a minute. It says legend? "Brwak, brwak, brwak, [*Cheep!*]."

ANGELA   "Colorful legend." That's what it says.

FRANCIS   Well, golly! All those years I thought I was actually talking to animals.

MIKE   Well, obviously we're talking, so obviously it's not a legend.

FRANCIS   Oh. That's true. Phew! Thank you, Mr. Vulture!

MIKE   Whoo, he's dim.

ANGELA   When is he gonna die?

MIKE   Shh, shh...

ANGELA   *I'm gettin' peckish again.*

MIKE   So you're a, what did you call it, a "saint"? What is that?

FRANCIS   Oh, it's just a job, really. My own particular area is telling my bestial brothers and sisters about the miracle of creation.

MIKE   "Miracle of creation..."

ANGELA   "Miracle of creation..."

MIKE   And what is that, exactly?

FRANCIS   Actually, I was walking along contemplating the miracle of creation when I fell into this gully. I must've twisted an ankle or something. Nothing too serious.

MIKE   Nope. Nothing serious.

ANGELA   Only total extinction.
[*The two of them snicker and high-five.*]
Does any of this saint stuff explain the antenna on your head?

MIKE   *Mafioso.* Hey! Hey! Gumba! Are you wearin' a *wire*?
[*He finds that very funny.*]
Are you wearin' a wire?

ANGELA Funny, Mike.

MIKE [*Readjusting* FRANCIS*'s halo.*] How's the reception with that thing? Look in his eyes. I think I'm gettin' the Food Channel.

FRANCIS It's called a halo. It wasn't my choice. They just sort of issue you one after a while. Standard issue, really. You might call it a metaphysical good-conduct medal.

ANGELA Is it edible?

FRANCIS I don't honestly know.

ANGELA We'll find out soon enough!

[*The birds slurp their tongues.*]

MIKE There's always room for halo!

[*They find that funny.*]

ANGELA You say good-bye, I say *ha-lo*!

MIKE *Hel-lo-oh*! Ha-*lo*-oh!

FRANCIS Anyway, the glow sure makes it great for reading in bed. You can turn it up, too. And if you put a pot on it? It boils water for pasta.

MIKE Pasta? What is that?

ANGELA You know.

MIKE What, that stuff? Don't get me started.

ANGELA Not unless it's got a meat sauce.

MIKE Not unless it *is* a meat sauce.

ANGELA So why do you do all this saint stuff? Or should I say, *don't* do all this stuff?

FRANCIS So that I can meet God.

MIKE Oh, uh-huh. "God." God...?
[ANGELA *shrugs.*]
God...

FRANCIS *You* know. The highest power in the universe.

MIKE   Oh, *the highest power in the universe.*

ANGELA   "God," remember?

MIKE   Sure. "*God*." You go around not doin' this and not doin' that so you can meet *God*.

FRANCIS   That's right. And so that I can get to paradise, where God is.

MIKE   Whoa, whoa, slow down, Frank. You're throwin' around a lotta technical terms here.

FRANCIS   Paradise is where you go after you die.

ANGELA   Oh, you mean like six feet under.

FRANCIS   No...

ANGELA   You mean nowhere.

FRANCIS   No...

MIKE   You mean dumped in a river.

FRANCIS   No, *paradise*. Traditionally paradise is up in the sky.

ANGELA   Oh yeah? I frequent the sky and I'm a stranger to paradise.

[*The birds hum the "Stranger in Paradise" theme.*]

FRANCIS   Ha, ha, ha. Paradise is invisible, of course.

ANGELA   Oh, it's *invisible*.

MIKE   "Of course."

ANGELA   Well, this explains everything.

MIKE   Small wonder my confusion.

ANGELA   And you yourself have talked to this higher power? Person to highest person?

FRANCIS   Not exactly talked, as such. I once got a stuffed turtle I wanted, named Mr. Murphy.

MIKE   Okay, so the highest power in the universe lives in a garden in the sky and he dispenses toys.

ANGELA   This is possible.

MIKE   And what do you do once you get there?
[*To* ANGELA.]
I can't wait.

FRANCIS   Well, many people claim you sit on a cloud and play the harp.

ANGELA   Mm-hm.

MIKE   You sit on a cloud and play a *harp* . . .

FRANCIS   The sitting on clouds has caused some discussion. But don't forget that a spirit is lighter than the water droplets that make up a cloud, so it actually is physically possible for a spirit to sit on, or at least, hover over a cloud.

MIKE   And these harps are *helium* harps?

FRANCIS   The harps are a bit sticky, scientifically. These days some theologians say it's not harps, it's guitars.

ANGELA   Yeah. Air guitars.

FRANCIS   I have my own theory, taken from scripture, that Hawaiian luau music is quite popular Up There.

MIKE   Francis, lemme get this straight. You spent your life talking to raccoons and you gave up [*Pumps his fist horizontally and makes a suction sound.*] for Waikiki in space?

FRANCIS   Uh-huh.

MIKE   Luau music?!

[*The birds collapse in laughter.*]

FRANCIS   Anything is possible.

ANGELA   Yeah, anything is possible—including zip zero nada *nothin'*. Which is slightly more probable.

MIKE   May I speak frankly, Frankie? You ain't headed for the clouds. You're *living* in 'em.

ANGELA   Is this a rich kid talkin', or what?

MIKE "Anything is possible." Wake up to social conditions, brother. Think about *this* world for a change.

ANGELA You coulda been anything, and you picked what? Idiocy. You're a loon! You're a kook! You're a fruitcake!

FRANCIS We all have our beliefs.

MIKE Yeah, some of us have the *leisure* to have beliefs. You get to sit on your arse and contemplate cloud life, *we* have to move from place to place and feed off rotten, stinking, putrescent carcasses. Not that we don't *like* rotten, stinking, putrescent carcasses...

ANGELA But we didn't have any choice in the matter. We *had* to eat rotten, stinking, putrescent carcasses.

MIKE I didn't want to be a vulture. I wanted to be a director.

FRANCIS Film director?

MIKE Funeral director. My mother says to me, "You're a vulture, Mighaele, you eat carrion and fertilize the desert with your shit, so siddown and take your place in the food chain." My sister wants to study French, that's okay. Spring at the Sorbonne, that's *fine*. Reading dead authors instead of eating 'em. *That's* purposeful. I go to Avis with a fresh concept. Avis Rent-a-Carcass. Do they bite? No. Can I get financing? No. Why?

FRANCIS Because you're a vulture?

MIKE Because I'm a vulture. I shoulda been *capo di capo* and soared with the eagles. Instead I got life as a buzzard and I flew with the sparrows.

FRANCIS Well, you're a vulture.

MIKE Actually, I'm only one-thirty-second vulture. The rest? Pedigreed buzzard.

[MIKE *weeps.*]

ANGELA No!

MIKE *Si!*

ANGELA *No!*

MIKE *Si!*

ANGELA NO!

MIKE *SI!* It's true! It's true! I'm a miserable friggin' lowlife buzzard!
[*Abruptly snaps out of it.*]
But what's the difference. Buzzard or vulture, did I ever have any options? You had everything and you threw it all away!

FRANCIS But I wanted to help the poor.

MIKE You didn't help the poor. You *joined* the poor. You *are* the poor. You spent your whole life as a scavenger on creatures who *work* for what they have. You're pathetic. You're a loser. You're a dickhead. And what have you done? Nothin'! You fell sucker for a concept, Frankerino. For a line. I say there's nothin' out there but oxygen, so gulp it while ya can.

FRANCIS A fairly bleak worldview...

MIKE Us vultures at least got a purpose. We fertilize the earth. We excrete nitrogen-rich turds. What did *you* ever do?

FRANCIS Well, maybe nothing as tangible...

ANGELA You done zip zero nada nothin'.

MIKE Period!

FRANCIS Well, listen, I'd love to stop and talk some more, but I've got a bullfrog waiting down the road for confession.
[*Tries to get up, but can't.*]
It was really nice meeting you two. Mike. Angela.
[*Tries to get up, but can't.*]
Arrivederci.
[*Tries to rise, but can't.*]
Whoo, hey, am I stiff.

MIKE "Stiff" is the word all right.

[*The birds find that funny.*]

ANGELA   Is that rigor mortis, or are you just glad to see me?

[*Even funnier.*]

MIKE   So how do you say "croak" in bullfrog?

[*Even funnier.*]

FRANCIS   I see I have a slight stomach wound here...
[*Takes a lamb chop out of the wound.*]
Maybe I'd better have that looked at.

ANGELA   [*Taking the meat from him.*] Thank you. I'll just pick.

MIKE   [*Holds out a "microphone," talk-show-host-style.*] So tell the folks at home, Frankie. Any near-death experiences? Do you see a long tunnel of light with your dead grandmother at the end of it?

FRANCIS   A long tunnel with my dead grandmother...? No. Should I? Where is it?

ANGELA   "Answer your beeper! It's the Reaper!"

FRANCIS   Reaper...My dead grandmother...

MIKE   You oughta be seeing her in about, I'd say six minutes.

FRANCIS   I'd love to see her. She used to make the most wonderful Jell-O molds.

MIKE   Mm-hm. Really.

FRANCIS   Lime on the bottom, orange on top, with these teeny-tiny marshmallows floating inside.

ANGELA   Fantastic.

MIKE   You oughta be tastin' that Jell-O anytime soon.

FRANCIS   [*Realization.*] Oh. *Ohhhhh*...You're not implying that I'm about to, um...?

MIKE   Die? Yes. Bingo!

[*The two birds start filing their beaks.*]

FRANCIS   Ah. Oh. Mm-hm. Yes. Is that what this is. Right, of course. I'm in the middle of the desert with a gaping stomach wound and there's nobody for miles. A few major organs missing. Death would certainly seem inevitable. Ah, well. Comes to us all, doesn't it.

[*Suddenly screams.*]

HELP! HELP! I HAVE A GAPING STOMACH WOUND AND I'M MISSING SEVERAL MAJOR ORGANS! I'VE ONLY GOT SIX MINUTES TO LIVE!

MIKE   Tops.

FRANCIS   *TOPS*! I'M GOING TO DIE AND BE EATEN BY BUZZARDS!

ANGELA   We are *not BUZZARDS*!

FRANCIS   Who GIVES A SHIT what you are?! AND YOU ATE MY FAVORITE SHEEPDOG!

MIKE   I hope you're tastier.

FRANCIS   Why, I oughta...I'M DYING UP HERE! HELP ME! HELP! HELP!

ANGELA   Sure took him long enough.

FRANCIS   IS ANYBODY OUT THERE? IS THERE ANYBODY OUT THERE? HELLO!

MIKE   Now who is gonna respond to a scream like that?

ANGELA   Too much vibrato.

MIKE   Narrow range.

ANGELA   Nobody's got a good scream anymore.

MIKE   Sure sounds like "a sissy" to me!

FRANCIS   WILL SOMEBODY HELP ME? I'M A DICKHEAD! I'M A TOTAL DICKHEAD! AND I'VE DONE NOTHING WITH MY LIFE! NOTHING! NOTHING!

ANGELA   Zip zero...

FRANCIS ZIP ZERO NADA NOTHIN'! I HAVEN'T LIED OR CHEATED OR STOLEN OR COMMITTED ADULTERY! WHATEVER THAT IS! Oh God, oh God! What God? There is no God. There's nothing. Nothing! NOTHING!

MIKE He's good.

ANGELA Now watch, here's where he begs us for help. Watch this.

FRANCIS Won't you help me, please, please, pretty please with sugar on top? Help me live! Please! Don't let me die! Help me LIVE! *I WANT TO LIVE!*

MIKE Um. Sorry.

FRANCIS [*A cry of total despair.*]

ANGELA Now the weeping.

[FRANCIS *weeps.*]

Now the gnashing of teeth.

[FRANCIS *gnashes his teeth.*]

Now the tearing the hair.

[FRANCIS *starts tearing his hair.*]

Right. Good. Biting the knuckles.

[FRANCIS *bites his knuckles.*]

Uh-huh. Now the rocking and moaning.

[FRANCIS *rocks and moans.*]

Very well done. Now the fast breathing and the sweating and the panic attack.

[FRANCIS *has a panic attack.*]

Good one. Now the calling for Momma.

FRANCIS *UNCLE BRUNO!*

ANGELA A variation.

MIKE Now here's where he gives up all hope. Total panic and despair. I love this part.

[*They wait for it. Instead*—FRANCIS *stands up.*]

FRANCIS *WOW!*

MIKE and **ANGELA** [*Fluttering around, flapping their wings in fear.*] *Brrrrwaaaaak! Brrrrwaaaak! Brrrrwaaaak!*

FRANCIS Wow! Is this not the most spectacular day you've ever seen? *Shazam!*

ANGELA Am I on peyote, or did he just stand up?

FRANCIS Will you look at this place? Is this gorgeous? I mean, the rock, the cactus, the *skull.* Kazowie! Guess I went through a bad patch there for a second. Sorry about that.

MIKE Must be hysteria.

ANGELA This too will pass.

MIKE Yeah, and so will he. Any second.

FRANCIS Five minutes to live, huh. Isn't that something. Five whole minutes to enjoy all this. And then—PSHOO!—blast off!

MIKE Yeah, blast off, all right. To *nowhere.*

FRANCIS All right, so I'm going nowhere! There's nothing waiting out there for me? Fine. No higher power in the universe? I'm all right with that. But even the chance to have experienced nothing is not nothing. It is not nothing to have seen this desert. It is not nothing to have tasted a purple plum plucked from a bough in Tuscany. It is not nothing to have met two creatures as glorious as you on this, the final day of my life.

ANGELA Glorious creatures . . . ?

FRANCIS Yes, you are two beautiful, radiant creatures. And I say it is not nothing for us three to be here together on a great round rock flying through a void a trillion light-years wide. I say that is a miracle. And we are standing on that rock right now, not another time, right now, not some other time, but now. This very moment. When I am filled with joy, even awaiting annihilation.

[*Hawaiian Luau music is heard.*]

It's sort of too bad there's no higher power. And I did sort of have my heart set on an afterlife ... But hey. Them's the breaks, right? Maybe another time. Do you hear something?

MIKE Is somebody holding a *luau* near here?

FRANCIS You know, it's funny but ... I could swear I see a long tunnel of light with my dead grandmother at the end of it.

[*His* GRANDMOTHER *appears on a cloud, holding a plate of Jell-O.*]

Yes! She's waving to me! And she's holding a plate of Jell-O with the teeny-tiny marshmallows floating inside! Hello, Babba! Hello, Babba!

GRANDMOTHER [*Italian accent.*] Francesco! Francesco! Long time-a no see!

FRANCIS Babba, you're standing on a cloud!

GRANDMOTHER This is because I am spirit, lighter than the water droplets I am-a standing on! But come, there are all these beautiful people here! All day we go [*Pumps fist and makes suction sound.*]. But *viene*! *Viene*! Your Jell-O she's-a melting!

[GRANDMOTHER *disappears.*]

FRANCIS Isn't this cool? Well, aloha, Mike. That's Hawaiian for "hello" and "good-bye."

MIKE Yeah, yeah, yeah. I know what *aloha* means.

FRANCIS Will you give me a hug? Come on.

MIKE Good-bye, Francis.

[*They hug.*]

FRANCIS Aloha, Angela.

ANGELA Aloha, Francis.

[*They hug.*]

FRANCIS Thank you for keeping me company today, you two. And hey—keep those nitrogen-rich turds coming! You're doing a fantastic job!

CACTUS [*Voice from behind the stage.*] Good-bye, Francis!

FRANCIS Good-bye, Mr. Cactus! Isn't that wonderful? I finally learned Cactus! Good-bye, Mr. Rock! Goodbye, Mr. Skull! I love you! Aloha, everybody! Aloha, world! Aloha!

[FRANCIS *disappears. Hawaiian music fades. All quiet.*]

MIKE I knew we shoulda had the smorgasbord. So you think there's really...*you* know...after we die?

ANGELA Anything is possible.

MIKE Obviously.

ANGELA Obviously. I tell you this, though: I'm goin' on pasta *tomorrow*.

MIKE So, Ange, you forgive me for bein' a miserable, lowlife buzzard?

ANGELA Yeah, I forgive you the buzzard. I do not forgive you the green wall-to-wall shag you put in the nest.

MIKE I'll change it soon as we're home. I swear to [*points upward*], even if there ain't one.

ANGELA *Caro bellissimo!*

MIKE *Mio tesoro!*

[*They join talons.*]

ANGELA Y'know, honey, I think this desert is slightly underrated.

MIKE I would say highly.

ANGELA I would say highly, vastly underrated.

MIKE Looks like it's gonna be quite a night, huh. Lotta stars...

ANGELA Yeah. And you know what I say? I say: delicious.

[*We hear birds and crickets and tree frogs as the sun sets in a gorgeous array of reds and golds. The stars come out.*]

[*The lights fade.*]

• • •

The Stormy Waters, the Long Way Home

Carey Lovelace

Carey Lovelace

Carey Lovelace has had over fifty productions of her works, including at 59E59 Theaters, Ensemble Studio Theatre, Bay Street Theatre, the Samuel French One-Act Festival (2006 finalist), and the BMI Music Theatre Workshop. Her 16-scene dark comedy, *Couple Counseling*, recently played to sold-out houses at the 2009 Edinburgh Fringe Festival. It received its world premiere at the REDCAT Theatre in the Walt Disney Concert Hall in Los Angeles, and was produced in 2008 by the Manhattan Rep Theatre. She has been a finalist, semi-finalist, and won honorable mentions in numerous competitions, including winning the Maxim Mazundar One-Act Play Competition. At BMI, she is a member of the Librettists Workshop and audited the Lehman Engels Music Theatre Workshop; she is a member of the Actors Studio P/D Workshop. For many years, she participated in Ensemble Studio Theatre's Citylab, under the direction of the late Curt Dempster. She is a co-principal in the theater company Loose Change Productions. She is also an art journalist and served as co-president of the International Association of Art Critics. She has written about the art world for over a decade and a half and has curated exhibitions at the Bronx Museum, The Drawing Center in New York, and the Los Angeles Museum of Contemporary Art.

character

    RENATA, late 40s to early 50s, beautiful in a wistful, childlike way

• • •

[*Empty stage. Sound of waves—maybe a foghorn. It is morning, a beach, very early summer, before it warms up. Woman, late 40s, early 50s, beautiful in a wistful, childlike way, comes over sand. Huffing and puffing, as if she's walked a long way. She carries a basket.*]

RENATA   God! Sorry. I've lost my breath here!

[*To unseen "friends" in the distance.*]

Come on! Hurry up!

[*Peering in the direction of the audience.*]

Oh. Hi! There you are. The fog is so thick. You got here before the others.

[*Waving offstage.*]

Over here!

[*A beat.*]

Hey! Listen.

[*A beat.*]

God, I love that sound!

[*As if struggling to regain her breath.*]

It gets harder every year!

[*She puts out different thermoses in the sand.*]

Okay. Barley soup. Juice. And this is *elixir vita*. My own recipe. Designed for anything that ails you.

[*Looking out, again, offstage.*]

I can barely see them. Can you? I hope he's okay! I get so impatient sometimes. I know I shouldn't. He's just so . . . you know! Slow!

[*She smells in the different thermoses, pours out of one of them, offers it.*]

You sure you won't have some?

[*She sips, makes a face.*]

No, it's great. Really. Full of vitamins! Listen, I need to ask you something. I'm glad we're alone for a moment. I . . .

[*She shivers.*]

God, a chill. Did you feel that? Like a ghost passing through the room. Isn't that the, what, old wives' tale? Old wife. I wonder where that expression came from. They never talk about "old husbands."

[*Singing.*]

"By the sea, by the sea, by the beautiful sea." You forget how long it takes for summer to come. I'm just so cold all the time now! I'm not complaining! Anyway . . . it's no use pretending things haven't changed a lot recently. Do you think I've changed a lot? Be frank. I want to know things the way they really are. And I know I can trust you. Can't I?

[*A beat.*]

Winter is still with us.

[*She takes another sip, again makes a face.*]

You know, there would have been a time I wouldn't be caught dead drinking this garbage. Give me a big, fat joint! Now, I'm ready to do a cookbook. *The Power of Juicing.*

[*She looks in the cup.*]

Seaweed. See? Nothing better. Iron. Vitamin A. Japanese mystics swear by it. That's a nice sweater. Is it a sweater? I can barely see it. You're fading into the sand there! Whoa! Ha! Ha! Don't go away! Please! God, suddenly I had that . . . déjà vu. Like I've been here before. Do you ever get that? Anyway, what I needed to ask . . . oh, it's so hard. So hard to . . . I've been thinking about T. S. Eliot a lot recently. Do you read poetry? Does anyone anymore? "The tolling bell measures time, not our time." "I hear the mermaids calling each to each." When I was little, we had a house by the beach and my father used to tell me to listen to the sound of the waves, listen very hard, actually, to the sound in between the waves. He'd say, "Can you hear? That's the sound of the sounds of the mermaids calling. Listen. There they are." And I would listen. He said they were calling out to me, that they were sad, trying to bring back their life. He used to say I had hair the color of sand. I would lay my head in his lap and he would stroke my hair. I dreamed last night I saw my father. I had a conversation with him, the way he was when he was young. And then he turned into my husband. Then into T. S. Eliot. Then everything vanished; it was like looking through a telescope the wrong way. It's very weird, this whole experience. Suddenly, it's happening to you. I wish I could see you! Don't hide from me! You'd think they'd be here by now! Anyway, what I wanted to say was ... I just wonder what he's going to do without me. You know, he's gotten worse and worse. He got so angry when he first heard. "Who's going to take care of *me*?" he said. He was right. It's been slow, over the years, and I never thought there would be a problem, because I never thought it would be me first, you see? He's still brilliant, of course. Have another drink of this?

[*She toasts, drinks, makes a face, tries to recover.*]

At first it changed my skin. That was the most shocking thing. To watch your body change. Fast. To look at your arm and have it be somebody else's. Then the loss of hair. You hold on to hope, some kind of thought it's going to reverse itself. It's incredible how strong that hope is. But, now, it's strange, I feel great! It's like I'm back to normal again! I'm afraid of the dark. At first there was pain. And fear. But then ... it stopped. Are you there? They say I'm still beautiful. Am I? Always beautiful.

[*She drinks again.*]

"In the end is my beginning." I don't really trust Western medicine. But, frankly, Eastern medicine isn't much better. Wouldn't it be nice if this were a nice, fat joint? Actually, that's why I'm glad we have this time. I need you to ... take care of him. I need someone to do that. And to tell people ... how much I love them. Can you do that? Whoa! You faded out there for a moment. What did you say? What? I can't hear you. Can you speak louder? Please! I don't mean to be upset. It's weird, this feeling. Waiting for friends to arrive. Always waiting. Waiting for friends.

[*Slow fade to black.*]

• • •

Early Morning

Eric Lane

Eric Lane

Eric Lane is an award-winning playwright, filmmaker, and book editor. His plays include *Heart of the City* (Theatre at 30th Street), *Ride* (W.H.A.T.), *Times of War* (A.T.F.), *Cater-Waiter* (HERE), and *Dancing on Checkers' Grave*, which starred Jennifer Aniston. Lane wrote and produced the short films *First Breath* and *Cater-Waiter*, which he also directed. Both films screened in over forty cities worldwide. For TV's *Ryan's Hope*, he received a Writers Guild of America Award. With Nina Shengold, he has edited twelve contemporary play anthologies for Penguin and Vintage Books, earning a Lambda Literary Award nomination. Honors include the Berrilla Kerr Playwriting Award, the Lamia Ink Award, and the La MaMa Playwright Award. Fellowships include Yaddo, VCCA, and St. James Cavalier in Malta. Lane is an honors graduate of Brown University and artistic director of Orange Thoughts, a not-for-profit theater and film company in New York City. For more information, please visit: www.ericlanewrites.com.

characters

DORIS HANSON, sixties to early seventies. Her grandson, Kenny, has just died. Her world has been turned upside down. She is experiencing a strong range of emotions—from grief to rage to relief. She is forced to protect herself and Kenny's memory.

DIAMANTINI, a detective. Working class, with a slight belly. Married, and the father of three girls. Has been on the force since his twenties. Having solved many disturbing cases, he still cares in spite of himself. A strong sense of right and wrong. While sometimes appearing casual, he drives the investigation and knows exactly what he is doing.

setting

Police precinct

time

1994. Fall to winter.

> Midnight, our sons and daughters
> Were cut down and taken from us
> Hear their heartbeat...
> We hear their heartbeat
> —U2, "Mothers of the Disappeared"

• • •

prologue

[*Preshow music, U2's "Mothers of the Disappeared," ends.* DORIS *stands, isolated in light.*]

DORIS   In times of peace, children bury their parents. In times of war, we bury our sons.

[*A moment.* DORIS *enters the police precinct.*]

scene one

[*Police precinct.* DIAMANTINI'*s desk. 1994. Fall. The office is decorated in no style other than functional. Detective* DIAMANTINI *slices and toasts a muffin in a toaster oven in need of repair.*]

[DORIS *sits. She is experiencing a strong range of emotions—from grief to rage to relief.*]

DIAMANTINI   You want yourself a muffin maybe? How 'bout a muffin?

[DORIS *shakes her head "no."*]

You want a muffin, we got. Or some pie. Piece a pie and some coffee. Me, I can't drink it. Bad stomach, but you want, we got, so . . .

[*He turns on a tape recorder.*]

DORIS   What is that for?

DIAMANTINI   This. Ah, it's nothing. Standard, you know. You say something, we wanna know what you said. Exact. Nobody making it up. No words being put in your mouth. You don't want anybody thinking you said something you didn't so— It's standard. Just procedure. You know—

[*The toaster bell rings. Ding.*]

This thing, you gotta press it three times before it toasts. Set it dark. Light. Doesn't matter. Tried a microwave once. You got one of those?

[DORIS *shakes head "no."*]

Don't bother. Bread, it's no good. Muffins, forget. You wanna heat up, like a piece of chicken, from the night before, OK. But bread, it makes it kinda doughy. Chewy. You know. It's like—

[*Toaster rings. Ding. He presses it again.*]

Like you wanna stay away. It's fast but it stinks, so what's the good of that. You got your toast but—

DORIS   [*Straightforward.*] I did not kill my grandson.

DIAMANTINI   No?

DORIS   No. I had gotten there this morning at six-fifteen.

DIAMANTINI   [*Sits.*] How come so early?

DORIS   Kenny would wake up. Maybe the noise. Or just being there, in the hospital. Two and a half months this time. This time, two and a half months. If I was there, he wouldn't— He would be, well, calmer. Maybe talk. Just a few—words.

[*Toaster. Ding.* DIAMANTINI *doesn't move.*]

Your muffin.

DIAMANTINI   That's OK.

DORIS   No, get it, Detective.

[*He does, careful not to burn himself.*]

Smells good.

DIAMANTINI   You want, Mrs. Hanson?

DORIS   [*Shakes her head "no."*] Doris.

DIAMANTINI   Doris. You sure?

[DORIS *nods. He sits.*]

He'd be calmer if you came. You were saying—

DORIS   Aren't you going to eat?

DIAMANTINI   Too hot. Bad stomach, you know. So, Kenny—

DORIS   Kenny. Do you have any children?

DIAMANTINI   Three girls. Play the violin. I hate that instrument. All strings.

DORIS   Kenny played the piano.

DIAMANTINI   Was he good?

DORIS   [*Nods.*] I used to listen. I liked listening, when he played.

DIAMANTINI   [*Hates classical.*] Classical?

DORIS   Classical. Pop. All different. I taught him.

DIAMANTINI   You still play?

[DORIS *nods.*]

Me, I got no musical ability.

DORIS   Everyone has some musical ability.

DIAMANTINI   I play you sixteen bars on trumpet, you'll think different. So it's just you this morning. Alone with Kenny. You'd talk.

DORIS   [*Nods.*] Like every morning.

DIAMANTINI   Me, six-fifteen, I'm not saying much. That's just me. What'd you talk about?

DORIS   It was his birthday. Twenty-nine years old. I brought him a cupcake with an electric candle in it. Turned it on and sang "Happy Birthday."

DIAMANTINI   I bet he liked that.

DORIS   Blew out the candle. I helped him. Took off his oxygen mask and blew it out. He saw it was electric, but still . . .

DIAMANTINI   What'd he wish for?

DORIS   I don't know. Even if I did, can't tell or it won't come true. Aren't you going to eat your muffin? It must be cool by now.

[DIAMANTINI *nods, gets muffin, offers it.*]

No, thank you.

[*He starts to eat.*]

Saturn Return. You asked what we talked about.

DIAMANTINI   What's that?

DORIS   This time of big change. Once every twenty-nine years. Kenny read all about it.

DIAMANTINI   You believe in that stuff?

DORIS   [*Nods.*] Do you?

DIAMANTINI   What do I know? There's all kinds of reasons why people do what they do. So you're in the hospital with Kenny. Two and a half months now.

DORIS   This time.

DIAMANTINI   This time, two and a half months.

DORIS   Yes.

DIAMANTINI   This morning, in his room, singing "Happy Birthday." By yourself the whole time.

DORIS   Nurses would come and go, but yes, I was there. Until I left the room at eight-thirty.

DIAMANTINI   You knew what time it was?

DORIS   I looked at my watch. It was eight-thirty. I went to the pay phone to call my daughter. Margie was at work by then.

DIAMANTINI   Kenny's mom.
[DORIS *nods*.]
And nothing seemed unusual.

DORIS   No.

DIAMANTINI   Was Kenny upset?

DORIS   He seemed calm, relaxed. He said he had a good night's sleep.

DIAMANTINI   You believe him?

DORIS   Why shouldn't I?

DIAMANTINI   It seems we got a couple of questions.

DORIS   What kind of questions?

DIAMANTINI   When his nurse—

DORIS   Carole.

DIAMANTINI   When Carole came in the room there was a pillow across Kenny's face. This is when you're making your call. His hands are at his side. His oxygen mask off and on the night table just out of his reach. Not impossible to reach, just slightly beyond. Do you understand what I'm asking?
[DORIS *says nothing*.]
Do you want to call your lawyer?

DORIS   I'd like some water, please.

[*He nods, gets her some.*]

DIAMANTINI   Nobody else was in the room. The curtain was drawn around the bed.

DORIS   People look in. You want your privacy.

[*He offers her the water.*]

Thank you.

[*She drinks some.*]

They didn't want to let me back in the room. His doctors. I made them. Kenny lying there. The safety rail's down, and I get in beside him. He's cold. I hold him to my breast. It's his birthday. Saturn Return. This time when Saturn returns to the exact position when you were born. It's like I see him hanging up there in the sky. His legs, like he's hugging his legs to his chest, and me, and Margie, and Nanna Jean, we're forming these three rings around him. Up high. Just hanging in the dark, the three of us trying to hold on. And we finally let go. Outside that body that hurt him for so long, and how happy he must be to leave it. He's gone, I think. Who he really is is gone. And anything that follows doesn't scare me—what they say or think, doesn't matter, 'cause I know he's safe. Ask your questions, Detective. Ask away.

[DIAMANTINI *looks at her. A moment. Lights fade.*]

scene two

[DORIS *and* DIAMANTINI *address the audience. They hear what each other says.*]

DORIS   There is no word. I'm suspected of a crime without a word. A son kills his mother—

DIAMANTINI   Matricide.

DORIS   A mother kills her baby—

DIAMANTINI   Infanticide.

DORIS   But the thought of a woman killing her child's child. It's not even part of the language. Because no one would believe it. No one.

[DIAMANTINI *looks at her. A moment. They enter the precinct.*]

[*Later that day.* DIAMANTINI *removes toasted muffin from toaster, puts it on a plate. Mid-conversation.*]

DIAMANTINI   You're in the room. Eight-thirty. And you're heading to . . .

DORIS   The pay phone.

DIAMANTINI   Which is—help me out here—which way?

[*He offers muffin. She shakes her head "no." He leaves it to cool.*]

DORIS   [*Indicates.*] Down the hall and to the left.

DIAMANTINI   OK. You reach the pay phone.

DORIS   The lounge is empty—TV on but empty, and I call Margie. Nothing important, just to say hello. She sends him her love. "Tell Kenny happy birthday and I'll see him later tonight."

DIAMANTINI   So you get off the phone and head back to the room.

DORIS   I watch a minute of the talk show. There's a commercial for orange juice and everyone seems happy. They're drinking orange juice around a table and everyone is glad.

DIAMANTINI   So you head back to the room.

DORIS   Head back, only everything feels different.

DIAMANTINI   Different how?

DORIS   Outside. The hall feels like—I don't know. Movie time. Slower. Just not me, but away, and this part of me— Just this part has this feeling like—

[*Searches for the words, can't find them.*]

DIAMANTINI   And when you get back to the room.

   [DORIS *looks away.*]

   When you get back—

DORIS   When I get back to the room there are people. Nurses, doctors. The door's closed and I know, well—think. Just bits of words each time someone runs—not runs but that fast hospital walk—we don't run, we just walk fast, calm but screaming inside because I know. In the time it took some little girl to drink a glass of orange juice. For me to call Margie and tell her everything is fine, Kenny died. And you think I did it.

DIAMANTINI I didn't say that.

DORIS No?

DIAMANTINI No. I'm just trying to figure out what happened.

DORIS Don't you think I want to know?

DIAMANTINI Then help me out here. All makes sense, only I got one question. Why'd you leave the room?

DORIS To use the phone.

DIAMANTINI Phone in the room.

DORIS I wasn't going to talk in front of Kenny.

DIAMANTINI Why not? He's your grandson.

DORIS And he's dying. Do you think I want to talk about that in front of him?

DIAMANTINI You were calling your daughter. Nothing important. Isn't that what you said?

DORIS Like every morning.

DIAMANTINI So you're gonna walk down two long hallways. Pay twenty-five cents, when a phone's right there in the room.

DORIS Yes.

DIAMANTINI Doesn't add up.

DORIS You have daughters.

DIAMANTINI We're talking about your grandson.

DORIS Your daughter's lying in bed, and you're watching her. Pretending nothing's wrong. Like nothing's been wrong the past three years. Watching her weight go down to ninety. Barely able to lift her head. Two and a half months this time. This time two and a half months in the hospital. Every morning at six-fifteen. You sit in that hospital room. You sit in that chair and watch and wait and pray and you tell me. You tell me if you'd step out of the room for five minutes.

DIAMANTINI   Maybe I would. Maybe I'd want it to end. Her suffering like that. Did you?

DORIS   Did I what?

DIAMANTINI   Want it to end?

DORIS   You seem to have all the answers. You tell me.

DIAMANTINI   I'm just trying to understand. Did you want him to die?

DORIS   No.

DIAMANTINI   Sitting in that chair. Watching and waiting. Praying. You must've thought about it.

DORIS   No.

DIAMANTINI   Blowing out that candle, there must've been something you wished for.
[DORIS *looks away.*]
Maybe he wanted it, too. Even asked you to help him.

DORIS   No.

DIAMANTINI   Three years and not once . . .

DORIS   You don't think. You just do what you have to do.

DIAMANTINI   Whatever he needs.

DORIS   Yes.

DIAMANTINI   To stop the pain.

DORIS   If I could. Yes. If I could make him more comfortable. We'd watch movies together. They have VCRs chained up in all the rooms. It'd help him forget.

DIAMANTINI   Forget what?

DORIS   Guess what Kenny's favorite movie is.

DIAMANTINI   I don't know.

DORIS   Come on. Guess.

DIAMANTINI   [*Shrugs, doesn't know.*] *Rocky.*
> [DORIS *shakes her head "no."*]
> *Gone with the Wind.*

DORIS   *The Wizard of Oz.*

DIAMANTINI   That was my next guess.

DORIS   [*Realizes he's joking with her.*] You're just saying that.

DIAMANTINI   You want some water?

DORIS   Some water, yes. I'd like some water.
> [*He gets her some. Checks his muffin, which has cooled.*]

When he was a little boy we'd watch on TV every spring. Whenever the witch would come on, he'd grab hold of me tight, hiding his eyes with his hands. So tight he'd hold on. "Should I turn it off?" I'd ask him. "No, she'll be gone soon." We'd watch it together. In the hospital. Knowing in the end she'd make it home. Where everything was brown and safe. We'd just watch.

> [*He hands her water; she takes it.*]

Thank you.

> [DIAMANTINI *nods.*]

Your hands are so small. The fingers fat. Like a little boy's. Sausages.

> [DIAMANTINI *smiles awkwardly.* DORIS *smiles.*]

Your wedding ring. Three different bands. I never saw that.

DIAMANTINI   Three different golds. My wife, she says it's like yesterday, today, and tomorrow. She's always coming up with stuff like that.

> [DORIS *nods. A beat.*]

Every Easter.

[*She looks at him.*]

The Wizard of Oz. My daughters would watch it, too.

DORIS That's right. Around Easter.

[DIAMANTINI *nods. A beat.*]

A miracle.

[*He looks at her.*]

You asked what I wished for. When I blew out the candle. I wanted a miracle.

[*A moment. Lights fade.*]

scene three

[DORIS *and* DIAMANTINI *re-enter the precinct. Three days later.*]

[DIAMANTINI *slices a muffin.* DORIS *sits in a chair.*]

DIAMANTINI So after three months, Kenny moves into a private room.

DORIS We've been over this.

DIAMANTINI Who's decision was that?

DORIS The staff.

DIAMANTINI Not you.

DORIS If you're asking if I wanted him in a private room, the answer's yes. But no.

DIAMANTINI Yes, but no?

DORIS Yes, you want your privacy. Someone sick sharing the room, no, you don't want that. But what it means, what it meant. I mean, I could see.

DIAMANTINI [*He starts to toast a muffin.*] You want?

[DORIS *shakes her head "no."*]

What'd it mean?

DORIS The sicker you got, the more likely a private room. If you went into a private, they thought it was bad.

DIAMANTINI   But you didn't request it.

DORIS   No.

DIAMANTINI   So that morning, Kenny makes his wish. Takes off his oxygen mask. Blows out the candle. Then puts it back on.

DORIS   Yes.

DIAMANTINI   Why not wait?

DORIS   For what?

DIAMANTINI   Me, I'd wait. 'Til later. Other people around. Presents.

DORIS   It was his birthday. I thought it might cheer him up.

DIAMANTINI   Was he depressed?

DORIS   He was in the hospital. What do you think?

DIAMANTINI   But you said he wasn't. He had a good night's sleep. Isn't that what you said?

DORIS   Yes.

DIAMANTINI   Then he wasn't depressed.

DORIS   No.

DIAMANTINI   You just said he was.

DORIS   I said—

DIAMANTINI   He was. He wasn't.

DORIS   [*Mispronounces his name.*] Detective Damanitini—

DIAMANTINI   [*Corrects her pronunciation.*] Diamantini.

DORIS   [*Repeats.*] Diamantini.

DIAMANTINI   [*Nods.*] Italian. It means little diamonds.

DORIS   You're Italian?

DIAMANTINI   On my father's side. Before, when I asked about the room, you said—

DORIS What about your mother?

DIAMANTINI Russian and Irish.

DORIS That's unusual, isn't it?

DIAMANTINI Yeah. You said, "When I left the room, I started—"

DORIS Any brothers or sisters?

DIAMANTINI A brother.

DORIS Does he live nearby?

DIAMANTINI Yeah, he does. Doris, it's getting late. I'm sure you're gonna want to be getting home—

DORIS For what?

DIAMANTINI Before it gets too late. If we could just—

DORIS I just thought it was interesting, that's all.

DIAMANTINI Before you said—

DORIS You don't look Russian.

[*Or: "You don't look Italian," depending on actor.*]

DIAMANTINI "When I left the room..."

DORIS [*Imagining in the sky.*] Little diamonds.
[*The bell on the toaster rings. A moment. DIAMANTINI presses it again.*]
He was about five-eleven, black wavy hair. I saw him just as I was leaving the nurse's station.

DIAMANTINI Who?

DORIS This man. I'm leaving the nurse's station and turning to head down the hall. And I see him go into Kenny's room.

DIAMANTINI And you don't think to say anything about it 'til now.

DORIS He was dressed like staff. I thought nothing of it at the time.

DIAMANTINI Three days of questioning and bammo, suddenly you remember.

DORIS   People were always coming in and out of the room. No more than a glimpse. A moment of seeing him from behind. I had no reason to think anything was wrong. Would you?

[DIAMANTINI *looks at her.* DORIS *holds the look. The toaster rings. Ding.*]

[*Fade out.*]

scene four

[DORIS *and* DIAMANTINI *address the audience.*]

DORIS   Word is out. About Kenny and me. The newspapers.

DIAMANTINI   TV.

DORIS   I get calls for interviews.

DIAMANTINI   A book deal.

DORIS   Movie of the Week and Betty White is to play me. I change my number. But word is already out. It's like Dorothy's house has landed on the Wicked Witch. Now everybody in Oz feels like it's OK to come up and tell her what they think about it.

DIAMANTINI   People start writing letters to the editor. Stories about the two of them.

DORIS   Day of the funeral, town paper, big headline above the fold, "GRANNIE-CIDE."

DIAMANTINI   Same day, one of the tabloids runs a story with color photos of a man entering a hospital room.

DORIS   Five-eleven.

DIAMANTINI   Black wavy hair.

DORIS   From behind, a white jumpsuit can look a lot like a doctor's lab coat.

DIAMANTINI   It wasn't suicide.

DORIS   It wasn't the grandmother.

DIAMANTINI   No. He was visited by Elvis.

[DORIS *and* DIAMANTINI *enter the precinct. Several hours later. He has been questioning her a long time. Their nerves are frayed. Toaster is on. They're in the midst of a heated argument.*]

DIAMANTINI   Was he wearing sneakers or shoes?

DORIS   I don't know.

DIAMANTINI   When he entered the room. You must've seen.

DORIS   They were white. What difference does it make?

DIAMANTINI   White what?

DORIS   I don't remember.

DIAMANTINI   Try to see—

DORIS   Put yourself in my position—

DIAMANTINI   Doris—

DORIS   If it were your daughter—

DIAMANTINI   I just need the facts—

DORIS   If she had been sick—

DIAMANTINI   It's a simple question—

DORIS   If she had been dying—

DIAMANTINI   Sneakers?

DORIS   Lying there—

DIAMANTINI   Shoes?

DORIS   If it had been you?

DIAMANTINI   But it's not!
　　　[*Quietly.*]
　　　It's not me.
　　　[*A moment.*]

My brother. He's got it. Nobody knows. My wife, she doesn't want him near our girls. Like they can get it just by being near him. Like it's his fault if he gets sick.

DORIS   I'm sorry.

DIAMANTINI   Yeah . . . Yeah . . . Anyway—

[*Toaster rings.* DIAMANTINI *doesn't go for it.* DORIS *goes to toaster, takes out muffin, puts it on a plate. She brings it to him.* DIAMANTINI *eats his muffin.* DORIS *watches. Lights fade.*]

scene five

[DORIS *and* DIAMANTINI *address the audience.*]

DORIS   People talk. Friends call. Appear. Disappear. I'm asked for my autograph and refuse. Cursed at for spoiling a woman's day. Now her husband's never going to believe she saw me. Girls in gym uniforms wave as I drive by, then scream to their friends in disbelief. "It was her."

DIAMANTINI   "Really."

DORIS   "Gross."

DIAMANTINI   "It was."

DORIS   "No way."

DIAMANTINI   "As if."

DORIS   "Her." A group of high school boys pulls up to the house and waits. They throw a pillow on the lawn, gun the engine and laugh hysterically as they drive off into the night. The nights are lonely. The morning. Afternoon. Margie, she keeps busy with work, but me . . . I go for a walk. Come home. Sit. Wait for something to do. To take care of. The laundry takes so long to pile up. Maybe shopping. I drive myself to the supermarket.

DIAMANTINI   Half hour later, we get a call to come pick her up.

[DORIS *and* DIAMANTINI *move into the precinct. A few weeks later. Late afternoon. She looks off, somewhat dazed, not saying anything. He toasts a blueberry muffin.*]

DIAMANTINI   You want half . . . ?

    [*No response.*]

    You want half a muffin, it's yours. Four o'clock, they're half price.

    [*Toaster rings. Ding. He presses it without missing a beat.*]

    All baked goods. I guess they wanna get rid of them for tomorrow. You know, fresh. For the morning. Not that it's stale. I'm not offering you stale goods. You toast it up, especially you toast it, you can't even tell. You want . . . ?

    [*Toaster rings. Ding. He presses it again.*]

    You like blueberry . . . ? Blueberry's good. Cranberry, I don't like. Too sour. They add sugar, but still—

DORIS   She spit in my face.

DIAMANTINI   At the supermarket?

    [DORIS *nods.*]

    Somebody you know?

DORIS   I'm walking down the aisle. My cart in front of me. This woman heads toward me. Her five-year-old son sitting in the cart.

    [*Enjoys this brief image.*]

    He's got a big chocolate mustache from a Ring Ding over his nose and mouth. I look at him and smile. She sees me and our eyes meet. Lock for that moment. Time stops. The music. The fluorescent hum it covers. Just her and me. Her son's fingers covered in chocolate. She looks in my eyes, spits in my face, walks down the aisle, turns and leaves.

DIAMANTINI   You go after her?

DORIS   I stand there stunned. Like her son must be each time she hauls off and whacks him one. Just stand there between the boxes of Cheerios and Pop Tarts. Frozen for a moment. Then start to scream. Loud. So loud women start running from other aisles to see what's wrong. Children whose eyes they shield from this crazy woman grabbing at boxes of cereal, Froot Loops, Lucky Charms, and tearing open the box. Circles of pink, yellow, moons and stars flying across the aisle and I yell. Loud. "You didn't know him." Grab a woman by the jacket as she backs away. "You didn't know him." The screaming so loud the manager turns off the music. "You didn't know him. You didn't know him. You didn't know him. You didn't know him. Sit with him at three a.m. beside the bed and wipe his shit. Fix his meals so maybe, just maybe he would have an extra bite. You didn't know him. Watch his weight go down to ninety. Watch your grandson, my grandson— You didn't know him. You didn't know him. You didn't know him."

[*A moment.*]

[*He takes a box of tissues. Offers it to her. She takes one. Wipes her eyes. He gently touches her shoulder. Toaster rings.*]

You should get that fixed.

DIAMANTINI   I kinda like it. The challenge, you know...

[*Offers her water.*]

You want?

[DORIS *nods her head "yes." He pours her water. She notices his wedding ring is gone.*]

DORIS   What happened to your wedding ring?

DIAMANTINI   [*Not wanting to talk about it.*] It's a long story.

DORIS   I'm sorry.

DIAMANTINI   Yeah, well, what're you gonna do.

DORIS   Must be hard on the girls.

DIAMANTINI   They'll be OK. That's what they tell me.

[DORIS *nods.*]

Yeah...

DORIS   How's your brother?

DIAMANTINI   He's doing all right. Thanks. How 'bout you?

DORIS   [*She just shrugs. Wipes her nose.*] Past few days I keep thinking about *The Wizard of Oz.*

DIAMANTINI   Watching it with Kenny.

DORIS   About the end. You know, where Dorothy finds out she could have gone back to Kansas all along. You remember, all she has to do is click her heels three times and say, "There's no place like home." "I should've thought of that for you," the Scarecrow says. "I should've felt it in my heart," the Tin Man says. "No," says Glinda. "She had to learn it for herself." I think somebody should've told her.

[DIAMANTINI *stays with her a moment. Lights fade.*]

scene six

[DIAMANTINI*'s office. A week later. Late night.* DIAMANTINI *hands* DORIS *a plate with a toasted muffin. She tastes it as he toasts one for himself.*]

DORIS   This is awful.

DIAMANTINI   It's low fat.

DORIS   Low taste is more like it.

DIAMANTINI   You really think it's bad?

DORIS   It tastes like old socks.

DIAMANTINI   You'll get used to it.

DORIS   I don't think so.

DIAMANTINI   You want the berry?

DORIS   No.

DIAMANTINI   You sure?

DORIS   No. Thank you.
[*Drinks water.*]
My lawyer thinks you're dangerous. That I shouldn't be talking to you.

DIAMANTINI [*Dismissing it.*] Ah, lawyers.

[*Turns on radio. "Moonlight Serenade" plays.*]

DORIS Are you?

DIAMANTINI Am I what?

DORIS Dangerous.

DIAMANTINI Me . . . ? I'm a pussycat.

> [*He laughs. So does she. Re: more water: You want? She nods. He pours water, gives her cup. A brief moment as they connect. He returns to the radio as "Moonlight Serenade" plays.*]
>
> Hey, you know this one?

[DORIS *nods. He turns it up slightly.*]

DORIS You know what the hard part is, with Kenny . . . ? It's like you get used to loving somebody. It's like you still have all this love and no place to put it.

DIAMANTINI Maybe you'll meet somebody.

> [DORIS *just laughs.*]
>
> Could happen.

DORIS I can just see them lining up for a date with the town's most eligible murder suspect.

[*He goes to her. Half-joking, half not.*]

DIAMANTINI May I have this dance?

> [DORIS *laughs.*]
>
> What?

DORIS Why are young men always trying to get me to dance with them?

DIAMANTINI C'mon.

> [*Amused,* DORIS *shakes her head "no," waves him away.*]
>
> What? There's nobody around.

DORIS But—

DIAMANTINI [*Takes her hand.*] C'mon.

[*She joins him. They dance, awkwardly at first, then with slightly greater ease.*]

DORIS   I haven't done this in years.

DIAMANTINI   You should. Keeps you young.

DORIS   You think so?

DIAMANTINI   What do I know.

[*They laugh slightly. Dance.*]

DORIS   I met my husband at a dance hall. Karl. Knew the moment I laid eyes on him. He had the most beautiful eyes.

DIAMANTINI   What'd you like about them?

DORIS   This beautiful chocolate color. And it wasn't so much the color, but the way he'd look at you. Like he was seeing you.
[*Looks at* DIAMANTINI. *A beat.*]
That was a long time ago.

DIAMANTINI   Never know. You could be throwing out the garbage, bammo, your life changes forever.
[DORIS *just shrugs, not really believing it.*]
What?

DORIS   I guess.

DIAMANTINI   I had a dream about you.

DORIS   When?

DIAMANTINI   Last night.

DORIS   What kind of dream?

DIAMANTINI   A three a.m. dream. You're on this train. You dream like that?

[*They stop dancing. He turns off radio.*]

DORIS   Like what?

DIAMANTINI   Train. Desk. Muffin. My wife, she used to dream, like, this glowing circle hangs over this red triangle. What's that about?

[*He sits on edge of desk.*]

DORIS   I walk a lot.

> [*Sits on edge of desk beside him.*]
>
> My arms reaching out. To the men in my family. Only lately they dissolve into the ground.

DIAMANTINI   The men?

DORIS   [*Nods.*] Into the earth. And standing behind them, where they used to be, is me. Only me back then. The girl who lost them. Her arms reaching out to me now.

DIAMANTINI   Is it a good dream?

DORIS   I don't know. So I'm on this train...

DIAMANTINI   Gray day. Clouds. You know, cold. And there's all these people looking in.

DORIS   At me.

DIAMANTINI   As you go past. The train picking up speed. People trying to catch a glimpse, but all they get's some blur. Maybe the color of your dress. Or your hair.

DORIS   What about you? What do you see?

DIAMANTINI   The train pulls into the station. End of the line, everybody out. There's another train across the platform, to go on further. You're heading to it. 'Til you realize you left your scarf behind and go back to get it. Before you know it, bammo, the doors shut and you're trapped inside. I see your face, like in close-up, from the other train. This look like fear. Helpless, you know. Stuck. And the train pulls off, with just you inside.

DORIS   Where are we headed?

> [DIAMANTINI *shrugs. He doesn't know.*]
>
> Do you help me?

DIAMANTINI   There's nothing I can do.

DORIS   Nothing?

DIAMANTINI   No.

DORIS   Do you try?

    [DIAMANTINI *says nothing.*]

    Maybe he's right. My lawyer.

DIAMANTINI   You think...?

    [DORIS *says nothing. Tosses out the uneaten muffin. Just looks at him. Starts to leave.*]

    Doris—

[*She exits. Lights fade.*]

scene seven

[DIAMANTINI *and* DORIS *address the audience.*]

DIAMANTINI   When a murder case goes to trial, a jury's got two choices: guilty and not guilty. Not guilty doesn't mean you didn't do it.

DORIS   Innocent would mean you didn't do it.

DIAMANTINI   Not guilty means there are enough questions, you can't say beyond a reasonable doubt she did it. So you get a smart lawyer, he raises enough questions, enough doubts...

DORIS   In our court system, innocence isn't an option. Even after I'm acquitted, the same questions remain.

DIAMANTINI   The oxygen mask...

DORIS   It's possible Kenny took it off and tossed it aside.

DIAMANTINI   He could've put the pillow over his own face. I had a case like that only a couple of months ago. Yeah, Kenny's hands were at his side, but they could've fallen. After he suffocated.

DORIS   It's possible someone came in the room. It's possible, they say, it was me.

DIAMANTINI   No fingerprints show up but Kenny's, hers, and the hospital staff.

DORIS   No one you could point to. To say how did this get here.

DIAMANTINI   No smoking gun.

DORIS   No bloody glove.

DIAMANTINI   No angle of the body, the neck, arms, that couldn't be explained at least three different ways, and in each of those, another three explanations. An act of mercy. Desperation. Violence. A grandson's request.

DORIS   A grandmother's love.

DIAMANTINI   Her fear. All possible. Questions with no single answer.

[DIAMANTINI *and* DORIS *enter the precinct. Around Christmastime. Late afternoon. He sits at his desk, working. After a moment, she enters, carrying a small paper bag.*]

DIAMANTINI   Doris—

DORIS   Don't get up.
[*He does.*]
I was just passing by. I knew you'd be here so, I, um, I brought you this.
[*She hands him the paper bag. He looks inside. Takes out a blueberry muffin.*]
It was after four. I thought...

[*He starts toward toaster, where he cuts muffin and puts it in to toast.*]

DIAMANTINI   You want half?

DORIS   No thank you.

DIAMANTINI   C'mon. Take two seconds.

DORIS   I can't stay.

DIAMANTINI   [*Sings.*] "I simply came to say I must be going."
[*She looks at him blankly.*]
The Marx Brothers. You know that one?

DORIS   My lawyer thinks it's in my best interest not to speak with you.

DIAMANTINI   Your lawyer.

DORIS [*Takes out lawyer's business card, awkwardly tries to give it to him.*] You have his number.

DIAMANTINI I have it.

DORIS His card. In case you need it. If you have any questions, you should call him.

DIAMANTINI Right.

[*He doesn't take the card. She leaves it on his desk. A moment.* DORIS *turns and starts to leave.*]

You ever try snorkeling?

DORIS [*Stops.*] I don't see what—

DIAMANTINI Vacation. Five years ago. The wife and me, we go down to Mexico. You ever been?

DORIS No.

DIAMANTINI Cozumel's nice. Cancun you wanna stay away from. Like one big shopping mall. Unless that's what you want. But Cozumel's nice. People friendly, you know.

[DORIS *shrugs, nods.*]

Water's this beautiful blue. Not blue, but blue-green. Like the inside of a pool, only better. You get in and it looks like, what? It looks like water. But you put on your goggles, you go under, and all these fish, like hundreds of them, swimming around—just beneath the surface. You wouldn't even know, even think, 'til you put your head in and suddenly this whole world going on under. You see what I mean?

DORIS I can't tell you what to do.

DIAMANTINI We're talking about you.

DORIS I see. What is it you want to know?

DIAMANTINI There was no other man. In the room. We both know...

DORIS I know what I saw.

DIAMANTINI Off the record.

DORIS   Meaning...?

DIAMANTINI   Between us.

DORIS   If it were you, if it were your brother, can you honestly tell me what you would do?

DIAMANTINI   I want to know. Was it you?

DORIS   Between us?

DIAMANTINI   Between us.

DORIS   "Yes, it was me." Like at the end of one of those Perry Mason shows. Always at the end somebody stands up in the courtroom, who you thought was a bit part—the gardener or maybe the family cook—finally stands up and says they're really the murder victim's ex-husband or daughter. "Yes. Yes. I did it!" they cry out. "And you want to know why...!"

[*A moment. Then...*]

How often has that happened on one of your cases?

DIAMANTINI   Why won't you tell me?

DORIS   What you want to hear.

DIAMANTINI   The truth.

DORIS   A single answer.

DIAMANTINI   Yes.

DORIS   I remember a time when questions had a single answer. There was right and wrong. Good and evil. All this talk, it still doesn't bring Kenny back.

DIAMANTINI   Doris, that's just not fair.

DORIS   Fair? He was my grandson.

DIAMANTINI   So that's your answer?

DORIS   There is no answer. I've watched the men in my family die. Cut down, one after the other. And this is what we've become. In my day, we knew the enemy. But now... Good. Evil. Black. White. Now it's all shades of gray.

[DORIS *and* DIAMANTINI *look at each other. Lights out.*]

• • •

Sisters

Adam Kraar,
Maria Filimon, and
Tasnim Mansur

Adam Kraar, Maria Filimon, and Tasnim Mansur

Adam Kraar's plays include *New World Rhapsody* (commissioned by Manhattan Theatre Club, produced at H.B. Playwrights Foundation); *The Spirit House* (premiered at Performance Network of Ann Arbor); *The Abandoned El* (premiered at Illinois Theatre Center); *Storm in the Iron Box* (National Play Award runner-up); *The Lost Cities of Asher* (New River Dramatists Fellowship; finalist, 2005 O'Neill Playwrights Conference); and *Freedom High* (winner of the Handel Playwright Fellowship from the Woodstock Byrdcliffe Arts Guild).

Kraar was a playwriting fellow in residence at Manhattan Theatre Club. His plays have been produced and developed in New York by Ensemble Studio Theatre, Primary Stages, NY Stage and Film, NY Shakespeare Festival, Cherry Lane Theatre, The Lark, Abingdon, H.B. Playwrights Foundation, Urban Stages, Queens Theatre in the Park, and Theatreworks USA; and regionally at Geva Theatre, New Jersey Rep, NY State Theatre Institute, Bloomington Playwrights Project, Key West Theatre Festival, and others.

His awards include Sewanee Writers' Conference, Bloomington Playwrights Project, Virtual Theatre Project, and the Southeastern Theatre Conference. His fellowships include William Inge Center for the Arts and the Millay Colony. His plays have been published by Dramatic Publishing, Smith & Kraus, Sundance Publishers, and Applause Books' *Best American Short Plays*. Adam grew up in India, Thailand, Singapore, and the US, earned an MFA from Columbia University, and lives in Brooklyn with his wife, Karen.

Maria Filimon is twenty-two years old and originally from Romania. Her passion for advertising started with an internship in one of the advertising companies in Romania, Tempo Advertising. To progress, she decided to explore the advertising field and came to the United States. She loves to travel, meet new people, and learn about other countries' cultures. She is very interested in developing her skills in photography and acting.

Tasnim Mansur graduated from the New York Institute of Technology in May 2009, with a BA in communication arts. Currently, she works as an assistant manager at Astoria Federal Savings Bank. Originally, she was born in Bangladesh, but she was raised in New York City.

characters

RANI, 23

MALLIKA, 19

Both characters are immigrants from a South Asian country.

place

A subway car in New York City

time

The present

• • •

[*Two sisters,* RANI *and* MALLIKA, *get on a subway train.* RANI *sits down, takes out her date book, and tries to re-plan her day.* MALLIKA *hesitantly sits down near her, but not next to her.*]

MALLIKA Rani—

RANI I don't want to hear it.

[*Pause.*]

MALLIKA I just—

RANI [*With finality.*] Mallika: you don't want to talk to me right now.

MALLIKA I just want to say, I'm sorry. Okay?

[RANI *shakes her head and goes back to her date book.*]

. . . I'm sorry I messed up your day.

[RANI *ignores her.*]

. . . What do you want me to do?

RANI I want not to hear your voice. If I never have to hear your voice again, that's what I want.

MALLIKA Could I please just explain—?

RANI No!

[*Long pause.* MALLIKA *tries to lighten up the situation.*]

MALLIKA [*In a silly voice.*] . . . Wazzup?

[RANI, *appalled, moves to another seat.*]

You almost laughed. Admit it. *Wazzup*?!

RANI Leave me the hell alone.

MALLIKA You said hell.

RANI One more word, Lika, I guarantee you.

[MALLIKA *goes to a different part of the train and sits down. She is trying to give her sister space, but she's upset. To take her mind off things, she goes for her cell phone. She can't find it. She gets more upset. She goes back to* RANI.]

MALLIKA We have to go back.

RANI What?

MALLIKA The police took my phone. . . . They did! I had it when they . . . and now it's gone. We have to go back.

RANI You go back. Get used to jail.

MALLIKA Rani!

RANI I'm through.

MALLIKA I was just trying them on— You know I don't like sapphires— But these had a great setting, so I wanted to see—

RANI Do you really believe yourself?

MALLIKA —how that kind of setting would look, 'cause you know I have small ears, right?

RANI And you forgot to take them off?

MALLIKA Yes.

RANI Do you know what would happen if you did this back home?

MALLIKA They don't have earrings like that back home.

[RANI, *beyond exasperated, says nothing.*]

. . . They took my phone.

RANI The police did not take your phone. . . . You probably left it at a club, or some man's apartment. Always leaving things behind.

MALLIKA   I swear to you—

RANI   Don't. Save it for the judge.... Now would you please leave me alone, like for the rest of my life?

[RANI *takes out her date book and tries to organize her day.*]

CONDUCTOR'S VOICE   Stop is West 4th Street. Change here for the A express and the F and D trains downstairs.... Next stop, 14th Street.

[MALLIKA *suddenly throws her arms around* RANI.]

MALLIKA   ... Rani! It was horrible! They were so mean!

RANI   What do you expect?

MALLIKA   You don't know! This woman, in the jail, tried to put her hands all over me. And the other ones, did nothing. They just laughed. And the police, the police weren't even there.

RANI   [*Concerned.*] Are you ... ?

MALLIKA   [*Moves out of the hug.*] It was really, really horrible. I know I'm a pain in your neck, but you have to understand, I'm really...
[*Beat.*]
I hate this country. I hate my job, I hate the people, I hate our tiny, tiny apartment—

RANI   Then maybe—

MALLIKA   I won't go back! I hate it there, too. Yes! I hate my life. You're the good one and I'm the fucked-up one.... I'm sorry. I'm sorry.

[MALLIKA *cries. Pause.*]

RANI   Mallika ... Hey... Do you know how much sleep I lose because of you? Something has to change, radically. Maybe you're better off going home.

MALLIKA   No!

RANI   ... Dad is crazy about you. He doesn't show it, but when he calls, the first thing he always asks me: "How's Mallika?" Of course, he asks me if you're wearing the right clothes and doing your work, but you know the real reason he's crazy about you? . . . Because you make him laugh.

MALLIKA He never laughs at me.

RANI He hides it. But I've seen him. You're the only one.

MALLIKA . . . Are you gonna tell him what happened?

RANI I don't know. I should! Maybe I will.

[*Pause:* MALLIKA *looks at* RANI. *After a while,* RANI *takes out a cell phone and shows it to* MALLIKA.]

MALLIKA You . . . ?

RANI You cannot be taking things, and leaving things behind, and turning my life . . .

MALLIKA I swear!

RANI Don't swear.

[RANI *gives her the cell phone.* MALLIKA *impulsively hugs her.*]

RANI Okay. Okay.
   [*Pries* MALLIKA *off her.*]
   Now, I have to go to work. And you . . . We'll decide tonight. You'll be there, right?

[MALLIKA *nods.*]

CONDUCTOR'S VOICE 14th Street. Change here for the L.

[RANI *looks at* MALLIKA *for a moment, then gets up.*]

RANI I'll see you tonight.

[RANI *exits.* MALLIKA *looks at her as she leaves. Suddenly,* MALLIKA *gets up.*]

MALLIKA Rani! Wait!
   [*Calling after her.*]
   Thank you!

[MALLIKA, *not sure if she heard her, runs off after* RANI.]

• • •

Little Duck

Billy Aronson

Billy Aronson

Billy Aronson's plays have been produced by Playwrights Horizons, Ensemble Studio Theatre, Woolly Mammoth Theatre, Wellfleet Harbor Actors Theatre, SF Productions, and 1812 Productions; awarded a grant from the New York Foundation for the Arts and a commission from the Magic Theatre; and published in three previous volumes of *Best American Short Plays*. His TV writing includes scripts for Cartoon Network's *Courage the Cowardly Dog*, MTV's *Beavis & Butt-Head*, Nickelodeon's *Wonder Pets* (head writer first season), and PBS's *Postcards from Buster* (Emmy nomination). His writing for the musical theater includes the original concept and additional lyrics for the Broadway musical *Rent*, and the book for the Theatreworks/USA musical *Click, Clack, Moo*. He lives in Brooklyn with his wife, Lisa Vogel, and their children, Jake and Anna. His Web site is billyaronson.com.

··· production notes ···

Little Duck was originally produced by Ensemble Studio Theatre—William Carden, artistic director; Paul Alexander Slee, executive director—as part of Marathon 2009. The cast featured Paul Bartholomew, Jane Pfitsch, Julie Leedes, Steven Boyer, and Geneva Carr, under the direction of Jamie Richards. The music was composed by Stephen Lawrence.

characters

> **ROBERT**, the president
> **HOLLY**, the intern
> **ANNE**, the writer
> **RJ**, the artist
> **DR. JILL**, the director of content

···

scene one

ROBERT   It's sweet and lovely but it's really smart, right, and funny?

HOLLY   It's so great, Robert.

ROBERT   And isn't it great that it's about how we can all work together and get along? Read me Darcy's note again?

HOLLY   "It's so sweet and funny and original, we at the network have the highest hopes for *Little Duck*."

ROBERT   The highest hopes.

HOLLY   She totally loves it.

ROBERT   She ordered a pilot and twelve episodes based on a ten-page bible, when does that happen?

HOLLY   Have you heard from the people who helped with the bible?

ROBERT   They're all on board.

HOLLY   All of them?

ROBERT   RJ'll do the designs, Anne'll be head writer, Doctor Jill'll be educational advisor and director of content.

HOLLY   Wow.

ROBERT   You'll give them total support. This takes priority over all your office duties.

HOLLY   Oh, could I ask something about that? One thing? Cheryl said you said she could do the one-on-ones with the *Little Duck* people?

ROBERT   She'd asked about that a while ago.

HOLLY   Cheryl's so great, she's been a total friend, but to meet with those people one on one, to go back and forth between them and you about the creative stuff, that's like my dream.

ROBERT   Cheryl's been here longer.

HOLLY   I know and normally I wouldn't say anything, but on this one project I think I could really contribute 'cause when I was reading your bible I totally felt the character [*She demonstrates.*] how he waddles into the yard, taking in the day, dippin' his tail into the pond, feeling the cool droplets all tingly and sparkly in the sun, then stretching his feathers out as far as they'll go and givin' that little wet tail a shake-a-shake-a-shake.

[*She shakes her tail.*]

ROBERT   You can do the one-on-ones with the *Little Duck* people.

HOLLY   [*Yelps for joy.*]

ROBERT   Cheryl won't like it. But this is *Little Duck*.

scene two

DR. JILL   It's super. I just love it.

ANNE   Oh good.

DR. JILL   I can't believe you turned a ten-page bible into a totally fleshed-out pilot script.

ANNE   It really worked for you?

DR. JILL   It really gets the content across, and it's so funny.

ANNE   It's so hard getting characters to talk for the first time, plus there was all this pressure to impress Robert, and you.

DR. JILL   With your resume I'm the one who should be nervous.

ANNE   Right. Anyway. Whew.

DR. JILL   So can I show you my notes? They're mostly tiny.

ANNE   I want them, I need them.

DR. JILL   Here you go.

ANNE   [*Reads.*] Okay. Good. Good. You didn't like the jelly?

DR. JILL   Kids might really do that at home.

ANNE   Okay.
[*Reads.*]
Sure. Good.

DR. JILL   The one other thing is, I think the pig should be physically challenged.

ANNE   The pig is a main character.

DR. JILL   Uh-huh.

ANNE   Did you run this by Robert?

DR. JILL   Holly said he wants us to go ahead on our own, he'll take a look at what we come up with.

ANNE   The show is supposed to be funny.

DR. JILL   Funny and sweet.

ANNE   I guess I, huh.

DR. JILL   I know it's a big change, but kids who are physically challenged get so many clues that they should be hidden. In the way people avoid eye contact or withhold a greeting. This would put them front and center in a way that's really groundbreaking. So give it a try?

ANNE   But the thing is, the script has a balance between the characters, it's a pure, complete thing, like a plant, you can't staple a nose on a flower, and what does that teach kids, that a message has to be forced, you see?

DR. JILL   I guess when you talk about keeping the show pure I think of how in some societies undesirables were hidden away or even done away with, I know you're not saying that, but you see what I'm saying.

ANNE   No, no, I know, but the thing about the Nazis was that in the name of their ideology they went around butchering people and lopping things off and squeezing things in where they didn't belong, so, yeah.

DR. JILL   Anne. You've done so much great work. So let's see if we can't take it to the next step and make it really great. Okay?

ANNE   Sure. Anyway.

DR. JILL   Okay, then.

> [DR. JILL *goes to hug* ANNE, ANNE *gives* DR. JILL *a violent shove.*]
> Did you just—

ANNE   Weren't you about to—

DR. JILL   I was going to hug you because—

ANNE   Sorry, sorry, shit. Should we—

[*Offers to hug.*]

DR. JILL   No, no, that's okay.

ANNE   Okeydoke.

scene three

DR. JILL   So you have this feeling, and your hand is drawing, and are you thinking?

RJ   Yeah.

DR. JILL   You're thinking and feeling, and do you have some idea what you're going for?

RJ I have a picture in my head.

DR. JILL A picture in your head. Wow. Does what comes out ever
surprise you?

RJ Sure.

DR. JILL You're open to discovery, and out comes a new character
who'll charm kids around the world and become part of their
lives. Do you feel proud?

[RJ *shrugs*.]

You should. You have a gift. Anyway, I had this idea that Little Pig
should be physically challenged in some way. If you could do one
of your amazing drawings, it would be a huge help in getting the
character approved.

[*He puts his hand on her breast. She slaps him.*]

You think because you're this young guy who's a big deal you can
just put your hand on my breast? I should report you. Or pinch
you, see how you like it.

[*She pinches him.*]

Do you like it when I pinch you? Do you?

RJ No.

DR. JILL I didn't hear you.

[*She pinches him again.*]

RJ [*Louder.*] No.

DR. JILL That's right you don't. Now give me that pig.

scene four

ANNE Robert's meeting with Jill to go over the script before he's
meeting with me?

HOLLY Yeah.

ANNE I'm the writer. So why's he going over the script with her first?

HOLLY Well, I know he's really excited about this drawing of the pig RJ
did for Jill.

ANNE RJ did a drawing for Jill's idea?

HOLLY Uh-huh.

[ANNE *stands up, bites her fist, sits down.*]

ANNE I need to be in that meeting with Robert and Jill.

HOLLY Okay, Anne. I'll try and get you into that.

ANNE Good. Thanks.

HOLLY So since I'm doing this for you, would you do one thing for me? Now I feel weird asking you, ugh!, anyway I wrote this script for *Little Duck* and I know it's a total dream that it could ever get on the show but—oh God, it's the first thing I ever wrote and you've been writing for TV longer than I've been alive but—ugh! ugh!— okay, just go for it—could I show you my script?

ANNE Of course.

HOLLY [*Hands over script.*] So what do you think?

ANNE It looks good, Holly.

HOLLY You're not laughing.

ANNE I never laugh out loud at these things but—

HOLLY You hate it, don't you?

ANNE No, I don't, it's really funny.

HOLLY Where?

ANNE Here.
> [*Points to script, laughs.*]
> And here . . .
> [*Laughs and laughs.*]

scene five

[*They nibble on cupcakes.*]

DR. JILL Mm.

ANNE   Mm.

DR. JILL   I love the ducks on top.

ROBERT   The feathers are coconut shavings.

ANNE   This one's cream-filled.

ROBERT   So how's everything going?

ANNE   Really well.

DR. JILL   It's an amazing team.

ROBERT   Everybody working well with Holly?

ANNE   She's a pleasure.

DR. JILL   How can she be so young and so sharp?

ROBERT   One day we'll all be working for Holly.

DR. JILL/ANNE   I think so. Yeah.

ROBERT   Anyway, I love where you guys are going with the script.

ANNE   Oh good.

DR. JILL   Anne's a wonderful writer.

ANNE   Jill's notes have been a big help.

DR. JILL   It's easy when the material's so clear.

ROBERT   As far as the question about the jelly, let's just have it be mud.

DR. JILL   Mud?

ROBERT   Yeah.

DR. JILL   I wonder if that would encourage kids to bring mud into the house.

ROBERT   I don't think so.

ANNE   Mud is funny.

ROBERT   And I love the idea about having the pig be physically challenged.

DR. JILL   Really?

ROBERT   It's so brave and original.

DR. JILL   It means so much to me that you think that.

ANNE   I admire a lot about it, but I guess I wasn't sure how it would fit with what you created.

ROBERT   We have to be willing to change anything at any point to make the show great. I'm so proud of you, Jill.

DR. JILL   Oh thanks, Robert.

ROBERT   I think it should be the raccoon, though.

DR. JILL   Little Duck's best friend should become a raccoon?

ROBERT   No, I'm talking about the raccoon character who visits the barn sometimes.

DR. JILL   So we'd have a minor character be physically challenged?

ROBERT   I thought instead of physically challenged he'd be overweight.

ANNE   Interesting.

ROBERT   That's a problem kids deal with. They worry about it. They make fun of it. They don't understand.

DR. JILL   Having it be the pig wouldn't work?

ROBERT   You can't have an overweight pig.

ANNE   You really can't.

DR. JILL   Right. Oh yeah. But the physically challenged major character, you didn't like?

ROBERT   It just doesn't feel *Little Duck*.

ANNE   It somehow doesn't.

DR. JILL   I see what you mean, I guess.

ROBERT   We can get the overweight raccoon in the pilot, right, Anne?

ANNE   Really?

ROBERT   I think we should.

ANNE   So much in the pilot is already set.

DR. JILL   I have an idea for how to fit him in.

ANNE   I'll fit him in.

ROBERT   Great. It'll be great.

DR. JILL   Definitely.

ANNE   It will.

ROBERT   You got coconut on your nose.

DR. JILL   Oh thanks.

ANNE   I got gooped.

ROBERT   [*Eating.*] Mm.

DR. JILL   [*Eating.*] Mm.

scene six

[*Words "in quotes" are screamed in a whisper.*]

ANNE   It "fucking sucks," it makes "no fucking sense," the instant he
said it I thought what the "fuck is he talking about," but I acted
like I liked it because I'm a "fucked-up piece of fucking shit."
Anyway, I don't know how you feel about the character, but if you
have concerns too, we could go in to Robert together and—

RJ   I hate the fucking raccoon.

ANNE   Really.

RJ   He never ran the concept by me. He just said we're doing it.

ANNE   Shit.

RJ   I didn't get it. At all. So I had to try like twenty times 'til he found
one he likes.

ANNE   He's settled on a drawing?

RJ   Yeah, the one that sucks the worst.

ANNE   Oh God.

RJ   It's rancid. It's cute. I don't want my name anywhere near it.

ANNE   If you can't make the character good, I don't have a chance. Everything you do is—

[*He puts his hand on her breast.*]

Wow.

[*She holds it there, leans in toward him to hide the hand, looks around.*]

Too bad we don't have private offices like he does, huh? So, did you go to art school?

RJ   Shh. Close your eyes. Imagine this.

[*She closes her eyes as he massages her.*]

You have a friend who's in touch with Darcy. Darcy's always asking him how things are going here. She gets a sense Robert's struggling, so she considers taking the show away from Robert, doing it in-house at the network with your friend taking the lead. He plans to bring Jill along, and you too. So it's the same creative team, but suddenly everything's different. You don't have someone telling you to do stuff that sucks. You can do what comes naturally. What feels right and good, you know it's good and the others know it's good too, and you know they know because of what they're doing with it, you love what they're doing with what you're doing, so you love doing it even more, putting it out there, feeling it good, getting it right and strong and good, every day you can't wait to go in.

[*He stops massaging her.*]

Okay?

ANNE   [*Opening her eyes.*] Okay.

scene seven

HOLLY   You really like *Cumfy Mumfy* better than *Bruno's World*?

DR. JILL   Bruno's too wild and crazy for kids.

HOLLY   He is really wild.

DR. JILL   To do stuff that's titillating or clever for adults, that kids can't even get, it can give them nightmares.

HOLLY   For sure. How do you feel about Robert's idea for the overweight raccoon?

DR. JILL   Well, Holly, I'm disappointed. He'd said he wanted to really do something bold with the show, I had an idea for how to do that, and his response seems like such a tiny step.

HOLLY   But you wouldn't complain outside the company, right?

DR. JILL   What do you mean?

HOLLY   Somebody's been complaining to Darcy about the character.

DR. JILL   You think I did?

HOLLY   Robert thinks maybe it was RJ.

DR. JILL   So you came to ask me about RJ's private conversations? Why would you do that?

HOLLY   Well, you and him, you know.

DR. JILL   No, I don't know.

HOLLY   I guess, I just thought, since he did those drawings for you.

DR. JILL   Robert changed the way the duck walks for you, so don't go making assumptions.

HOLLY   I'm not making assumptions.

[DR. JILL *snaps her fingers and stomps her foot.* HOLLY *gasps.*]

DR. JILL   You should think about what you said to me.

HOLLY   I'm sorry.

DR. JILL   I expected better from you.

[HOLLY *cries.*]

HOLLY   I didn't want to ask you this stuff, Robert made me. I totally respect you, I want to learn from you and work with you and help with your book, you're my total role model, but Robert's putting me in this position and now I got you all angry.

DR. JILL   I'm not angry. Listen. Darcy's interested in RJ's career, so she asks him how things are going and he tells her. That's all.

HOLLY   Okay.
[*Sniffles.*]
Thanks.

scene eight

ROBERT   You're doing great work.

RJ   Thanks.

ROBERT   You take my ideas and run with them really well.

RJ   It's fun.

ROBERT   Oh good. So I was surprised to hear you complained about how things are going to Darcy.

RJ   That was just about the raccoon.

ROBERT   So you did complain.

RJ   About the raccoon.

ROBERT   What did you say?

RJ   I said I didn't get what you were thinking.

ROBERT   You told her that.

RJ   Yeah.

ROBERT   Why didn't you tell me?

RJ   I did.

ROBERT   You didn't. You had questions. But you didn't say you had no idea what I was thinking. Why didn't you tell me before you complained to Darcy?

RJ   There's no point.

ROBERT   No point?

RJ   You always know what you want.

ROBERT   That's right, I know what I want. The show came from me, my gut, so I can see what it needs, so you have to trust me, and if something bothers you, don't tell Darcy, tell me.

RJ   But you just said you won't listen.

ROBERT   I said I will listen.

RJ   "You have to trust me." You just said.

ROBERT   That's right.

RJ   So if I see a problem—

ROBERT   You're a jerk. That's what you are. You're an arrogant little jerk. I spent years building this company, and you come along and try to mess things up. You think I wouldn't have a show without you? Is that what you think?

RJ   Yeah.

ROBERT   You think without you I wouldn't have a show? You really think that? You think that?

RJ   Yeah.

ROBERT   Let me hear you say it. Say it.

RJ   I think—

ROBERT   Let me tell you, I would have a show. It would be exactly the same show.

RJ   You wouldn't have the characters.

ROBERT   I'd have all the characters. They're all mine.

RJ   I made them.

ROBERT   I created them. I named them. I gave them personalities. I described how they look. Without you they'd look a little different and that's all, and let me tell you something else, you think you've done so much, you haven't done crap, those other shows you've worked on are crap, I don't care what the ratings are, everybody knows they're crap. This is your first chance to do something really good, I'm giving you a chance, so don't go shooting off your mouth. Okay?

[RJ *shrugs.*]

What? You'll keep talking to Darcy?

[RJ *shrugs.*]

I didn't want to use this.

[*He takes out a duck puppet.*]

Darcy gave us the duck puppets. I don't think she'd like to hear about the patch of worn-down fur inside yours.

RJ   Who knows about this.

ROBERT   Just the person who discovered it.

RJ   You know. So you discovered it.

ROBERT   Right.

RJ   The worn-down part is way up in the back of the head, the only way you could have found it is if you were using the duck for the same thing I was.

ROBERT   Damn it.

RJ   Do you go around the office at night checking them all out for softness?

ROBERT   [*Looks away.*]

RJ   Are they all wool?

ROBERT   [*Refers to a smaller puppet.*] This one's velvet.

RJ   Nice.

ROBERT   Yeah.

[*They stroke each other's ducks.*]

scene nine

[*They pretend to work on a script, speaking secretively to one another. CAPITALIZED WORDS are spoken loudly to throw observers off-track.*]

ANNE   Did RJ back down?

DR. JILL   He let Robert think he's backing down but he's not. And Darcy's close to making a move.

ANNE   REALLY GOOD NOTE.

DR. JILL   OH THANKS.

ANNE   Wow.

DR. JILL   How do you think RJ would be as a boss?

ANNE   Better than Robert. Why?

DR. JILL   RJ decides things by impulse, what he feels in the moment. I wonder how we'd work with that.

ANNE   Right.

DR. JILL   You and I can always talk things out.

ANNE   We disagree but—

DR. JILL   We always—

ANNE   Talk things out, sure.

DR. JILL   So. What if we tell Darcy we'll only stay on if RJ shares control with us three ways.

ANNE   You and me would be a majority of the three.

DR. JILL   Exactly.

ANNE   What would you want to do about the raccoon?

DR. JILL   Lose it.

ANNE   Great.

DR. JILL   As long as one character, at some point, is physically challenged.

ANNE   Make the call.

DR. JILL   GOOD MEETING.

ANNE   GOOD MEETING.

[*As* DR. JILL *tries to hug* ANNE, ANNE *shoves her away.*]
Shit, shit, sorry.

DR. JILL   We have trust issues.

ANNE   I'm so fucked up, please let me try again, we need to get through this.

DR. JILL   All right, but slowly, okay?

[*They slowly go into a hug.*]

ANNE   [*Gasps when they make contact.*]

DR. JILL   We did it. Okay. You can let go now.

ANNE   You're really tense, Jill.

DR. JILL   Am I?

ANNE   Like a rock.

scene ten

[ROBERT *sits frozen, hyperventilating.*]

HOLLY   So Darcy wants you to show everybody the rough cut of the pilot, get their feedback, get things out in the open, it doesn't mean she's taking the show away from you. They'll love what they see and they'll stop complaining to her.

ROBERT   They're going to hate the pilot. I redid everything they gave me.

HOLLY   Maybe if you just change the one character they don't like—

ROBERT   That would be like replacing my brother.

HOLLY   The rough cut'll be done Friday, so should I schedule a showing for then?

ROBERT   They'd love the pilot if I were dead.

HOLLY   She's holding back the budget 'til we do this.

[ROBERT*'s entire body shakes.*]

ROBERT   Can I see your bare foot?
>   [*She shows him her foot. His shaking subsides.*]
>   Okay, Friday.

scene eleven

[RJ *draws.* HOLLY *walks past, drinking juice from a small carton. They pretend not to see each other.*]

HOLLY Jill and Anne.

> [*Makes hand gesture of gabbing mouth while making two-beat clucking sound with her tongue.*]
> To Darcy.

[RJ *smacks a desk.*]

RJ This shakes things up. On Friday, after we speak truth to shit-head, if things go my way—

HOLLY [*Whispers.*] Oh God.

RJ They're out, you're in.

[HOLLY *squeezes her juice, it squirts.*]

scene twelve

ROBERT How is everybody?

DR. JILL Good.

ANNE Good.

RJ Okay.

ROBERT Everything's going okay?

DR. JILL Sure.

RJ Mm-hmm.

HOLLY Did you want me to cut the cake?

ROBERT Um, maybe after the show. Anyway, listen. To say things about how things are going here, to anybody on the outside, if you can't say them to me, it's really bad form. So, does anybody have anything to say? Now's your chance.

DR. JILL I suppose if I had one comment, it would be that sometimes suggestions aren't given quite as much weight as they might be, so it feels like we might be being humored instead of really being part of a team.

ROBERT   Huh. Anybody else?

ANNE   [*Mumbles softly.*] I guess, yeah, the feeling, sometimes, of being given changes, and feeling like, yeah, like she said.

ROBERT   Hm. Any more?

RJ   You don't listen.

ROBERT   No, I do. I do listen. Right? Anyone? What do you think, Holly?

HOLLY   I think it's an amazing show, and their comments are good because it can always be more amazing, anything can.

ROBERT   Oh. Okay. Well, we don't need to watch this if you people aren't in the mood.

DR. JILL   Oh no, let's watch it.

RJ   Let's see.

ANNE/HOLLY   Sure. Yeah.

ROBERT   Okay, then.

[HOLLY *handles a remote control. They watch. We hear, but don't see, the TV.*]

FROM THE TV   "Hey, Little Duck." "Hey, Little Pig." "Wanna take a walk around the pond?" "Okeydoke!" [*Sweet music plays.*]

[*As the sweet music continues:* ROBERT *stands behind the other four, watches them watching. He picks up the cake knife, brings it to his throat, then his heart. He turns the knife away from himself, towards* RJ.]

[RJ *turns, sees* ROBERT *pointing the knife at him, lunges at* ROBERT. *They fight.* DR. JILL, ANNE, *and* HOLLY *struggle to pull the men apart.*]

[*The knife falls.* HOLLY *pulls* ROBERT *away from* RJ, *holds him back.*]

[DR. JILL *and* ANNE *hold* RJ, *kiss him.* ANNE *pushes* DR. JILL *away from* RJ, DR. JILL *pushes* ANNE, ANNE *and* DR. JILL *struggle and begin making out.*]

[RJ *watches* DR. JILL *and* ANNE *make out, picks up a duck puppet and rubs it against his body*]

[ROBERT *kisses* HOLLY. *She pushes him off and grabs on to* RJ. *As* HOLLY *kisses* RJ, ROBERT *pulls off her shoe and sucks her foot.*]

[RJ *gets free of* HOLLY, *grabs* ROBERT *from behind and humps him.* HOLLY *grabs on to* DR. JILL *and* ANNE, *who try to push her away.*]

"Hey, Little Duck."

[*All stop mauling each other and watch the screen, transfixed.*]

"Hey, Little Raccoon."

[*They give a small laugh, in perfect unison.*]

"I [*Hiccup.*]"

[*They give a bigger laugh.*]

"I think you're great."

[*They sigh.*]

"Wanna dance?" "Okeydoke." [*Music swells.*]

[*They gasp, blown away. As the music finishes, they sit in silence.*]

DR. JILL   Robert, when you took my suggestion for a challenged character and changed it to the raccoon, you were so right. It really does feel exactly like I'd hoped and I'm so proud.

RJ   It really does work in the context. It's like the coolest of all my characters.

ANNE   Oh thanks. Sometimes when you're at the computer a character just starts speaking, it's so amazing when that happens.

ROBERT   You've all done amazing work on my show.

HOLLY   I'm so happy with how Little Duck walks.

RJ   Me too.

DR. JILL   He's a tremendous character.

HOLLY/ANNE/ROBERT/RJ   Thanks.

HOLLY   Robert. I was bad. I guess I started thinking, maybe this wasn't the place for me. So I talked to someone. I was totally wrong.

DR. JILL   Me too.

ANNE   Yeah.

RJ   Sorry about that.

ROBERT   It's okay.

RJ   And sorry about just now, too.

DR. JILL   That was inappropriate.

ANNE   Yeah.

HOLLY   We got carried away.

ROBERT   Big groups get so crazy. I'll try to keep meetings smaller.

RJ   Definitely.

DR. JILL   Yeah.

HOLLY   For sure.

[*Pause.*]

ROBERT   I guess we can have cake now.

DR. JILL/HOLLY   Sounds good. All right.

[*Pause.*]

ANNE   How about a group hug?

ROBERT   Okeydoke.

[*They move together, slowly, embrace.*]

• • •

A Portrait of the Woman as a Young Artist

Meg Miroshnik

Meg Miroshnik

Meg Miroshnik's recent plays include *Bad Money* (March 2009, Perishable Theatre, Providence, RI, directed by Vanessa Gilbert), *Ah, Americans!* (December 2008, Yale School of Drama, directed by Charlotte Brathwaite), and *The Droll* (*Or, a Stage-Play About the END of Theatre*) (November 2009, Yale School of Drama, directed by Devin Brain). She is the recipient of the Dennis Johnston Award for Playwriting and holds a BA in English from Smith College. Miroshnik is currently studying playwriting with Paula Vogel at the Yale School of Drama (MFA expected 2011). *A Portrait of the Woman as a Young Artist* was first developed at the Yale Cabaret in April 2009, directed by Devin Brain and dramaturged by Tanya Dean. The workshop production featured Da'Vine Joy Randolph, Ben Horner, Tomas Andren, and Brett Dalton.

characters

(1 W, 2 M)*

LEDA/ DOCTOR CYGNUS/ WOMAN'S RECORDED VOICE. Tall,
strong, dark skin. A force of nature. Literally.

JOYCE/ MAN'S RECORDED VOICE (via gramophone). A literary
legend. Wears glasses with an eye patch.

MR. JAMES/ MAN'S RECORDED VOICE (via answering machine).
Pale and paranoid.

*Another actor may be necessary to operate puppets and provide the voice for the **SWAN IN
THE REFRIGERATOR**.

text

Slashes // indicate overlapping speech.

• • •

1. Odette

[*Lights up on a single bed, covered in filmy white.*]

[*The sound of a gramophone record: The scratchy, hollow tones of a man, a poet, reading.
The record skips several times.*]

MAN'S RECORDED VOICE   *A Portrait of the Artist as a Young Man:* A girl
stood before him in midstream, alone and still, gazing out to sea.

[*A stirring in the bed.*]

She seemed like one whom magic had changed into the likeness
of a strange and beautiful seabird.

[*A curve emerges in the silky whiteness.*]

Her long slender bare legs were delicate as a crane's and pure save
where an emerald trail of seaweed had fashioned itself as a sign
upon the flesh.

[*The shape becomes defined: The silhouette of a woman.*]

Her thighs, fuller and soft-hued as ivory, were bared almost to the hips, where the white fringes of her drawers were like feathering of soft white down.

[*The woman turns, languidly, sensuously.*]

Her slate-blue skirts were kilted boldly about her waist and dovetailed behind her. Her bosom was as a bird's, soft and slight, slight and soft as the breast of some dark-plumaged dove.

[*The woman turns again.*]

But her long fair hair was girlish: and girlish, and touched with the wonder of mortal beauty, her face.

[*Movement stops suddenly and the shape begins to change: Two peaks arise in the bed.*]

A girl stood before him in midstream.
A girl stood.
Her thighs
Her thighs
Her thighs

[*The peaks grow into outspread wings.*]

[*The record is jostled out of that groove.*]

Her thighs, fuller.
Bared.
Hips.
Her thighs, fuller.
Bared.
Hips.
The white fringes of her drawers were like.
The white fringes of her drawers were like.

[*The wings continue to grow; they are magnificent.*]

Her drawers were like.

[*The curve extends under the silkiness. A bill becomes distinct. The shape is now fully formed: A swan. It continues, improbably, to grow in all directions.*]

A girl stood before him in midstream.
A girl stood.
Her bosom

Her bosom
Her bosom.

[*The record is jostled. The swan rears its head beneath the fabric.*]

Her bosom was.
A bird's.

[*The swan is towering, twice human height. And then a sea change: The lights shift and the swan lets out a howl. The gramophone is slowed down and the sound is distorted—the poet's voice is suddenly deep and apocalyptic. The swan continues howling.*]

A girl stood.
Seabird.
Girlish.
Fair hair.
White fringes.
Featherings.
Soft white down.
Softhued thighs.
Fuller as ivory.
Her bosom.
Bared.
Pure, save.
A SIGN UPON THE FLESH.

[*Black out and silence.*]

2. The Tom Stoppard Play

[*Lights up on a bespectacled* JOYCE *seated next to the bed. His eyes are closed and he holds a manuscript copy of the serialized* A Portrait of the Artist as a Young Man. *Also present is a contraption from the early days of refrigeration technology.*]

[*A gramophone record plays a crackly version of the overture from "Swan Lake."*]

[*A moment of stillness. Then a stirring in the bed.*]

[*A shape emerges in the white silkiness. First, a hand, then an arm, and then a head. It is* LEDA. *She is not a bird, she is a woman. And she is not white.* LEDA *wraps the bedclothes around herself and addresses* JOYCE.]

LEDA   It's not a very good likeness.

JOYCE   [*Eyes still closed.*] Hmmmm?

[LEDA *snatches the manuscript from him.*]

LEDA   [*Opening it to the page in question.*] The likeness, Joyce. You said a
portrait. But it's not very like.

JOYCE   [*Unconcerned.*] Mmmmmm.

[LEDA *steps off the bed. The bedclothes trail behind her like a train as she walks to the
icebox, still holding the open manuscript, and takes out a glass bottle of milk, sniffs it
before drinking.*]

LEDA   I am neither birdish, nor girlish, sir. I've been rendered
unrecognizable.
[*She gulps milk.*]
And I was told you were … talented.

[JOYCE *opens his eyes.*]

JOYCE   You settled for secondhand sources on that subject?

LEDA   You're listening.

JOYCE   You have not formed your own opinion on the merits of my
work? I may have overestimated you, Miss Swansea.

LEDA   Unlikely. You've never seen the likes of me.
[*Shaking the manuscript at him.*]
But my likeness?

JOYCE   Wouldn't you rather pour the milk into a glass?

LEDA   Yes.
[*A long drink of milk.* JOYCE *waits.*]
You have no glasses.

[LEDA *wipes away a milk mustache.*]

JOYCE   Oh, I see.

LEDA   I looked earlier.

JOYCE My apologies. Housekeeping is not my strength.

LEDA [*Looking around the room.*] Worldly concerns are not your strength.

JOYCE Quite.

LEDA Quite.
> [*She laughs. It is at his expense.*]
> You are delicate and pure. Not to be sullied with the marketing and the washing-up. You are soft and slight. Not to be bogged down by the peculiarities and annoyances of the physical world.
> [LEDA *measures out the apartment in footsteps.*]
> You are *softhued as ivory*, Joyce.

JOYCE You're upset.

LEDA I'm confused. *Who* is your creation, Joyce? Who is this *bird*girl? You said a portrait.

JOYCE You are far too single-minded, Miss Swansea. Portraiture, happily, is not as narrow as you.

LEDA I am of average width.
> [*A beat.*]
> Your flat, on the contrary, is quite wide. There's such potential for *large-scale* work in here, Joyce.

[JOYCE *snatches back the manuscript.*]

JOYCE I work in words.

LEDA This expanse of *white walls*. It's a waste.

JOYCE An obsolete form! Visual art is constrained by the physical world, "fastened to a dying animal." That's one of Mr. Yeats's. You do know the great Mr. Yeats, Miss Swansea?

LEDA I'm familiar with his . . . *mythological* work.

JOYCE A girl mastered by the brute blood of the air. "Leda and the Swan." Good poem, that.

LEDA It climaxes with the *rape* of a *woman* by a *bird*.

JOYCE It's an inevitable ending, you see.

LEDA Birdrape—inevitable?

JOYCE Stories with swans always end in a despoiling. Cycle of history— Helen of Troy is conceived in that climactic moment.

[*A change of tack.*]

But my point: Yeats's father was a portrait *painter*, a tattered coat upon a stick, confined to representing the physical world in a clunky, physical medium. For anyone might look at a painted portrait and say, *No, no*, that is not quite the image of this or that piece of *flesh* that lives next door to me. But Yeats himself threw off that tyranny of likeness to create pictures in poetry. Portraits that need not live in a single room in a single museum, but can fly around the world, words light as air. That's progress.

LEDA Progress? You have made a likeness that's nothing like me. That seems to me a failure.

JOYCE A person with some technical abilities might replicate you as you are, Miss Swansea. But an artist. It is the business of an artist to make you more.

LEDA I'm plenty.

[LEDA *puts the empty bottle down heavily.*]

JOYCE But as an artistic expression—

[*Seeing* LEDA *put the empty bottle back into the icebox.*]

Why would you put the empty back?

LEDA You hold your guests to housekeeping standards higher than your own? Your hypocrisy is sharper than your prose, sir.

JOYCE Which is duller still than your wit, Miss Swansea.

LEDA You mean that?

JOYCE Oh, come. You are more keenly aware of your intelligence than anyone, I'm sure.

[LEDA *advances toward him somewhat aggressively.*]

LEDA   Yes, but do you *mean* that?

JOYCE   I'm not sure I understand. I think that it is very common to compliment one's conversational partner—

LEDA   What I meant WAS: You are admitting my superiority? You are granting that you are not my equal? *Your talent is slight, Joyce, and your mind is soft.*

[LEDA *hovers over him in the chair;* JOYCE *leans back, nervous. Maybe she grabs the manuscript back and rips the passage in question out at this point.*]

[*The record comes to a screeching halt: The sound of a swan barking. Lights shift.*]

3. Odile

[*The rush of beating wings. After an initial crescendo of purpose, the sounds settle into an aimless pattern (swans in an aviary with no particular place to go). They are very close, just behind the stage.*]

[*Lights up on the room. The glare should give the impression of a time at least a century later than the previous scene.*]

[A MAN'S RECORDED VOICE. *The sound is still mediated, but less scratchy than before—a voicemail message, not a gramophone record. The* VOICE *is still authoritative, but it is more paranoid than before.*]

MAN'S RECORDED VOICE   A girl stood alone and still I was a sucker midstream. Saw her gazing out to sea this was some ballet-type shit and I had to have her had to master her brute blood in the how would you say the love at first sight delusion. But I swear to God she's not the girl I married or I married the wrong girl or something I don't know you gotta get me out of here I'm not gonna make it.

[VOICE *lower, an urgent whisper-yell of conspiracy.*]

Listen to me: THEY ARE ORGANIZING. I CAN'T TALK NOW, BUT BELIEVE ME, *they are putting on the knowledge with the power and* THEIR PRESENCE WILL SOON BE FELT. DISMISS ME AT YOUR OWN PERIL. THEY WILL *NOT* BE PLACATED.

[*Faster.*]

I don't have much more time. *Pay attention:* A GIRL STOOD ALONE IN MID—

[THE MAN *is interrupted by a rush of wings, this time on the recording, which cuts out with a hiss. A beat of stillness. And then . . .*]

[*Slowly, the icebox door opens. A beat. And suddenly, a giant black wing is visible over the top of the door. A hiss, then the door is slammed shut.*]

[*A beat. The icebox door opens again, faster this time. The empty milk bottle is pushed out. Lights down on the sound of shattering glass.*]

4. TS:2

[*The gramophone record playing the overture to "Swan Lake." Lights up on* LEDA *hovering over* JOYCE *in the chair. The broken milk bottle lies in front of the icebox; neither seems to notice it.*]

[*Behind them, there is now a huge stroke of black paint on the white surface. There are distinguishable feather-marks in the design, as though it had been made by the sweep of a wing dipped in paint.*]

LEDA I SAID: YOUR TALENT IS SLIGHT, *JOYCE*, AND YOUR MIND IS SOFT.

[*A beat.* JOYCE *looks as though he might be sick. And then* LEDA *starts laughing.* JOYCE *laughs, too.* LEDA *curls up onto the bed.*]

JOYCE You are spirited, Miss Swansea. That was a very good joke, equality.

LEDA You were telling me of your artistic expression, Joyce.

JOYCE Indeed. Artistic expression.

[JOYCE *stands, excited. He takes the needle off the record. If* LEDA *has torn out the passage, he tries to salvage it.*]

You must understand: This particular . . . portrait, this . . . passage is of great value. This was a *sublime* moment. Seeing *you* like this. Or rather, as we have established, I did not actually *see* you like this. But this double vision! Seeing you on the beach yesterday, and at once *seeing* you—

LEDA In your mind's eye.

JOYCE In my mind's *eye*. A girl stood—

LEDA I am not a girl.

JOYCE A girl stood before me in midstream, alone and still, gazing out to sea. And she was lovely and captivating and all the things people say about pretty girls. But from a molecular standpoint you could say she was just a girl. A mortal, fallible, fleshy *girl*.

LEDA [*Low, but insistent.*] I am *not* a girl.

JOYCE In my mind's eye, I bent the girl's molecules to my will. I ravished their form completely, I ravaged that particular composition of particles entirely, I negated her being! I destroyed you, Miss Swansea.

And then I set to work to put it all back together. I reconfigured that figure into something new. Something more than a girl. Still a girl, but something more. As if by magic...

[*Reading.*]

A strange and beautiful seabird.

LEDA I am not a bird.

JOYCE But I could *make* you one. Make: To create and to compel. It was overwhelming, the thought of such...

LEDA Godliness.

JOYCE Yes, godliness, exactly. In the sense of *divinity*, not piety, there was nothing lowly or pious about it. Because I realized, in that moment, as I began to recompose you and compose that passage at the same time. I realized that I am the *creator*.

LEDA An artist.

JOYCE I am an *artist*. It was awful. In the sense of awe-inspiring, you understand. But you cannot understand! What a moment this was. This was Wordsworth's "huge peak, black and huge," with its upreared head.

LEDA It seems to me that that moment was rather white and small.

JOYCE   A metaphor, Miss Swansea. For the elation an *artist* must feel at that summit of confidence, that expansion after years and years of constricting self-doubt. You cannot understand.

LEDA   But I think I do.

JOYCE   How is that possible?

LEDA   I have been *constricted* myself.

JOYCE   You have ambitions, Miss Swansea? You hope to become an authoress? Or perhaps a poetess? You would not be alone amongst my female readers.

LEDA   No, *Joyce*, you need not feel threatened. My artistic aims are not literary.

JOYCE   Oh?

LEDA   I'm a painter.

JOYCE   Oh. You wish to be a … *paintrix*. I imagine that your art is, for the most part, representational?

LEDA   [*Looking back at the black paint on the wall.*] My art is *large-scale*. Too large to be contained. That was a … problem in my former habitation, though I have hopes for a new space. My art is large and truthful.

JOYCE   Oh?

[LEDA *rises on the bed, slowly, menacingly.*]

LEDA   I am God, too, *Joyce*. But I am just. I am a *creator* and a *destroyer*, too, *Joyce*. I giveth and I taketh, but I do so *justly*, *Joyce*. My likenesses are like and my destruction is always deserved. I am taking you apart—in *my* mind's eye—right now. I am bending you to my will, I am ravaging and ravishing *you*, *Joyce*, right now. I am recomposing *you* and composing my masterwork, as I speak and there is *nothing you can do about it.* You approached me on the beach, your skirts kilted boldly about your waist, dovetailing behind you, and you called me a girl, with a hope in your white down breast, and you promised me immortality: A portrait. You begged me for inspiration: *long slender bare legs fuller thighs hips bare bosom breast.* You *blanched* me and *bleached* me and made me into a *bird* in words. *Does this look like a birdbody to you, Joyce?*

[LEDA, *facing* JOYCE, *towers over him, her arms outstretched in the white fabric to look like wings. A beat.*]

[JOYCE *takes hold of her and guides her down to sitting on the bed.*]

JOYCE   There, there. I see now. I have wounded your feelings, haven't I? You have gone to such extreme lengths of immodesty and you feel that in my recreation I failed to pay tribute to this display. But I must assure you, Miss Swansea, your beauty has not gone unnoticed. I would not have been able to *create* such sublimity without your *compelling* beauty as counterpoint.

[JOYCE *touches her, gently.*]

But you are quite right. I owe you a compliment, Miss Swansea.

[JOYCE *caresses her as he helps her recline.*]

You are very *fair*, Miss Swansea. You are captivating, you have made me a prisoner to your loveliness, Miss Swansea.

[JOYCE *finds something under the fabric, on* LEDA'S *leg.*]

What is this?

[JOYCE *pulls a large feather out; it comes out with a tug, as though it had been attached to* LEDA'S *skin.*]

LEDA   A sign upon the flesh.

JOYCE   Ah, you see? I will make of you a *bird* yet.

[JOYCE *kisses her.*]

You will be my dove, Miss Swansea. Or perhaps we are closely acquainted enough that I might know your given name?

[LEDA *arches back so that her head is hanging off the bed.*]

LEDA   Leda.

[*She smiles.*]

[*Lights down as the sounds of the aviary filter in.*]

5. The Swan in the Refrigerator

[*Sterile lights up. Again, the icebox door opens slowly. A beat. Flapping inside the appliance. Another beat, and then...*]

THE SWAN IN THE REFRIGERATOR [*A hiss.*] Tssssssssssss.

> [*A beat.*]
> Tssssssssssss.
>
> [MR. JAMES *bolts upright in the bed and looks around for a moment, and then sees it. The thing that we cannot see. In the refrigerator.*]
> Tssssssssssss.

[MR. JAMES *is galled, offended by this hiss. He looks around quickly to make sure no one is looking, then...*]

MR. JAMES Tssssssssssss!

[*A flapping of wings in the refrigerator. And then a bark.*]

THE SWAN IN THE REFRIGERATOR Haarrrrrrrrrrh.

[*This is an even greater affront to* MR. JAMES. *He hops into a crouching position, looks around, leans forward, and then barks.*]

MR. JAMES Haarrrrrrrrrrrrh!

> [*Wings flap in refrigerator.*]
> Haaarh! Haarh! Haarh!

THE SWAN IN THE REFRIGERATOR Haarh! Haarh! Haarh!

> //Tssssssssssssssssssssssssssssssssssssssss.

MR. JAMES //Haarrrrrrrrh! Tssharh! Tssharh!

THE SWAN IN THE REFRIGERATOR //Tsss! HaarrrrrrhTsss. Haarh!

> Haarh! Haarh! Tss!
> Tsssshaarh! Tssshaarh!
> Haarh! Tsss! Haarh! Tsss! Haarh!

MR. JAMES //Haarh! Tssssshaarh. Tsss!

> Tsss! Tsss! Haarh!
> HaarhTsss! Haarhtsss!
> Haarh! Tsss! Haarh! Tsss! Haarh!

MR. JAMES   Tsssssssssssss . . .

> [MR. JAMES *realizes that he is hissing alone and looks around to see if he's been overheard. Beating wings in the refrigerator:* THE SWAN *laughing its ass off.* MR. JAMES *furiously crawls on hands and knees toward the refrigerator.*]
>
> [*Urgent whisper-yell of the voicemail message.*]
>
> Oh, yesssss? You think that's sssssoooo funny?
>
> [*Wings flapping. Yes, the* SWAN *does think that's so funny.*]
>
> Lisssten to me. I'm *on* to you. I saw a *girl* she stood alone midstream I know what I saw some ballet-type shit. Still I was a sssucker midstream had to have her to master her brute blood in the air love at first sssight delusion. I know what *I saw.*
>
> [*Wings flapping in protest.*]
>
> Oh, *no.* NO. I *KNOW* what I saw.

THE SWAN IN THE REFRIGERATOR   [*Admitting the possibility.*] Hmmmph.

MR. JAMES   Lissten: I'm not a complete asssshole I tried to do the right thing by her.

THE SWAN IN THE REFRIGERATOR   Haaa!

MR. JAMES   Maybe not at first at first there was inspiration long slender bare legs fuller thighs hips bare bosom breast the white fringes of her *drawers* were like soft white down *oh, down there,* there was inspiration.

THE SWAN IN THE REFRIGERATOR   Tsssssss.

MR. JAMES   Tsss! But then. Tsss. Then.

> [*Wings flapping in refrigerator.*]
>
> I made it official Tsss! I took her in marriage I reconfigured her as a wife I mastered her legally I was a sucker midstream.

THE SWAN IN THE REFRIGERATOR   Haarh!// Haarh! Haarh!

MR. JAMES   //Haarh! Haarh! They slipped another one in there haarh! thought I wouldn't notice the difference haarh! and truth be told I didn't not until it was too late haarh! haarh! but *then* what I was left with? Stories with harh! always end in *despoiling*.

THE SWAN IN THE REFRIGERATOR   [*A response, annoyed.*] Hmmph-haarh.

MR. JAMES   *I married the wrong one.* Tssssssss! They *made* (compelled) me to marry the one they *made* (created) and here I am stuck midstream with this *haarh* you have no idea and then it's inevitable cycles of history.

[*Wings flap and a few feathers fly up.*]

HAARH YOU LIKE THAT TSSSSSSS? AM I AMUUUUSSSING YOU? TSSSSSSSSS TO HELL.

[MR. JAMES *reaches out and slams the icebox closed. He turns away, sulkily, and starts to crawl back under the bedclothes.*]

[*A beat. The sounds of the aviary grow as loud as they were at the beginning of the scene—still aimless flapping.*]

[*Then, slowly, the icebox door opens a crack. A tube of paint is thrown out, next to the broken glass bottle.* MR. JAMES *snaps around, on the defensive. He looks at the tube of paint and then at the icebox, still open just a crack.*]

Hmmmph?

[*No reply.* MR. JAMES *edges toward the refrigerator, warily.* THE SWAN IN THE REFRIGERATOR *makes a kindly, soft, quavering sound.*]

THE SWAN IN THE REFRIGERATOR   Wooo-oooo-hooo. Wooo-oooo-hoooo.

[MR. JAMES *looks at the icebox, unsure.*]

[*Reassuringly.*]

Woooo-hooo-ooooooo. Hoooo-ooooo-wooooo. Hoo-Hooo. Hoo-Hooo. Woooo-ooo.

[MR. JAMES *reaches out his hand tentatively to pick up the paint tube.* THE SWAN IN THE REFRIGERATOR *urges him on, seductively. The sounds are still animal, though; think a sexed-up version of the tundra swan's flight call.*]

Wooo-hoooo-ooooo. Oooo-oooo-oooo. Ooooo-hoooo. Ooooo-hooooooo. Oooooo.

[*Satisfied that it is safe,* MR. JAMES *picks up the paint tube and inspects it.*]

MR. JAMES What—what is this? Why do I know this?

> [*No response.*]

> Do you—do you . . . use *this*?

THE SWAN IN THE REFRIGERATOR Woooo-hoo-hoo-hoo.

MR. JAMES [*A suspicion he can't name.*] How do you use this?

THE SWAN IN THE REFRIGERATOR Wooo-hoo-hoo-hoo. Ooo-ooo.

MR. JAMES Oh. I had no idea. I never guessed you had these interests . . . well, I guess I mean that I had not guessed you had so . . . *evolved.*

THE SWAN IN THE REFRIGERATOR Wooo-hoo-ooooo. Ooooo-hoooo.

MR. JAMES There's more?

THE SWAN IN THE REFRIGERATOR Ooooo-woooo. Wooo-oooo.

MR. JAMES I don't hear anything.

THE SWAN IN THE REFRIGERATOR Woooo-hooooo-hoooo

MR. JAMES Still nothing.

THE SWAN IN THE REFRIGERATOR Ooooo!

[MR. JAMES *concentrates. Just the general noises of the aviary. Then a sharpening: The sounds of wings flying in lockflap. Disciplined, purposeful, organized flying. Getting louder. Perhaps there could be a snare drum added to this sound. Anything to emphasize the revelation that there is a swan army headed this direction.*]

MR. JAMES No.

THE SWAN IN THE REFRIGERATOR TSSSSSSSSSSSSSSS.

MR. JAMES NO.

THE SWAN IN THE REFRIGERATOR [*Sweet call turned diabolical cackle.*] Wooo-hooo-hooooTSSSSSSSSS.

MR. JAMES NOOOOOOOOOOOOOOOOOOOO!

[*A knock from offstage and a steady* WOMAN'S VOICE.]

WOMAN'S VOICE Mr. James? Mr. James? Is everything all right?

[*The icebox slams shut and the lights shift.*]

6. Mr. Straussler: The Change

[*Lights up on* JOYCE. *He is on his hands and knees, sweeping up the broken glass on the floor.*]

[*Another huge stroke of black paint has been added to the white surface.*]

[*Offstage, a gramophone plays a few seconds of the "Swan Lake" score and then the sound of a rush of beating wings. The two sounds alternate, a second or two of each, the same few bars of music repeated over and over. The effect is grating.*]

JOYCE   LEDA, TURN THAT OFF!

> [*Regaining composure.*]
>
> Darling, my dove, my lovebird? Why don't you join me out here? Keep me company?
>
> [*The record is scratched as it is turned off. Then smashed.* JOYCE *cringes: More to clean up.*]
>
> *Leda.*
>
> [LEDA *enters. She is dressed all in long white; the dress drags on the floor, hiding her feet. The style is conservative, old-fashioned—it is period even in this period.*]
>
> Why did you have to go and smash the record, darling? I don't understand your sudden passion for breaking everything even remotely fragile in the flat. It's just so *unnecessary*.
>
> [LEDA *says nothing.*]
>
> And the . . . stain?
>
> [JOYCE *and* LEDA *both look back at the painted wall.*]
>
> I pretended not to notice its unsightliness earlier, dove, told myself it must be an accident, a sign upon the flesh, but . . . It's growing larger, lovebird, and now it really *cannot be ignored*.
>
> [LEDA *starts tracing the shape, caressing the paint with her hands.*]
>
> And while you've been up to God knows what kind of mischief in the WC, I've spent half the morning trying to tidy the place up. I have to follow around after you to take the paints out of the icebox. The energy this has diverted is . . . shameful. Just when

inspiration for a new work has struck, I'm on my hands and knees like a housemaid.

[LEDA *goes to the icebox and retrieves a bottle of milk, which she drinks as he speaks.*]

Did I tell you my idea for a new work, Leda? Another portrait! Of Helen of Troy. She is buying stockings, but in the background we may see "the broken wall, the burning roof and tower," as Yeats had it. That's from your favorite, darling, "Leda and the Swan." My work will be quite comedic, I expect—death and destruction and the most beautiful woman in the world on a shopping excursion. I will make much of the historical anachronisms, of course.

[LEDA *says nothing.*]

[*Incredulous, interpreting her silence as lack of understanding.*]

Of the stockings? Even you must know that the ancients did not have stockings?

[LEDA *gives him a withering look.*]

Of course, of course. You've just been so ... reticent lately, my strange and beautiful seabird. I don't quite know what to make of you.

[LEDA *drinks more milk.*]

But the stockings! Perhaps Helen will have a flash of her conception as she fingers the silky fabric on display.

[LEDA *puts down the bottle of milk and begins circling the room, arms out.*]

That inevitable ending, her beginning: An entanglement of girl and god, female and fowl. Yeats saw "Her thighs caressed / By the dark webs, her nape caught in his bill, / He holds her helpless breast upon his breast." Oh, Leda! You must promise to be good, I feel my artistic will drain like dishwater with every chore. I must concern myself with Yeats, not washing plates.

[LEDA *knocks the milk bottle on the floor; it shatters. It's possible it could have been an accident? Maybe? JOYCE looks crushed.*]

LEDA! *Not again.* Now you *lissten* to me. This is *it.* There will be no more of *this.*

[LEDA *gives him a pitiable look.*]

Oh, no. Bird, forgive me.

[LEDA *turns away from him.* JOYCE *scurries to clean up the new mess.*]

My Helen! I will mine your knowledge of shopping and stockings and model Helen, the loveliest mortal, after you.

[LEDA *again looks intrigued.*]

Of course, there will be some...factual differences. I think it is generally agreed that Helen's hair was *long* and *fair*, yes, I think that classical scholars believe her to have had long fair hair, so that will be a small difference.

[LEDA *returns to her painted wall, annoyed.*]

And her legs. Her legs are thought to have been long and slender when bare, delicate as a crane's and pure. Your lovely legs will fill out Helen's stockings. Oh, and there is the matter of her fuller thighs, softhued as ivory, classicists are unanimous on the subject of her fuller thighs softhued as ivory. So. But we shall have no complaint with her bosom, which was reputed to have been soft and slight, slight and soft, the breast of some dark-plumaged dove. That is just right.

[*Something occurs to* JOYCE.]

Leda? You have been so terribly quiet. And your dress of late has also been quite demure. There is a charming femininity to it all, of course, but I'm wondering if it might not be better practiced in moderation? Women do show their ankles and quite a bit more in polite society nowadays. And it is very well to share your opinions sparingly, but not speaking at all? For...

[*Not sure how long it's been.*]

...days, perhaps? That seems a bit excessive.

[LEDA *has her back to* JOYCE. JOYCE *approaches her slowly.*]

Darling, is everything all right? You seem somehow...changed.

[JOYCE *reaches a hand out to touch the nape of* LEDA's *neck. She pivots instantly at his touch and snaps at his hand with her mouth. She barks, much like* THE SWAN IN THE REFRIGERATOR.]

LEDA   HAARRRRH!

JOYCE   [*Shaking his hand.*] Sssshit! LEDA! FOR CHRISTSSAKE.

[*He advances toward her.*]

LEDA   Tssssssssssssssssss.

[JOYCE *jumps up on the bed, trying to get away from her.* LEDA *circles the bed, hissing.*]

Tssss. Tssss. Tssss. Tssss.

JOYCE   Leda! For godsake, *lissten* to yourself! What are you doing? Leda!

LEDA   Tsss. Tssss. Tssss.

[JOYCE *looks around for an escape route.*]

JOYCE   Leda, darling! It's me. It's your Joyce.

LEDA   TSSSSSSSSSSSSSSSSSSSSSSSSSSSSS!

[LEDA *lunges at him and* JOYCE *jumps off the bed, headed offstage to the bathroom. He slams the door shut. A beat.*]

JOYCE   [*Reacting to something in the bathroom.*] Oh dear GOD.

[LEDA *relaxes, smiles. She walks to icebox, opens it. Takes out a bottle of milk, sniffs it, then takes a little sip.*]

[*Quietly, muffled gagging.*]

Leda?

[LEDA *lunges toward the bathroom in an exaggerated manner.*]

LEDA   TSSSSSSSSSSSSSSSSS!

[JOYCE *yelps a little in response, as though there were not a door between them.*]

JOYCE   Oh God, no!

[LEDA *smiles, drinks a little more milk.*]

[*Again, gagging.*]

Oh my God, Leda?

[LEDA *laughs, swan-style, to herself.*]

LEDA Hmmp-haarh!

JOYCE [*Gagging.*] Leda, God! Lisssten, YOU GOTTA GET ME OUT
OF HERE OR I'M NOT GONNA MAKE IT.

[JOYCE *starts gagging more violently. The gags gradually begin to sound more and
more like swan barks.*]

LEDA Haarh!

JOYCE Leeeeeeeda. You. Haarh. Have. Haarh. To. Promise. Haarh.
Haarh. Haarh.
[LEDA *takes another drink of milk. She's starting to get bored with this.*]
You. Haarh. Won't. Hmmphmmphmmp. Hurt. Me. Hmmp. If. I.
Haarh. Come. Haarh. Haarh. Haarh. Out. Haarh.

[LEDA *rolls her eyes.*]

LEDA Hmmmp.

JOYCE Promise. Haarh. Meeeeeeee. Leeeeeee-
[LEDA *walks offstage and opens up the door. JOYCE falls out, gasping for
air. JOYCE crawls on after* LEDA, *breathing heavily.*]
Leeeeeeeeda.

LEDA [*Half-heartedly.*] Tssss.

JOYCE You. Promissssed.

LEDA [*Okay, fine.*] Hmmph.

JOYCE [*Catching his breath.*] The. WC. Hmmmph. Leeeda. The. WC.
What?

LEDA Hmmmph.

JOYCE Oh, the sssstink. So many of them. Leeeda.

LEDA Hmmmph.

JOYCE Droppings. Everywhere. The droppings, Leda.

LEDA [*A laugh.*] Haarh-hmmmph!

JOYCE WHAT IS GOING ON HERE? My darling, my *bird*—

LEDA [*Vicious.*] Tsssssssss.

[JOYCE *scrambles to his feet.*]

JOYCE Leda. What is happening? What are you—why are you wearing that dress? Show me your legs, Leda.

LEDA Tsssssssss.

[JOYCE *moves slowly toward her.*]

JOYCE Show me. Your legs. Leda. Your long slender bare. Legs. Delicate as a crane's and pure. Pure, save. Show me your.
[JOYCE *reaches out his hand toward her skirt, slowly.*]
Slender bare. Thighs fuller. Pure, save.

[JOYCE *makes a quick move to snatch the skirt, but* LEDA *jumps out of the way.*]

LEDA Tssssss.

[JOYCE *lunges for her again and catches hold of some fabric.*]

JOYCE SHOW ME. //SHOW ME. SHOW ME YOUR PURE, SAVE FOR.

LEDA //TSSSSSSSSSSSSSSSSSSSSSSSSSSSSSSSSSSSSSSSSSSS.

[JOYCE *manages to pull up her dress around her waist. Her thighs are covered in black feathers and her feet are revealed: Huge, three-toed, webbed.* JOYCE *is stunned.*]

[*Black out on the sound of beating wings.*]

7. A Sudden Blow

[*Sterile lights, aviary sounds.* MR. JAMES *in bed, wrapped up in the sheets in a manner reminiscent of a straitjacket.*]

[*The icebox is closed. Another stroke of black has been added to the wall and the painting is starting to take shape.*]

MR. JAMES NOOOOOOOOOOOOOOOOO.

[*Knocking. A steady* WOMAN'S VOICE.]

WOMAN'S VOICE Mr. James? Mr. James? Are you all right?

[MR. JAMES *listens: Aimless aviary flapping. He looks at the icebox and then looks down at where the paint and glass had been.*]

MR. JAMES [*Not convincingly.*] Quite all right?

WOMAN'S VOICE Mr. James, I'm coming in.

MR. JAMES Oh, no, no need, nurse.

> [*Enter* DOCTOR CYGNUS, *played by the same actress who plays* LEDA. *She wears a white lab coat over her white gown, a white surgical mask, a white hairnet, and surgical goggles. She has been rendered unrecognizable.*]

I'm quite all right, there's no need, nurse—

DOCTOR CYGNUS Doctor.

MR. JAMES Sorry?

DOCTOR CYGNUS I'm a doctor, Mr. James. You know that.

MR. JAMES Oh. I do?

DOCTOR CYGNUS Do you?

MR. JAMES No, yes, yes, I do.

DOCTOR CYGNUS Interesting.

MR. JAMES What? What's going on?

DOCTOR CYGNUS That's what I've come to determine. You were making quite a racket, Mr. James. You woke some of your neighbors.

MR. JAMES Fucking loons.

DOCTOR CYGNUS Why would you talk that way about your neighbors, Mr. James?

MR. JAMES Because they are, everyone in this place is a fucking loon. I gotta get out of here or I'm not gonna make it.

[DOCTOR CYGNUS *inspects the room; she wears white rubber gloves.*]

DOCTOR CYGNUS Why would you say that, Mr. James?

MR. JAMES *They* will see to it, ignore me at your own peril.

DOCTOR CYGNUS Who are *they*, Mr. James?

MR. JAMES   The same ones that set up the marriage, they made sure I married the wrong, one that she was not the one I married—

DOCTOR CYGNUS   I think it's significant that you bring up your wife, Mr. James.

MR. JAMES   You do?

DOCTOR CYGNUS   Don't you?

MR. JAMES   I don't know, I—

DOCTOR CYGNUS   You know why you're here, Mr. James.

MR. JAMES   I saw a girl standing alone midstream and I had to have her had to master her brute blood in the air a love at first sight delusion.

DOCTOR CYGNUS   Yes, that's right. You were sexually attracted to her, Mr. James.

MR. JAMES   She was one species during the day, something else entirely at night.

DOCTOR CYGNUS   You are describing a Madonna/Whore Complex.

MR. JAMES   No no no, she was another *species*.

DOCTOR CYGNUS   It's not uncommon, Mr. James, for people to change significantly over the course of long-term relationships.

MR. JAMES   She was what would you say rendered *unrecognizable*.

DOCTOR CYGNUS   These physical changes, Mr. James? Did they decrease your sexual desire for your wife?

MR. JAMES   Pay attention please: *she was not my wife*.

DOCTOR CYGNUS   I'm disappointed in you, Mr. James. You are negating the progress we've made.

MR. JAMES   It's *them*, not me. *They* put me in here, *they* pulled the rug out from under me—

DOCTOR CYGNUS   Mr. James, that is a fictional story. A very famous one, in fact.

MR. JAMES   I saw a girl standing alone midstream, it was some ballet-type shit—

DOCTOR CYGNUS   Very good, Mr. James. It's a ballet, isn't it?! A girl stood alone midstream, girl by night, but by day...

MR. JAMES   What?

DOCTOR CYGNUS   You know this, Mr. James.

MR. JAMES   I do.

DOCTOR CYGNUS   By day, a swan.

MR. JAMES   [*Excitement in the recognition.*] Yeah. Yeah, that's it, that's right.

DOCTOR CYGNUS   That's "Swan Lake," Mr. James, you know that. You experienced what clinicians call the delusion of love at first sight and hastily arranged a wedding. But it turned out that a sorcerer bent on destroying you had sent a doppelgänger.

MR. JAMES   [*This is valuable intel.*] A sorcerer?

DOCTOR CYGNUS   His daughter. Odile to your Odette. A black swan to your white. He slipped in his black swan for your white swan bride. The marriage rites were performed before you noticed the difference in hue. And it all ends in a dramatic drowning.

MR. JAMES   That's it, exactly.

DOCTOR CYGNUS   Mr. James, *you know why* you're projecting the story of "Swan Lake" onto your marriage.

MR. JAMES   I do?

DOCTOR CYGNUS   Yes, you do, Mr. James. You are trying to excuse your own actions, rationalize the... incident with the excuse that you *didn't really know your own wife.*

MR. JAMES   *Lissten to me*, I'm telling you, she was another species.

[DOCTOR CYGNUS *approaches the bed.*]

DOCTOR CYGNUS   Listen to *yourself*, Mr. James. She was another species? Think rationally, Mr. James. How would that work? How would you imagine that you might engage in sexual intercourse,

Mr. James, with a . . . bird? Anatomically, how would a man and a bird copulate?

MR. JAMES [*A little flustered.*] I, uh—

[DOCTOR CYGNUS *leans over the bed.*]

DOCTOR CYGNUS Do you think about that a lot, Mr. James?

MR. JAMES I think—

DOCTOR CYGNUS Does that image cause you to become aroused? Do you frequently masturbate to that thought, Mr. James?

MR. JAMES I think—

[DOCTOR CYGNUS *leans in closer.* MR. JAMES *squirms a little.*]

DOCTOR CYGNUS Do you think of long slender bare legs, delicate as a crane's and pure, white fringed drawers like soft white down, and a bosom soft and slight, slight and soft as the breast of a dark-plumaged dove, is that what stimulates you sexually, Mr. James?

MR. JAMES Could I have a glass of water?

DOCTOR CYGNUS Yes, of course, Mr. James.

[DOCTOR CYGNUS *has gone to the icebox and is about to open it.*]

MR. JAMES No, don't do that!

DOCTOR CYGNUS You asked for a glass of water, Mr. James.

MR. JAMES Don't. Open. That.

DOCTOR CYGNUS Why do you say that, Mr. James? What will I find inside it?

MR. JAMES There's a [*Something inaudible.*]

DOCTOR CYGNUS I'm sorry, what was that last part, Mr. James?

MR. JAMES There's *one of them* inside.

DOCTOR CYGNUS You think that there is a *swan* hiding inside the antique icebox, which—against the better judgment of the staff and the state—you were allowed to bring into the facility *yourself*?

MR. JAMES   I saw...

DOCTOR CYGNUS   What do you think you saw, Mr. James?

MR. JAMES   I—I don't know.

DOCTOR CYGNUS   Well, let's have a look, why don't we?

> [MR. JAMES *braces himself as* DOCTOR CYGNUS *opens up the icebox. A beat. Nothing at all.*]
>
> You see there, Mr. James? Nothing to be afraid of, is there? What do we have here? How about a cold glass of milk?
>
> [DOCTOR CYGNUS *takes out a bottle of milk, looks around.*]
>
> Where is your little plastic cup? Where is it, Mr. James?

MR. JAMES   I—I don't know.

DOCTOR CYGNUS   All right, I'll let you have the milk in the bottle if you promise to be very, very good. The staff refuses to clean up after you anymore, Mr. James. Do you promise? To be very, very good?

MR. JAMES   Uh-huh.

[DOCTOR CYGNUS *returns downstage bedside.* MR. JAMES *wriggles a little in his straitjacket sheets.* DOCTOR CYGNUS *responds by lifting the bottle to his lips. Throughout, she helps him drink, occasionally wiping a dribble of milk from his face.*]

DOCTOR CYGNUS   Now, isn't this nice? Don't you enjoy this, Mr. James?

> [MR. JAMES *nods as he swallows milk.*]
>
> We could spend all our time together like this, Mr. James, wouldn't you like that? It's so simple, Mr. James. All you have to do is own up to your actions. All you would have to do is recount the incident, Mr. James.

MR. JAMES   The incident.

DOCTOR CYGNUS   You woke up that morning and saw your wife, standing alone midstream, and, for the first time, Mr. James, you really *saw* her. And her skin appeared to be covered in paint, you noticed for the first time that her skin appeared to be covered in a layer of paint.

MR. JAMES Tubes and tubes of black paint.

DOCTOR CYGNUS That's right, Mr. James. So you tried to wash it off, didn't you?

[*A subtle shift in the sounds—the aviary becoming more ordered. It's barely perceptible.*]

MR. JAMES I did?

DOCTOR CYGNUS You did. You tried to scrub the black paint from her skin. You washed her off in the water standing together midstream, you held her down, trying to blanch and bleach her, but it wouldn't come off, would it, Mr. James?

MR. JAMES No.

DOCTOR CYGNUS Oh, yes. You held her under Swan Lake ten minutes too long, Mr. James.

MR. JAMES No, Lisssten!

DOCTOR CYGNUS I think you need to listen, Mr. James.

MR. JAMES Lissten to *them*.

[*A beat. Wings are a bit more organized.*]

DOCTOR CYGNUS Oh, that? That's our aviary, Mr. James, you know that. You've always found it very soothing.

MR. JAMES No, it's not the aviary, you gotta believe me, the aviary keeps them locked up, they fly around without purpose, they have no plans, I am safe from them when they are in the aviary. This is *different*.

[*The wings are flying in lockflap; maybe the drums start to come in.*]

DOCTOR CYGNUS [*A shift, icy.*] Oh, yes, *Mr. James*? They have a plan? And what would you say *their* plan is?

MR. JAMES [*Urgent whisper-yell.*] They've militarized—it's—it's an army or I guess an air force. They are organizing, believe me, *they are putting on the knowledge with the power and* THEIR PRESENCE WILL SOON BE FELT.

[*The wings grow louder.*]

DOCTOR CYGNUS And where do you think *they*, this militarized presence, are heading?

MR. JAMES They'll come for me first, but after that? Oh, God, you gotta get me out of here or I'm not gonna make it.

[*The wings are very, very close.*]

DOCTOR CYGNUS *They will not be placated, Mr. James.*

MR. JAMES No, no, they won't!

DOCTOR CYGNUS THEY ARE PUTTING ON THE KNOWLEDGE WITH THE POWER and after that? Oh, *GOD.*

[DOCTOR CYGNUS *lets out a sweet swan call cackle that sounds exactly like* THE SWAN IN THE REFRIGERATOR.]

Wooooo-hooooo-ooooooo.

MR. JAMES What did you say your name was, nurse?

DOCTOR CYGNUS DOCTOR.

MR. JAMES Sorry?

DOCTOR CYGNUS I'M A DOCTOR, *Mr. James*, YOU KNOW THAT.

MR. JAMES Oh. I do?

[*Back to the audience,* DOCTOR CYGNUS *removes her mask and goggles, so that* MR. JAMES *can see her face.*]

DOCTOR CYGNUS I'm Doctor Cygnus, James. You remember me.

MR. JAMES Oh, God, I DO.

[*Wings/drums grow deafeningly loud.* DOCTOR CYGNUS *puts a hand over* MR. JAMES's *mouth as he starts to yell out* ("NOOOOOO" *as in the beginning of the scene). They struggle. He knocks the bottle of milk out of her hand as the icebox door blows open. Feathers stream out of the icebox. The room shakes, the icebox and bed move, the walls are crumbling. The wings' bass grows louder.*]

[*Just as it seems that the center cannot hold, a white curtain falls over the scene and the sound cuts out abruptly.*]

8. The Swan Air Force Off-duty

[*USO night for the swans. Lights up on the white curtain. Behind it, we can see the silhouettes of a swan audience, off-duty swan soldiers. They drink beers and some of them still carry their weapons. There is grunting and barking throughout and the occasional fight breaks out amongst them. A black-and-white film is projected on the screen: "Swan Lake." The music is somewhat distorted, like the sound at a drive-in movie theater.*]

[*On the screen, Prince Siegfried enters. The hum of audience noise, no one is paying attention. But then the swan maidens enter. There is catcalling (Wooo-hooo) and honking and wing nudging. Odette gets a huge response. Perhaps some of the swans hum along with the score?*]

[*The projector cuts out. There is much hissing (Tssssssss!) and a few swans throw beer bottles at the curtain. And then the movie starts up again and there is a chorus of honking appreciation.*]

[*Downstage of the curtain, MR. JAMES peeks out. He looks like he has been through hell: clothes shredded, bloody scratches everywhere. He jumps back at the sight of the swans, but then, seeing that they cannot see him, he edges out further. The movie ends and a* SWAN ANNOUNCER *comes over the loudspeaker.*]

SWAN ANNOUNCER Haarh haarh haarh hmmph hmmph haarh haarh hmmph. Hmmph Hmmph . . . Leeeeeeeeeda!

[*Crazy honking from the crowd. LEDA enters. We can see in shadow that she is largely swan now, though she may still wear some part of her dress from earlier. She waves a wing to the swan audience and they go mad.*]

LEDA Wooo-hooo-ooooo. Hooo-ooo-hooo woo-hoo woo-hooo.

> [*LEDA gives a speech in trilling but serious tones; the swan audience is rapt. As she speaks, MR. JAMES is drawn closer to her shadow on the curtain until he is finally compelled to reach up and touch a wing. When he does so, the lights shift so that it is clear that the swan audience can now see him. LEDA barks orders to them.*]
>
> Haarh haarh haarh . . . Haarh!

[*The swan audience scrambles into formation, throwing away their beers, grabbing their weapons, etc. LEDA has turned to face MR. JAMES. He is frozen. The audience, now a disciplined army, starts to mobilize and the drums start in. Weapons are pointed at the screen.* MR. JAMES *lets out a small cry.*]

[*Lights down.*]

9. Tomáš: The Feathered Glory, Loosening Thighs

[*White curtain up.*]

[*The bed is askew and the icebox lies flat on its back, door open.*]

[*The light has a new quality: For the first time in the play, we see natural light. The white walls have crumbled and have been replaced by an expanse of sky. The painted portrait remains, however, and it has been completed: A giant black swan on a backdrop of sky.*]

[*The bedclothes are rustled by the breeze. A beat.*]

[*A sound inside the icebox.* JOYCE *emerges from it. His glasses are missing one lens. He clutches something tightly in his fists as he scampers out of the box.*]

[*He crawls over to the bed, nestles in some of the fabric, and looks around quickly before revealing his treat: A tube of open paint.* JOYCE *begins greedily eating the paint. There is a thud offstage.* JOYCE *jumps in response, hiding the paint. He waits a beat. Nothing.* JOYCE *returns to eating the paint.*]

[*He talks to himself as he eats.*]

JOYCE   Helen Helen Helen Helen Helen, I said. Helen Helen Helen Helen. Silky fabric fingering terrified vague fingers push Helen which pair shall you purchase? Flash of conception, terrified vague fingers push the the the *feathered glory.*

[JOYCE *looks back at the portrait.*]

THE FEATHERED GLORY THE FEATHERED GLORY THE FEATHERED GLORY. After that? Oh, *GOD.*

[JOYCE *turns away from the portrait, rocking himself for comfort. A happy place.*]

Oh, your drawers, Helen, the white fringes of your drawers featherings of soft white down. Your drawers your drawers your drawers, Helen. *I will save the lingerie counter,* the broken wall, the burning roof and tower, do not worry, Helen, I am the *salvation* of your drawers Helen Helen Helen Helen Helen. I was *God.*

[*Buoyed by this thought,* JOYCE *makes an attempt at the old language.*]

Just think, Miss Swansea, of the . . . *sub-lime.* The *sub-lime.*

[*Excited, maybe he's on to something.*]

Yes, Miss Swansea, the less than lime, the citrus of sinners, the preoccupation of . . . [*What?*] Yeats and gates and and hates and mates and and. I, I. *Helen.*

[JOYCE *gives up on this intellectual pursuit and crawls back over to the icebox. He throws out a few empty tubes of paint, and then finds one that seems to have a small amount left in it. He squeezes paint desperately onto his tongue.*]

Droppings! The housekeeping, Miss Swansea. The housekeeping.

[JOYCE *sees the gramophone, inspects it warily. He places the needle on the record.* The MAN'S RECORDED VOICE *(from the voicemail in scene 3) recording comes from the gramophone.*]

MAN'S RECORDED VOICE   *Listen to me:* THEY ARE ORGANIZING. I CAN'T TALK NOW, BUT BELIEVE ME, *they are putting on the knowledge with the power and* THEIR PRESENCE WILL SOON BE FELT. DISMISS ME AT YOUR OWN PERIL. THEY WILL *NOT* BE PLACATED. I don't have much more time. *Pay attention:* A GIRL STOOD ALONE IN MID—

[*As he hears a sound offstage right,* JOYCE *takes the needle off the record. He waits as the noise comes into focus: The Swan Air Force, moving quickly. He thinks. Curls up into the icebox and shuts the lid. A beat. Then he opens the lid, having reconsidered, and scurries off toward stage left.*]

[*A sound offstage left.* JOYCE *perks up and again waits as it comes into focus. The Swan Air Force, of course.* JOYCE *runs back toward stage right. He thinks for a moment, shrugs a what-the-hell, then jumps back into the icebox and closes the door.*]

[*The sound of the Swan Air Force surrounds the stage. They are now holding their flight pattern, just offstage.*]

[*A commanding bark and* LEDA *enters. She is magnificent. Her feathers are an iridescent black and they are everywhere. She has a shockingly orange bill that may move, or not, when she speaks.*]

[*She walks around the stage, lifting her webbed feet high. As she nears the edge of the stage, she turns her long, curved neck back to look at the icebox; the rest of her body remains motionless. She walks slowly back to the icebox, looks at it a moment, then opens it suddenly with her bill. She laughs at* JOYCE.]

LEDA   Hoooo-hooo-hooo!

> [JOYCE *scrambles out of the icebox, trying to use the door as a shield from* LEDA. *She laughs at him again.*]

> Hooooo-hooo-hoooo!

JOYCE   *Pleeease.*

LEDA   Hoooo-hooo-hooo!

JOYCE   *Pleeease, Misss Ssswaan—*

LEDA   Tsssssssss!

JOYCE   Leeeeeeee-da. Pleeease.

[LEDA *reaches out for him with a wing. He cowers, expecting a blow. Instead she touches him gently. He lets out a cry—a whimper of orgasm. She laughs.*]

LEDA   Hoooo-hoooo-hooooo.

JOYCE   Leeeeee-da. Helen! Helen! The portrait!

LEDA   Tsssssssssssss!

JOYCE   I'm—I'm sorry if the portrait . . . displeased you if you were not pleased by the likeness if you didn't like I'm s-s-sorry if—

> [LEDA *makes a dismissive noise. She looks at her own portrait, mirroring its pose.* JOYCE *is terrified.*]

> The the the feathering of no the white fringes of no the the the FEATHERED GLORY, THE FEATHERED GLORY, after that? Oh, *God.*

[LEDA *silences the waiting forces, still mirroring the portrait. She makes soft, quavering swan noises throughout (the* WOMAN'S RECORDED VOICE *provides the English translation for these sounds).*]

LEDA Woooo-hooo. Hooo-hooo.

[*Offstage, the* WOMAN'S RECORDED VOICE *begins. It is a gramophone record played through a loudspeaker.*]

WOMAN'S RECORDED VOICE A sudden blow.
> A sudden blow.
> A sudden blow.

JOYCE Is that ... *Yeats*, Leda?

[LEDA *turns to* JOYCE. *There is a burst of bass from the swan troops, then nothing.*]

WOMAN'S RECORDED VOICE The great wings beating still.

> [LEDA *begins to raise her wings very slowly.*]

> Above the staggering child.
> His thighs
> His thighs
> His thighs
> His thighs

JOYCE [*Overlapping with the repeating record.*] That's Yeats, but Leda. It's *her thighs*. Yeats had *her thighs*.

[*The record is jostled out of that groove.* LEDA's *wings are outspread. She is enormous.*]

WOMAN'S RECORDED VOICE Caressed by the by the dark webs.

> His nape
> His nape
> His *nape*

JOYCE But that's *her nape*—

[*The record is jostled out of that groove.*]

WOMAN'S RECORDED VOICE Caught in her bill.

JOYCE And *his bill*—

LEDA [*Slowly starts beating her wings. Her webbed feet leave the floor half an inch.*]

> She holds his helpless breast.
> His helpless breast
> His helpless breast

[*She ascends a few inches from the floor.* JOYCE *cries out.*]

JOYCE   The inevitable end to stories with harh!

WOMAN'S RECORDED VOICE   She holds his helpless breast.
Upon her breast.
How can those terrified vague fingers.

[JOYCE *begins to recall something.*]

WOMAN'S RECORDED VOICE   //Those terrified vague fingers.

JOYCE   //Those terrified vague fingers.

WOMAN'S RECORDED VOICE   How can those terrified vague fingers
push
The *feathered glory* from his loosening thighs?
And how can body, laid in that white rush,
But feel the strange heart beating where it lies?
[LEDA *rises higher in the air; her wings beat faster.*]
Terrified vague fingers.
The feathered glory.
His loosening thighs.
The feathered glory.
A shudder in the loins.
Engenders there.

JOYCE   The broken wall, the burning roof and tower!

WOMAN'S RECORDED VOICE   And Agamemnon dead.

[LEDA *moves higher, wings beat faster.*]

WOMAN'S RECORDED VOICE   Being so caught up.
So *mastered* by the brute blood of the air
Did he put on *her* knowledge with *her* power
Before the indifferent beak could let him drop?

[LEDA *is now very high off the ground.* JOYCE *knows exactly what will happen to him. She continues to make swan noises under the record.*]

JOYCE   The inevitable harh! To stories with harh! The harh!
despoilment harh! harh! harh!

WOMAN'S RECORDED VOICE   Terrified vague fingers.

His helpless breast.

His loosening thighs.

His body laid in white rush.

He engenders

He engenders

He engenders

He engenders

He engenders

[*The record is jostled out of that groove and there is a sky change: It is suddenly overcast and the record speeds up. The* WOMAN'S RECORDED VOICE *becomes distorted, a harbinger of destruction. The Swan Air Force begins flapping.* LEDA *inhales a breath that pushes her up an inch higher, then dives down toward* JOYCE.]

WOMAN'S RECORDED VOICE   A sudden blow.

The great wings beating still.

Her dark webs.

Her bright bill.

The feathered glory.

Her portrait.

Her portrait.

Her portrait.

Her portrait.

[*Lights down just as* LEDA *swoops down on* JOYCE, *covering him in her great wings.*]

• • •

Slapped Actress

Emily Conbere

Emily Conbere

Emily Conbere is a playwright, lyricist, and composer. She has held playwriting residencies with East River Commedia, Mabou Mines Theater, and ALT Opera. Emily has had opera productions at the Kansas City Art Institute, Symphony Space, and PS 122 in New York. Her plays and musicals have been produced at PS 122, Ensemble Studio Theater, Southern Theater (MN), Collective Unconscious, and Williamstown Summer Theater. Emily's play *The Scholar* was presented at the State Theater of Bielefeld in Germany as part of the Voices from Underground Zero Festival. *The Scholar* was translated into German and published with S. Fischer Verlag in 2008. Emily's one-woman show *Broken Dog Legs* is currently being translated into German as well. Emily was a finalist for the Bay Area Playwrights Festival 2008 and for the Creative Capital Grant 2009. She was recently commissioned a Sloan grant and has been awarded a MacDowell Colony fellowship. She has an MFA in playwriting from Columbia University and teaches playwriting at ACT in Seattle.

• • •

[*Onstage, there is a single spotlight on the* EVANGELICAL THEATER CREEP (ETC). *Somewhere off and above the stage lives the* WOMAN IN THE WINDOW.]

ETC   One ticket, one hundred dollar. One ticket, one hundred dollar. Or get our special half-price ticket to this Broadway show for only two hundred dollar. One ticket, half price—two hundred dollar. Two hundred dollar to dance yourself down the Great White Way.

[LITTLE GIRL *comes onstage, dragging an old typewriter on a leash.*]

LITTLE GIRL   But I only have one sixpence, sir. And my little cat. Only one small coin and a little pet to get me through the rest of my life. Does that mean I have no access to theater?

ETC   That means you only have access to theater if you make it yourself. Two tickets for the price of one—three hundred dollar. Two tickets, price of one—three hundred dollar.

[*He keeps ranting while* LITTLE GIRL *cuddles with typewriter.*]

LITTLE GIRL   Come here, pet-pet. You love me, don't you? This little pet-pet is the only thing that loves me in the whole wide world.

[*The typewriter curls up on her lap.*]

ETC   Two tickets, price one, three hundred. Two tickets, price one, three—

WOMAN IN WINDOW   It's given me nothing! Why, you no good, good for nothing, nothing doing, do-gooders! All I do is hear you . . .
[*Deep crotchety intake of breath.*]
. . . all night long, yelling and carrying on with your lies, lies! Making up stories to suit yourselves! The world is the way it is and it is going to remain that way, so why do you have to go on there, go on and keep making the world different than the way it is, this beautiful—
[*Deep, crotchety intake of breath, then a dark cough.*]
beautiful world! Why do you keep pretending! Constantly. You liars! And it keeps me awake at night! Your view on reality keeps

me awake at night. This light in my window, always burning. And now I'm getting on to my later adult years, where I's can barely see and I's can barely walk and I's can barely breathe and you tell me you want me to come downstairs...

[*Sharp, loud, crotchety intake of breath.*]

...come downstairs!—when I can barely walk—and join your petty little theater company, you lowlife misdemeanors, keep me awake all night long.

LITTLE GIRL Why is she so angry, pet-pet?

ETC She used to be the star of the theater, and then one night, in all her glory, someone slapped her.

LITTLE GIRL Oh...well, sometimes actresses get slapped.

WOMAN IN WINDOW No, they don't! No, they do not! It is supposed to be pretend! Theater is supposed to be pretend, you stupid lying people! I hate you! You ruined me! You ruined my life!

[*She turns off the light in her window.* THE EVANGELICAL THEATER CREEP *begins again.*]

ETC My friends, what the woman says is true! We are all liars, here! Liars! And doesn't it feel goddamned good to say whatever the hell you want to say—

LITTLE GIRL But we don't get to say whatever we want to say, do we? We have to say what the playwright wants us to say?

ETC And do you want that power, little girl? CAN YOU HANDLE the power of the playwright—the all mightiful, usually merciful god, that godforsaken playwright—the power of the playwright is that who makes old men cry (onstage), that who makes young men act like grown-up women impersonating terrible children, that who turns people into asses and asses into candy—CAN YOU HANDLE the kind of responsibility where you turn asses into candy?

LITTLE GIRL What kind of candy?

ETC What kind of ass candy you create depends upon the play.

LITTLE GIRL   I think so, sir. I think I could handle that kind of responsibility. Why, my mother, God bless her soul, taught me well.

ETC   Then you, *you* shall be the god of the playwrights! When will you give me your play so that we can get on with things, now—

LITTLE GIRL   Why, I have one with me, sir!

ETC   Let me see it.

LITTLE GIRL   Here.

[*She takes the piece of paper out of the typewriter.*]

ETC   But this is only one sheet of paper.

LITTLE GIRL   But it is a play.

ETC   But it is a short play, then?

LITTLE GIRL   No. Why don't you read it.

ETC   If it is only one page, it is going to be a short play.

LITTLE GIRL   Why don't you quit being so judgmental about the play and just read it for what it is. What did you say your job was?

ETC   I'm a director.

LITTLE GIRL   Yeah. See.

ETC   Alright, I'll read it, oh, powerful playwright. But then you need to keep recruiting. You need to keep convincing them to come to the theater. Can you do that?

LITTLE GIRL   Sure.

[ETC *sits down and starts reading the play.*]

[LITTLE GIRL *speaks calmly and rationally to audience. She is sweet and little and everyone loves her. She should be very endearing and speak in a little girl voice.*]

LITTLE GIRL   Please come see my play. You see. I have very little. My mother is gone, may she rest in peace, and my father left me long ago, as fathers do, don't they, most of the time. I just want a little bit of attention. I am a very shy person and it is really hard for me to make friends because of that. The only time I really feel worthwhile or of any value is when a cast joins me on my play, when a director believes in my play, when a patron pays for my play and when an audience partakes in my play. It is the only time I feel like there is a reason for me to exist on this planet. If it weren't for my plays, I would believe myself to be utter trash and not worth anyone's time of day and I probably would be dead right now. So will you please come? Because in all actuality, I am a very loving person and I can write a real good play, I swear I can—won't you just believe in me? Won't you just believe in me for one second?

[*The light in the window turns on.*]

WOMAN IN THE WINDOW   Do you mean what you say, little child?

LITTLE GIRL   I mean what I say with all my heart, as liars always do.

ETC   This is amazing. Absolute truth. What I have in my hands here is absolute truth! Don't you want to be a part of it?! Don't you want to BE A PART OF THIS?! ABSOLUTE TRUTH! IT IS PAGES LIKE THIS—PAGES LIKE THIS THAT SAY THEATER WILL NOT DIE! THEATER WILL NOT DIE!

[PIA #1, *a person in the audience, stands up*]

PIA #1   I'd like to be part of the motherfucking play.

LITTLE GIRL   Oh boy!

ETC   Did ya hear that? That man wants to join the theater! He's on our side!

LITTLE GIRL   You're on our side now! You dear, dear man! You're on our side! Oh, did you hear him? He said he wants to be part of the motherfucking play!

WOMAN IN THE WINDOW   I'm coming down. As long as I don't get slapped.

LITTLE GIRL   She's coming down! Did you hear that?! I promise! I promise you won't get slapped!

ETC   Amazing! She's coming down! The star of theater is returning! Oh, glorious Great White Way—your goddess is coming home!

WOMAN IN THE WINDOW   Someone help me with my cane...

ETC   And that audience member! What an amazing man! You will not regret it, sir! Come on up here! Come on up here and be part of the motherfucking play!

PIA # 2   Why, I think I'd like to join the theater, too!

LITTLE GIRL   Do you mean it?

PIA #2   Why, I think I do! I *do* mean it! I'd like to join your crappy little theater!

LITTLE GIRL   Because what you will find here is the absolute truth! We might not have money, we might not have glory, but we have truth!

ETC   As liars always do—

PIA # 2   [*Stands, maybe even goes onto stage.*] That's always what I wanted!

LITTLE GIRL   Don't you see! It's us against them! It is US AGAINST THEM! There are people who believe! There is US! And then there are people who just *accept*! That's them! And I feel sorry for those people! I feel so sorry for the people who just accept! Won't you join us?! Won't you join us, please?!

WOMAN IN WINDOW   [*Making her way to the stage.*] I'm coming, I'm coming! I'm making my way back to the theater!

[*The song "Slapped Actress" might start to play.*]

PIA # 3   [*Stands.*] I'm coming! I'm coming to the theater! It's us against them!

LITTLE GIRL   Don't you see? We are the theater! They are the people!

PIA # 4   We are the theater! They are the people!

LITTLE GIRL   Come one! Come all! Join us! Stars will flip in the theater! Chain saws will orgasm! Faces will explode!

PIA #5 and **#6**   We are the theater! They are the people!

LITTLE GIRL People will fall in love! You'll go on road trips that spin out of control! You'll fuck your brother and you will love it! You'll make up your children! You'll kill a seagull! You'll kill yourselves here and everyone will clap afterwards!

[*More and more people stand and speak—either together or separately—over her monologue.*]

PIAS WE ARE THE THEATER! THEY ARE THE PEOPLE!

[*More and more people come onto the stage or stand up in the audience.*]

LITTLE GIRL Come to the theater! You can be narcissistic and talk in clipped sentences and beat the shit out of people for a nickel! You can be emerging! You can be constantly emerging!

PIA #7 I'm constantly emerging!

[ETC *slaps the old woman in the window amidst the chaos.*]

ALL We are the theater! They are the people! We are the theater! They are the people!

   [*Lights start to go on in the audience. More and more people stand up and join in, saying: WE ARE THE THEATER, THEY ARE THE PEOPLE.*]

[*The chant continues—the whole theater, stage and audience, is lit up . . . everyone is one, we all continue chanting: WE ARE THE THEATER, THEY ARE THE PEOPLE.*]

[*Lights out on everyone.*]

• • •

The Last Artist in New York City

Polly Frost and Ray Sawhill

Polly Frost and Ray Sawhill

Polly Frost and Ray Sawhill are a married couple. They often write on their own, but they also frequently collaborate on projects. Recently they co-wrote and co-produced the sci-fi burlesque Web series *The Fold* with the director Matt Lambert. Frost and Sawhill also co-wrote a satirical-erotic theater project, *Sex Scenes*, which they recently produced as an audiobook—"Detention," an episode from *Sex Scenes*, was just selected for Maxim Jakubowski's *Mammoth Book of Best Erotica 2009*. Frost's humor writing has been published in *The New Yorker*, the *New York Times*, *The Atlantic*, and *Narrative*. Her book *Deep Inside*, a collection of erotic horror monologues originally performed by actors in live performances, was published by Tor in 2007. Sawhill worked as an arts reporter for *Newsweek* and has written articles, reviews, and interviews about music, architecture, books, and films for many different publications.

Frost's Web site: pollyfrost.com. Sawhill's Web site: raysawhill.com.

Dedicated to Karen Grenke, Jason Jacobs, Jake Thomas, and Tim Cusack.

··· production note ···

First performed at PS 122 in Avant Garde Arama, produced by Theatre Askew (co-artistic directors Jason Jacobs and Tim Cusack), with Karen Grenke and Jake Thomas.

note

We intend this play to be specific to the circumstances of its production. Thus, the name of the theater space in which this play will be performed in your production should be substituted for "PS 122"—and the name of the actor who will be performing the main role in your production should be substituted for "Karen Grenke." (Karen acted in the first production of this play, which took place at PS 122.) We are also open to other substitutions for "New York City" and for the suburb "Metuchen" as long as we are consulted and give our agreement prior to performance.

···

scene one
Metuchen Mall

ANNOUNCER VOICE   Ladies and gentlemen, as the last performance at PS 122 before Chase/Wachovia–Whole Foods moves in for your financial and shopping ease, Theatre Askew presents Karen Grenke, "The Last Artist in New York City."

[KAREN *is moving into the theater space with a flashlight. Points it at walls, ceiling, people in the audience, at herself.*]

KAREN   [*To audience.*] Walking through the Metuchen Mall.... By my side, Xavier, my former lover in the Polyamory Art Collective.... You may know them as PAC.... Years ago, Xavier helped me find my current style.... Of course I helped him equally.... Metuchen? you ask. Central Jersey is the answer.... Central Jersey is always the answer.... My old partners had abandoned Williamsburg years ago....

[*Flashlight continues picking out things.*]

[*To audience.*]

Dark corridors . . . dried-up fountains . . . display windows for
Linens Etc. and Williams Sonoma now cracked and jagged. . . .
Sullen kids in tight pants and spikey hair camping out and
smoking. . . . We're inside an abandoned mall, but I'm reminded of
photos I once saw in a book about Astor Place in the '70s. . . .
Xavier is talking.

[*As* XAVIER.]

Why has it taken you so long to visit us in person? The time has
come for you to give up the big city dream. Baby, New York doesn't
care about art any more.

[*To audience.*]

Xavier pushes open a huge door. . . . Rave music up. People
dancing, flashing lights, pulsing electronica . . .

[*To* XAVIER.]

Oh my God, Xavier, this is the greatest scene ever! Retro-Hindu-
Trance, aren't I right?

[*As* XAVIER.]

Welcome to the Big Box, baby!

[*To audience.*]

When the day began I had no idea how momentous it would
prove.

[*Rave music continues for a few seconds, then stops.*]

scene two
Karen on Segway

[*Swirly pink-green light. Earlier that day. Hurrying between jobs.* KAREN *quaffs
Red Bull.*]

KAREN [*To audience.*] Floating through the city on my faithful Segway . . .
Between one job and the next. . . . Five day jobs and I barely get

by.... Bouncing.... Ah, the hallowed cobblestones of SoHo....
Paying tribute.... The greats of the past... Karen Finley, Eric
Bogosian, Spalding Gray... Then through Chelsea.... Once full
of galleries, now play date central for families.... In midtown, the
former sites of Sonnabend, Castelli, Pace Wildenstein.... I nod
silently.... Wavy... blue glass... high-rises... taking over
everywhere.... I hate those fucking things!

[*Ka-boop of iPhone e-mail notification interrupts.* KAREN *tries to keep balance as she pulls out iPhone and calls up e-mail.*]

[*To audience.*]

Stefani Symonds. Dot N-Y-Times? That's right, the *Times*. The
New York fucking *Times*! She wants to do a feature. That's right,
about me, Karen Grenke. "You're the last remaining artist in New
York City. You're a cultural landmark." Omigod, omigod,
omigod.... After all these years... all my sacrifices... my time as a
New York artist has finally come!

[*Twirls around on Segway in joy and—horn honks—almost gets run over.*]

scene three
Karen at Frank Gehry High

[*Hard white light up.* KAREN's *at desk in "teacher" mode—think Spalding Gray in eyeglasses. Takes a big swig of Red Bull.*]

KAREN [*To audience.*] There I was, behind my teacher's desk, at Frank
Gehry High for the Developmentally Gifted on the Upper East
Side. As my student settled in, I crafted a proud e-mail to my
former mates in the Polyamory Art Collective... PAC.... Been
years since I last wrote them. But I felt certain they'd be happy for
me.... The great artistic spirit that this city once had... embodied
now in me and me alone!... I was still buzzed as I began talking
about Warhol's immortal brilliance.

[*As student.*]

Screw immortality. How'd his paintings do at the most recent
auction?

[To audience.]

God, how I hated these new entitled brats! But it was my own fault, I was the one who'd persuaded the principal to let me replace Introductory Art History with Art as Recession Investment Strategy. It was time to steer the conversation in a productive direction.

[To class.]

Hey, I have a fun announcement this morning. The *Times* is doing a feature on me. That's right, me, your very own teacher, Ms. Karen Grenke. You never really believed I was an artist, did you? But now—

[As student.]

What's The *Times*?

[To class.]

You really don't know? It's what we used to call a major news source. It symbolized New York and its great cultural life.

[As student.]

Losing strategy. The underlying mortgage on that new Renzo Piano building is killing them. You should be targeting Collegehumor.com instead.

[To audience.]

Christ! After class, I was unlocking my Segway. I noticed this shy girl from class standing there. You know the type. Gaunt... dreamy... her hair a different color every week.

[As JESS.]

Sorry about my idiot classmates. Screw them. They know nothing about art.

[To JESS.]

Oh. And you do?

[To audience.]

She pulled out her iPhone.... It's a YouTube mashup showing Schnabel, Fischl, and Sherman mouthing the lyrics to "Sheena Is a Punk Rocker."

[*As* JESS.]

I did it by myself. AfterEffects. Flash. Final Cut.

[*To audience.*]

I started to lecture her about giving people you're stealing from credit, then...decided not to go there. Why squash creativity?

scene four
Karen on Segway

[*Lights change back to Segway-swirly.* KAREN *on Segway, a dreamy-pleased state, slurping Red Bull as she steers with one hand.*]

KAREN   [*To audience.*] So there's hope.... New York may have a cultural future after all!...Cruising home...me and my Segway merging as one....Crossing 14th...ah, my beloved East Village...home of the Beats...the punk rock revolution....

[*Takes big swig of Red Bull. It has its effect.*]

But even downtown the bio-morphing blue glass buildings are taking over.

[*Another big swig.*]

Fuckers!

[*iPhone e-mail goes ka-thump.* KAREN *calls it up.*]

[*To audience.*]

Eden, my rival for Xavier in the Polyamory Art Collective... PAC....I know what you're thinking—"rivalry"? Well, if you're polyamorous you know how it goes....All the blah-blah around who's sleeping with who....Ethical sluts talk more than they fuck!...But there was just no getting past our feelings of possessiveness....In the space behind Eden, the other members of PAC writhe in a naked heap....Rehearsal or orgy?

[*As* EDEN.]

Congrats! We'd help you celebrate in person but we never come to NYC any longer. Honey, today's real artists don't even know where Manhattan is.

[*To audience.*]

Once a bitch, always a bitch! Why can't Xavier see that!

[*Swigs Red Bull in fury.*]

scene five
Karen at Her Apartment

[*Swirly lights stop.* KAREN *now sitting on the desk, as though on sofa or bed. Many empty cans of Red Bull in a mess around her.*]

KAREN   [*To audience.*] The real trouble, I was starting to realize—I've been so busy maintaining life in New York that I haven't gotten much art done. None. Zero. Nada. What will I have to show when I meet with Stefani?

[*Takes big swig of Red Bull. Sets empty can down among others. Contemplates arrangement of cans. Rearranges them.*]

[*To self.*]

I was starting to see some real artistic possibilities. . . .

[KAREN *kisses the Red Bull. Fondles it. Runs the can of Red Bull over arms, head, legs, boobs, tummy. Starts to masturbate using the can of Red Bull. In big gesture of heedlessness, she sweeps all the other cans of Red Bull onto the floor. As she's starting to feel the heat—the iPhone makes its e-mail ka-thunk sound.*]

Oh, shit!

[KAREN *calls up e-mail.*]

[*To self.*]

Say it isn't so!

[*To audience.*]

Stefani's been downsized. The underlying mortgage really is causing hell at the *Times*! And worse—the article about me is off! What has my life been about!? I blasted off a woeful mass message to my entire e-mail list. The Collective got back to me instantly. . . .

scene six
Karen on Segway

[*This time we get a nightmare version of swirly pink-green Segway lighting and subjective movement. It's dark and stormy, and* KAREN *is despairing.*]

KAREN   [*To herself and the audience.*] Come join us, they say.... A performance in Metuchen, they say.... It's the old loyalties that help us out in tough times.... I throw on my old art-chick party clothes.... The first time in years.... The Segway and I are off!... Dodging potholes.... Steering around young families with their damn baby strollers.... Blind with emotion, we fly—fly!— through the rain.... Screw you, New York City.... Screw your SUVs... your endless bank branches.... I hate tourist-safe neighborhoods!... Screw your K-Marts... your Barnes and Nobles... your family-friendly Disney musicals.... I hate branding!... Trader Joe's I'll make an exception for.... Excellent prices on wine... and like that—

[*Lights go to black. Big whoosh sound.*]

[*To audience.*]

I was in the tunnel on my way to central Jersey.

scene seven
Metuchen Mall

[*Flashlight in* KAREN's *hand, as in opening scene. Sounds of flogging and moaning.* KAREN *stares offstage, takes big swig of Red Bull.*]

KAREN   [*To audience.*] In a room to one side of the dance space Xavier is laying into Eden.... When I was living with the Collective, flogging and suspensions weren't our thing. But ever since Kink.com took all those awards for BDSM porn everyone has been into it.... Ouch!... Still—oh, Christ, look at that.... So gruesome.... It really is beautiful.... Shit, that was a motherfucker of an orgasm!... I have to say that PAC is doing their best work ever.... Hanging exhausted from the rack, Eden is transformed into an icon of desire.... No! No! I can't keep watching.... Artistic jealousy.... Sexual jealousy.... It's a lethal combination!...

[*Rave lighting and music up as* KAREN *switches off flashlight and staggers back to desk. Starts to climb stairs up to desktop but she's so emotional that she stumbles. A strobe light pops off.*]

What the hell?

[*Looks around. Another strobe pops off, then another.*]

[*To herself and the audience.*]

Somebody shooting photos.... Right up between my thighs!

[*To stranger.*]

Hey, quit it!

[*To audience.*]

A woman. At least it isn't some pathetic frat boy.... We gasp. We look at each other in confusion.

[*To stranger.*]

I know you! You're Stefani Symons!

[*As* STEFANI.]

Karen, I'm sorry that the story didn't—

[*To* STEFANI.]

And I'm sorry about your job.

[*As* STEFANI.]

Don't be. I landed a gig with CollegeHumor.com two hours later. Between us, the *Times* is going to be bought out by CollegeHumor.com within the month anyway.

[*To audience.*]

Stefani snaps a couple more shots.... She promises to put them on CollegeHumor's site later in the evening.... Screw it. If I'm going to be here at all I should dance, damnit, dance... I give over to the wild spirit around me.... Pouring vodka into my Red Bull.... In the ladies' room taping on smart-drug skin patches....

Maybe I do need to throw aside my dreams. . . . Maybe it's time to move to Jersey. . . . The stall door swings open—it's Xavier. He glares at me. "Fuck polyamory" I mouth at him. . . . Ten minutes later I'm leaning against a wall. . . . Groups of people—anyone passing by—is writing on my legs, my back, my arms. . . . I'm being inscribed. . . . Someone is drawing on my tummy. A girl with pink hair stands up.

[*As* JESS.]

Ms. Grenke, please don't tell my parents you saw me here!

[*To audience.*]

It's Jess, the arty girl from Frank Gehry High!

[*To* JESS.]

How'd you know about this scene?

[*As* JESS.]

Everybody knows Metuchen is where it's at. I get out to the Big Box every week. I take the bus and change into my party clothes at the Metuchen bus station. God, it's so depressing to have to live in Manhattan! Did you see what I wrote on your left arm?

[*To self.*]

"You are my role model."

[*To* JESS.]

Really?

[*To audience.*]

We share a big hug. Jess looks deep into my eyes. We're naked to each other emotionally, spiritually, artistically. Then she can't help herself and bolts.

[*As* JESS.]

I gotta get home to boring Manhattan. But I admire you so much I'm gonna write about how great you are on you my blog! I get tons of hits!

[*Calling to* JESS.]

Sweetie, I haven't done any art in four years!

[*As* JESS.]

Don't you know what you are to me? What you represent? Check out your other arm!

[*Reads writing on the arm.*]

"Karen Grenke has stayed in New York. That is the performance. You are the art."

[*Inspired,* KAREN *waves bye-bye to* JESS, *then climbs stairs to desktop as music gets louder.*]

[*To self, audience.*]

I am my own art form. My life.... My art....

[*Up on the desk now, music louder,* KAREN *dances.*]

[*To audience.*]

OK, so immortality isn't in the cards. That dream is dead. But tomorrow I'll be the last artist in New York City once again. And I'll be showing up on CollegeHumor, and on a very cool girl's blog.

[*Pulls string attached to large can of Red Bull mounted on ceiling. Glitter falls from it all over her.*]

[*To audience.*]

There's always the chance that I could go viral!

[*Dances ecstatically, finally released.*]

scene eight

[*Music fades, house lights come up.* KAREN *shifts back into being "herself," awkwardly getting down off desk and picking up a stack of flyers.*]

KAREN   [*To audience.*] Thank you very much for watching my performance—

ANNOUNCER VOICE   [*Interrupts.*] Thank you for joining us at this final show at PS 122—

[KAREN *waves to stage manager to shut the announcer up, but construction-crew guys are coming onstage to initiate demolition. KAREN gives them an outraged look, hurries to audience, and starts handing out her flyers.*]

Join me on May 16, 2019, at 10 p.m. for a talk-back about the important issues that I've raised in this piece! Will there be any art at all in Manhattan by that time?

ANNOUNCER   Please ignore the artist and begin filing in an orderly fashion out the doors so that the construction crew can begin the transformation of this ratty disgrace of a building into a gleaming new retail space—

KAREN   We'll be meeting on the corner just outside no matter what blue glass piece of shit the fuckers have turned this building into! Please show up and help celebrate our legacy! Help me do it, so that art will not be forgotten!

ANNOUNCER   Be sure not to forget your personal belongings, and remember to return to enjoy Chase/Wachovia–Whole Foods, a new concept in banking/shopping pleasure, designed from the bottom up to suit you, and the way you tell us that you like to live....

• • •

The True Author of
the Plays Formerly
Attributed to Mister
William Shakespeare
Revealed to
the World for the
First Time by Miss
Delia Bacon

James Armstrong

James Armstrong

James Armstrong is a member of the Dramatists Guild of America. His plays have been performed by such theaters as The Attic Ensemble (*The Four Doctors Huxley*), the Abingdon Theatre Company (*Foggy Bottom*), the Epiphany Theater Company (*A Christmas Carol*), and Playwrights Forum (*The Metric System*). New York audiences have seen the premieres of a number of his short plays, including *The New Mrs. Jones, Searching for Saint Anthony, When Ladies Go A-Thieving, The Mysteries of the Castle of the Monk of Falconara*, and *Corpse*, as well as *The True Author... Revealed*. You can keep up with him at www.armstrongplays.com.

···production note···

The True Author of the Plays Formerly Attributed to Mister William Shakespeare Revealed to the World for the First Time by Miss Delia Bacon premiered at The Tank Theater on June 5, 2009, produced by Dawn Cardinale and Tap Monkey. It was directed by Ken Kaissar and starred Katherine Harte-DeCoux.

character

DELIA, a young American woman

time

The mid-nineteenth century. Evening.

place

An auditorium in the American Consulate in Liverpool, England

···

[*At rise,* DELIA *stands center stage at a podium. To her left is an easel with a placard that reads, "THE TRUE AUTHOR REVEALED." To her right is an empty chair. She is bursting with energy.*]

DELIA   Welcome. Welcome, ladies and gentlemen. I am truly honored that you have come to the American Consulate tonight. My name is Miss Delia Bacon. I'm from Connecticut; that's in America. Yes. I suppose you all know that, don't you?

[*Stops. Giggles. Returns to her talk.*]

Yes. Ever since I arrived in Great Britain, I have had one goal in my pursuits. To uncover the truth. And now, I am pleased to announce, that for the first time in history, I am able to reveal to the world the true author of the dramatical poems heretofore spuriously and falsely attributed to one Mister William Shakespeare. By the end of the evening, ladies and gentlemen, you shall know that name, that blessed name, of the true genius greater than all other authors. Now, before I begin, I must acknowledge the support of the man without whom I could not be here today. He has encouraged me in all my endeavors, and has even provided this lovely hall in the consulate tonight. He promised to be here this evening, so ... please allow me to thank my fellow countryman, famed writer and American consul to Liverpool—*Nathaniel Hawthorne!* Will you come up here, please, Mr. Hawthorne?

[*Motions to chair.*]

Here's the chair, just like we agreed. He's right there in back. I don't mean to pressure you. You could just wave or something. If you prefer. Will you wave to us, please, Mr. Hawthorne? Wave?

[*Waves. No response.*]

Mr. Hawthorne's a bit shy tonight. Pay him no mind, ladies and gentlemen. No mind at all. Though if you would like to come up ...

[*Stops. Smiles. Waits for approval.*]

Oh. I see. Mr. Hawthorne is a bit skeptical about my ideas, but perhaps we'll convince him by the end of the evening. After all, your chair is waiting. ... Well, I shan't keep you all in suspense any longer. I did have some notes here. Mr. Hawthorne advised me not to try to speak without notes. It's very important to be prepared, you see. That's what he told me. I just have to get these papers in order and then ... well ... Without adequate preparation, a speech is ... I'll be right with you, ladies and gentlemen. Just as soon as ... they were right here and WHERE ARE THE GODDAMNED—

[*Stops. Glances up at the audience. Smiles. Giggles.*]

Yes. Here they are. No, don't go! No! Please? Yes. Thank you. Sit down. I do apologize. I'm not a— I don't know what came over me. Well. Now we can begin.

[*Glances down at the notes. Looks up at the audience.*]

"Reason."

[*Smiles. Looks down at notes.*]

"Reason is the sole force which must motivate us in the quest for truth."

[*Glances up. Looks for approval. Uncertain. Turns back to her note.*]

"If we are to tear away from our attachment to the past, we must be willing to sacrifice everything, and head forward towards all the abundance that the future has to offer."

[*Beams.*]

We live in an age of progress, ladies and gentlemen, as I am sure our good friend Mr. Hawthorne would agree! As a matter of fact, if he would just...

[*Pats the back of the chair.*]

Well... I'm not as good as he is at articulating these things, but I'll do my best. You see, the Elizabethan Age began a trend towards scientific investigation, and we must bring that same investigation to the greatest texts of that age. Only then can mankind, and yes, womankind too, be freed from the shackles of convention, which prevent us from...

[*Quickly.*]

This is what I've been trying to get my brother Leonard to understand all these years. Of course he would just call me a— He could never appreciate it. Rationality. Why, if that scoundrel friend of his had been acting rationally, he never would have proposed and then— But I digress.

[*Smiles. Back to business.*]

Now, if we are to determine the true author of—he *did* propose to me by the way—the true author of... these most magnificent works... it follows that we must first reject the spurious claims of that *man* from Stratford. Yes.

[*With disgust.*]

William Shakespeare.

[*Shakes off the name.*]

There are many reasons for doubting the authorship of Shakespeare, but three in main:

[*Checks notes.*]

"One. William Shakespeare was the poor son of a common butcher."

[*Looks up. Panics.*]

Oh, come now, Mr. Hawthorne. I know what you're going to say. John Shakespeare was not a butcher per se, but a glover. But it's not much of a debate with you sitting out there in the audience now, is it? Why don't you...?

[*Looks back at her notes.*]

"Two. By all accounts, William Shakespeare led a sparse and altogether uninteresting life."

[*Turns back to audience.*]

An author of such distinction? Why was he not noticed?

[*Smiles.*]

Genius can only be ignored for so long, ladies and gentlemen. I myself have suffered from neglect. Been called names. Laughed at even! But it can only go so far. The human spirit is resilient, yes, but... Sooner or later, one is noticed.

[*Motions to the chair.*]

Are you sure you wouldn't...?

[*Waits. Smiles. Giggles.*]

"Three." Perhaps the most convincing. "In light of recent evidence stressing the importance of heredity, it seems impossible that a man of such genius could be the only individual of note in his family." Why are there no other geniuses with the surname Shakespeare? More on this later.

[*Smiles.*]

If our author was not a man of the theater, what was he? I suspect... he was not much different from you, Mr. Hawthorne! A man of both literary distinction and governmental service. A man of connection to individuals of import. A man, perhaps, with a dissatisfied marriage, waiting to share his affection with—

[*Pause. Smiles. Sudden panic.*]

Or perhaps... this is reading slightly too much into the situation.

[*Smiles.*]

Ah, but Mr. Hawthorne, do you not remember that noble sentiment from Hamlet? "Doubt thou the stars are fire . . . Doubt that the sun doth move . . . Doubt truth to be a liar . . . BUT NEVER DOUBT I LOVE!"

[*Smiles. Recovers.*]

Now what at first appears to be a simple love poem, at second look, aha! "Doubt thou the stars are fire? Doubt that the sun doth move?" Is this not a challenge to the very foundations of a Ptolemaic universe? Why, if the plays were in Italian, we would have to concede they were written by Galileo!

[*Laughs hysterically. Pauses. Very quickly.*]

Yes. Now it so happens that at that time, a new philosophy was taking root. The mind that created *Hamlet* and *Julius Caesar* and *Coriolanus* also perceived this new mode of thought. The new philosophy, which we have adopted as a practical philosophy, not merely in that grave department of learning in which it comes to us *as* philosophy, but in that not less important department in which it comes to us in the disguise of amusement, this Elizabethan philosophy is, in these two forms of it, not two philosophies, not two new and wondrous philosophies, but one—one and the same!

[*Stops. Catches breath.*]

Well, what of this conclusion? Will it be attacked? Certainly. Just as Galileo was blinded by the forces of the Inquisition, I doubt not that a modern Inquisition is forming as we speak. You know what they called Galileo, don't you? They said he was—

[*Calms herself.*]

I, however, cannot be silenced. And I can assure you, ladies and gentlemen, any evidence they may produce in opposition to my conclusions will not be of the least value. As for the internal evidence of the plays themselves, it is far too extensive for me to recount it here. I am at work, however, on a manuscript, which I hope, Mr. Hawthorne, you will condescend to read. Let it suffice for now to state that the author of the plays was none other than the discoverer of inductive reasoning himself, Sir Francis Bacon.

[*Smiles.*]

Yes, Mr. Hawthorne, Sir Francis Bacon. And yes, an ancestor of mine. You see now, I am not a *freak*. I come from a long line of great minds. Like yours. Perhaps you thought before that I wasn't worthy, but do you see now? So if you wish to...

[*Motions to the chair. Long silence. Nothing happens. Sudden panic.*]

But... could such a distinguished person, Sir Francis Bacon, allow his works to be performed upon the public stage? Upon the stage? Well, he wouldn't be onstage himself, ladies and gentlemen. Not sitting up there himself. But he would still support his works. What could a prestigious individual like Mr. Hawth— Bacon, have to fear?

[*Passionately.*]

Francis Bacon fought for a world based solely upon rational fact. Throw out Aristotle! Throw out Ptolemy! Throw out the Bible! Yes, Mr. Hawthorne, you mustn't be shocked.

[*Smiles.*]

Nothing should stop us. If we reject convention, if we put aside the doubts and hesitations that prevent us from seizing what we really want, we can create a whole new society. If the world were to see, if you were to stand up here with me and proclaim that what we have—

[*Quickly.*]

We can defy convention, Mr. Hawthorne. Traditions do not matter to us; marriage doesn't matter; forget about that New England cow of yours; I'll wear your scarlet letter! I may have gone too far last night, but you belong with me, not her! You were supposed to be here, Mr. Hawthorne! You promised! You said you'd be— OH DEAR GOD!

[*She screams and knocks over the lectern. Papers fly everywhere. She flings her arms in a mad rage and continues to shriek through tears. She stops. Opens her eyes. Looks out at the audience.*]

Oh. Oh dear. Well. I must say, I do ... I do apologize. Where was I?

[*Tries to gather up the papers and sort through them.*]

No, please don't go yet. I still haven't gotten to the best part. You see, the plays are inscribed with a secret code. If you look at the sequence of words in the second part of *Henry the Fourth*, and count off using the square root of ... It all makes perfect sense. Mr. Hawthorne? You are still out there, aren't you? You are ...?

[*Stares into the void.*]

I know ... you couldn't sit up here with me. I understand that now. But ... that was you I saw in the back. ... It was ... right? Mr. Hawthorne? Hello? Are you ...? Mr. Hawthorne ...?

[*The lights slowly fade to blackout.*]

• • •

The Lovers and Others of Eugene O'Neill

Marla Del Collins

Marla Del Collins

Marla Del Collins holds a PhD in arts and humanities in education, Department of Culture and Communication, an MA in educational theatre, Department of Music and Performing Arts Professionals, New York University, and a BFA in dramatic arts from the Creative Arts Center, West Virginia University. As a professional actor and published playwright, she holds membership in Actor's Equity, SAG, and AFTRA, and is an associate member of the New York Dramatist Guild. Her tenure at the Stella Adler Conservatory of Acting and her affiliation with the Actors Studio afforded her the opportunity to work with both Stella Adler and Lee Strasberg. She also apprenticed with Uta Hagen at the HB Studio, and studied Shakespeare with Mario Siletti at the National Shakespeare Conservatory. As a professional actor, she performed in numerous stage productions both States side and abroad. Her first published one act, *Houses of Jasper Streets of Gold* (celebrating a legacy of three generations of Irish American working women), appeared in *Ais Eire Journal* and was performed (as part of *A Tribute to Eileen O'Casey*) at Joseph Papp's Public Theatre, Walter Bruno Theatre at Lincoln Center, American Place Theatre, Labor Theatre, The Project Theatre (Dublin, Ireland), and at various community theaters and institutions of higher learning. She is an acting coach, and CEO of Dragonfly Dynamics, a consultancy specializing in creative problem solving and human communication skills.

• • •

scene one

[Lights dimly reveal a set that vaguely resembles a Victorian sitting room, a funeral parlor, and an opium den suspended in time; a place where dimensions and spirits collide and glide in and out as in a dream. There lingers the faint scent of myrrh and frankincense suggesting a Catholic Mass, or that some other form of religious ritual has just been completed. Downstage right the parlor is fitted with a large oriental rug and four distinctly styled chairs. Each chair represents and belongs to each of the four female characters in the play. Both the characters and their chairs reflect the wide range of styles in O'Neill's dramatic writing. His mother's chair is Gothic revival, and implies expressionism. His nanny sits on a kitchen chair, which represents caricature. AGNES, his second wife sits comfortably on a modern oak library chair that represents realism, and CARLOTTA, his third wife sits in a stuffed chair, which suggests melodrama. The chairs are arranged so that the most influential character in O'Neill's psychological development is nearest to him (O'Neill is in attendance through a photograph of the man himself on a draped table that looks remarkably like a coffin). The chairs are all arranged around a small Victorian card table. An Autoharp sits on the small table center. Directly behind the sitting area are four (larger than life) black wooden crosses. ELLA's cross is the only one twisted at an odd angle, reflecting her mental instability. On each cross hangs a plain white mask of a woman's face, along with the garments worn by each character so that the crosses take on a human shapes all their own with heads, arms, and torsos, and suggest visually that these women have all been crucified in one way or another. The first cross (CARLOTTA) wears a wide-rim black hat and is draped with a black feathered boa. The second cross (AGNES) wears a smart modern hat from the 1920s and a long string of pearls. A cigarette in a cigarette holder protrudes at a sophisticated angle, from the mouth of the mask. The third cross (SARAH, the nanny) wears a silly little black hat with a flower perched on the end, and a long white Victorian apron. Inside the apron is a small bottle of brandy. The fourth cross (ELLA) is twisted at an awkward angle. There are white gloves on each end of the cross, a black Victorian close-fitting bonnet that ties under the chin, a heavy black Victorian cape with white fur trim. An oversized black rosary dangles from one arm of the twisted cross. Upstage left on the draped table are five candles (one lit), and the 8 x 10 framed photo of Eugene O'Neill staring grimly out at the audience. Scurrying about before the show are three figures dressed in black monk robes, their faces obscured by the hoods make

them seem sinister. They go about their tasks uttering, gurgling, cackling inhuman nonsensical gibberish—sounds of mischief and cruel delight akin to the three witches in Macbeth. They have already lit the incense before the audience is seated and have lit one of the five candles. Each candle represents the spirits of O'Neill and the four women. These monk-musicians take their seats on pillows just offstage right, but are still clearly visible to the audience. Their presence and their music, chants, and bell-ringing are an intricate part of the play; in a sense, they represent in total, another character who interacts with the women as they materialize, voice their opinions and then de-materialize. One is the "bell ringer" while the other three play Irish music on bodhran, harp, flute, and fiddle. They play as the audience is being seated and during various interludes throughout the play. When the audience enters the musicians play "Endearing Young Charms" (chord E♭, note G), "Owen Roe" (chord A♭, note F),and finish with "Gene O'Dreams" (chord E♭). As the lights go up, the NARRATOR-GUIDE, *dressed in a mid-calf-length tailored dark suit, is seen sitting in one of the chairs. She takes up the Autoharp and begins to sing "Gene O'Dreams."]*

NARRATOR-GUIDE   [*Sings with Autoharp.*]
>Across the hills the sun has gone astray
>Tomorrow's cares are many dreams away
>Sleep is a river
>Flow down forever
>And for your boatman choose old Gene O'Dreams
>And for your boatman choose old Gene O'Dreams
>
>Both man and master in the night are one
>All things are equal when the day is done
>The prince, the plowman, the slave, the freeman,
>All find their comfort in old Gene O'Dreams
>All find their comfort in old Gene O'Dreams
>When evening comes, the stars will guide your way
>Through dreams of longing for a bright new day
>The stars are flying, your candles dying
>Lift up your darkness to old Gene O'Dreams
>Lift up your darkness to old Gene O'Dreams.[1]

---

[1] "Gene O'Dreams" is an altered version of the song "John O'Dreams," an Old English folk ballad, origin unknown.

[The monks chant a choral. They sound like the waves of the sea washing up upon the shore.]

It's home again to the sea, my brother
It's home again to the sea.
Where the seagulls cry and the land lights die
It's home again to the sea.[2]

[The NARRATOR-GUIDE *moves only when the bell is rung. The bell represents order, religion, oppression, judgment, authority, and criticism, a punishing male God, the director, etc. It rings characters on and off the stage. It moves the play forward. It rings in increments of three or four, as in the Catholic Mass. The* NARRATOR-GUIDE *moves downstage left to the table. She is an almost supernatural, nondescript entity soon to become each of the four women. As she glides, she joins the chanting. The musicians chant "Deus Meus" as the candles are being lit. The bell rings in increments. With each ring, she lights a candle, until five candles are burning brightly. She glides to center stage left, into a spotlight where she sings the first song fragment representing the next woman to come, and then speaks through the poem fragment written by Eugene O'Neill as a coaxing for the next woman to materialize.]*

[The NARRATOR-GUIDE *speaks (she/he is possessed by the spirit of O'Neill). She/he is the "medium" through which he expresses his feelings. His poem fragments represent the brighter side (lover) and darker side (other), his dual personality, and his relationship with each of these women. Each song and poetic interval is dedicated to the next woman to be revealed. The* NARRATOR-GUIDE *is also the embodiment of O'Neill himself, who does not appear like the others as a character with full-blown mannerisms. The words of O'Neill's poems create the picture and express his message. His language is simple, mechanical, dream-like, direct, and unembellished. He/she stands tall and speaks out to the audience, but not directly to the audience. His/her manner is formal, stiff, and void of animation. At the same time the* NARRATOR-GUIDE *is the fundamental unidentifiable, nameless entity from which the women take shape. They originate with O'Neill's romantic ideal of what a woman is, or should be. They express themselves still further through the characters in his plays. But they are masked ... still not completely human, still without their own voice or identity. It is not until the mask is removed do they speak*

---

[2] "So it's back to the sea, my brothers, Back again to the sea..." (from O'Neill's poem "The Call," printed under the heading "Laconics," in the *New London Telegraph*, November 19, 1912, Yale UP, *Poems of O'Neill*, 32, 33).

their true thoughts and feelings. The masks in this play represent man's shaping of the female identity, the socially constructed "feminine mystique," woman through the male gaze.]

NARRATOR-GUIDE   [*Sings a capella with* CARLOTTA *in mind.*]

    Me husband can dance and caper and sings
    And do anything that's fittin' for him
    But he cannot do the thing I want
    Because he has no courage in him

    O' dear oh, O' dear oh
    Me husband's got no courage in him
    O' dear oh!
    Me husband's admired wherever he goes
    And everyone looks well upon him
    With his handsome features and well shaped leg
    But still he's got no courage in him.
    O dear oh, O' dear oh
    Me husband's got no courage in him
    O' dear oh[3]

"THE OTHER"   [*Speaking through the poetry of O'Neill as O'Neill.*]

    A quiet man,
    In love with quiet
    Deep in my silent sea
    I am only a seagull
    Dolefully squawking
    When it would sing.[4]

"THE LOVER"

    Somewhere she waits to make you win
    Your soul in her firm white hand
    Somewhere the Gods have made for you,
    The woman who understands.[5]

---

[3] "My Husband's Got No Courage in Him," sung by Mady Prior and June Tabor on the CD *Silly Sisters*, Adonia Music Ltd./Chrysalis Music Ltd.
[4] Written by O'Neill at Tao House, August 17, 1942, O'Neill papers (Yale Univerity Press, *Poems of O'Neill*, 104).
[5] Poem written by O'Neill around 1915 and sent to Beatrice Ashe, Berg Collection of the New York Public Library, O'Neill papers (Yale Univerity Press, *Poems of O'Neill*, 101).

[*Music accompanies the next character transformation (allows time for the actor to costume). The musicians play "Humoresque" (chord E♭, 1st version, 2 phrases). They stop when she turns around masked. . . . CARLOTTA is taking shape.*]

CARLOTTA (EUGENE O'NEILL'S THIRD WIFE)   [*Masked.*] "Duty! How often I've heard that word in this house! Well, you can't say I didn't do mine all these years, but there comes an end."[6]

[*The bell rings. The mask is removed.* CARLOTTA *sits in her chair—first chair, stage right. She is in her late 40s, is wearing a large black wide-brimmed hat bedecked with ostrich feathers. She is the third and last wife of Eugene O'Neill. The brightly colored feathers are offset by her feathered boa that she drapes repeatedly over her shoulder. She is an actress (not a very good one) of her day, and is so accustomed to posing and indicating in third-rate, poorly written parts that these mannerisms have become habitual even off the stage. Her low, throaty voice pierces through the quiet like a knife. Her affected British accent grates on the ear. She is a woman used to getting what she wants when she wants it, and she has been known to throw a tantrum if she doesn't. Yet behind this facade, is a lonely, insecure woman, who both admires and resents the positions of power held by men. She needs to be needed and puts any of the creative energy she may possess into "the man." She understands his emotional neediness, self-preoccupation, and his artistic drive. She lives through his success, not her own. She does not let him forget this.*]

CARLOTTA   [*Unmasked. Directly to the audience.*] I suppose you've come to hear some titillating gossip about my life with Eugene O'Neill. Well, I do hate to disappoint you, but I have no intention of prostrating myself before a pack of plebeian spectators, especially those of the academic ilk! As for the other women in his life . . .

[*Motions to the masked crosses on display.*]

. . . they may do as they please. They can spill their guts out for all I care, but not I, no, my duty lies with my husband . . .

[*Walks over to the droll photo of O'Neill.*]

. . . even from beyond the grave. And if you had even a modicum of respect for the memory of the greatest American playwright

---

[6] Christine's line from O'Neill's play *Mourning Becomes Electra*.

who ever lived, you would rise up now and depart before this
morbid little melodrama begins.

[*She pauses...waiting for the audience to make their move as she has
directed, but no one does.*]

No? I see. Behind all your scholarly panache you are nothing but
the gawking public after all. Very well then...but don't say I didn't
give you ample warning! You shan't get your money back....

[*Addressing the bell ringer.*]

Ring me off the stage!

[*Bell rings. She snuffs out the first candle.*]

Oh, what must be careful here...I don't want to light my
feathers. What one won't do for cheap thrills. Playwright dear,
don't embarrass me now so early on. Have you fallen asleep at
your own play? Ring me off the stage!

[*The flute music begins.* CARLOTTA *removes her hat and scarf and places it on her
chair—first chair, stage right. She walks over to the spotlight, downstage left, and
digresses back into the narration.*]

scene two

NARRATOR-GUIDE   [*Sings a capella with* AGNES BOULTON *in mind.*]

As I walked out one mornin',
Mid the verden braes o'skeen
I lean my back to a mossy tree
To view the dew on the west country,
The dew on foreign strand.

O' sit you down on the grass, he said,
On the dewy grass so green
For the wee birds all have come and gone,
Since I my true love seen, he said,
Since I my true love seen.

Oh, I'll not sit on the grass, she said,
No lover I'll be of thine,
For I hear you love a Conought maid,

And your heart's no longer mine, she said,
And your heart's no longer mine.[7]

"THE OTHER" [*Speaking through the poetry of Eugene O'Neill as O'Neill.*]

I gazed in the mirror
And smiled at myself
But my eyes could not smile.
They were dead souls.
Imprisoned.
How could they smile?

Yet I must meet her—
And so I shaved,
And shuddered
At the horror
In the mirror.[8]

"THE LOVER"

A ledge of rocks that juts into the sea;
The swift gulls dip, I hear their mournful cry;
Far off the white sails of the ships glide by;
I sit and dream, and you are with me.[9]

[*Music accompanies next character transformation, allowing the actor to costume. The musicians play "Owen Roe" (chord A♭, note F, 8 measures).*]

AGNES (EUGENE O'NEILL'S SECOND WIFE) [*Masked.*] "And if you've suffered all these years, imagine how I've suffered? All this time—I loved. I've lain awake nights longing for you and knowing that you hated me and knowing that if I told the truth—and set you free—that you'd go—and I'd never see you again!"[10]

---

[7] An Irish ballad from Derry of unknown origin.
[8] Printed from a typed copy made about 1940 by Carlotta Monterey O'Neill. O'Neill has added "N.Y./Garden Hotel 1917." The O'Neill papers (Yale Univeristy Press, 89).
[9] Written January 9, 1915, and sent to Beatrice Ashe, Berg Collection of the New York Public Library (Yale University Press, *Poems of O'Neill*, 55).
[10] The role of Cora, from Agnes Boulton's (pen name: Elinor Rand) play, *The Guilty One*, act 4 (Bogard, *Unknown* 146).

[*The bell rings, the mask is removed.* AGNES *is a tall, lithe, attractive woman in her mid-30s. She is O'Neill's second wife and the mother of his children. She is fashionably dressed in a rimless hat, which hugs her pale aquiline face. She holds a short cigarette holder with an unlit cigarette at the end. She is a bit nervous...hesitant...perhaps a little high-strung. There is, however, a pragmatic steadiness in her voice that comes from dealing with the realities of life. Agnes is intelligent, articulate, and an artist in her own right. She seems flustered, a bit confused by not knowing where she is, or how she got here.*]

AGNES   [*Unmasked.*] Well, I do feel a little awkward.

[*She shrugs.*]

I mean here I am...Agnes Bolton, the wife who failed the great Eugene O'Neill!

[AGNES *walks over to the table where stand the burning candles. She is about to light her cigarette with one, thinks the better of it, and takes her seat—second chair, stage right.*]

You know, it took me many years to realize that our failed marriage was not entirely my fault, if in fact it was my fault at all.

[*Notices that the votive candles around the photo of O'Neill seem to be a shrine of sorts in the form of votive candles. Puzzled by what she sees, she sits down in her chair—second chair, stage right—her cigarette still unlit.*]

No, I think Eugene and I would have parted company with or without Carlotta in the picture. Well, let me see...

[*Pause.*]

...what can I tell you about him, I mean, that's why you've come, isn't it? Well, I can begin with the first time we met. It was at a little bar somewhere in the West Village, Bleecker Street, I think. I knew who he was, everyone did. But on this particular evening, he walked in, sat down at my table, and proceeded to stare at me for the longest time. Well, I was young enough to feel flattered. I thought he was intoxicated with my very presence, until I realized that was not staring at me, but at his own reflection in the mirror directly behind me! "Mr. O'Neill," I said, "why are you staring at yourself, people will think you're conceited." To which he indignantly replied, "I am not conceited. I stare at myself to make sure I'm still there." Well, it was always my innocent questions, my candid little remarks that would get me into trouble with Gene. He hated having anyone challenge his well-rehearsed public persona... "thee Poet." As a matter of fact, I don't think he ever liked me very much. He was jealous. Oh yes, he was! He could grow jealous just watching me smoke!

[*She attempts to draw on her unlit cigarette, frustrated glances over at the votive candles.*]

He was jealous of the fact that I too was a writer with a personality and an ego of my own. He hated my innocence, my sense of fun, my human fallibility... and on many an occasion he would strike out at me with his fists. His inner rage would strike out at my vulnerability.

[*She pauses.*]

You see, my vulnerability reminded him of his own. He was in love with his own tragic concept of life, so you mustn't pity him. He loved being tortured! And I cannot think of a more supreme torture than for him to have married Carlotta, the actress. Well, I have to admit, I was taken a bit by surprise.... I mean, after all, just between you and me, Carlotta was no intellectual genius. I thought he'd grow bored with her after a time... but apparently his need for a mother and caretaker far outweighed his need for a lover and intellectual companion. Oh, don't get me wrong, we did have our good times, you know. Lying on the beach... watching the seagulls gliding overhead. Gene used to imagine himself a seagull... free from domestic care and responsibility. But inevitably one of my irreverent remarks would bring him plummeting back down to earth again. "Gene," I'd say, "seagulls must land eventually, you know, dirty diapers, children's vomit on the backseat." That is the one thing I shall never for-give him for... the way he treated our children. It would have been better if he had abandoned them altogether, but he enjoyed holding power over them, even from a distance. There was no pleasing him, no matter how hard they tried. No one could please him. I certainly couldn't please him... so I gave my "artist" husband the freedom he said he so desperately needed. The illusion of freedom so often maintained by the male sex... and what does he do with it? He walks right through the open door and into captivity... into the waiting arms of Carlotta, his beloved jailer!

[*Looking over her shoulder at the photo of O'Neill.*]

Well, I'm sorry, Gene, but I do believe in telling it just the way it is. You know I've always been that way.

[*She walks over to the candles, lights her cigarette, and takes a satisfying puff, then turns again to the audience.*]

You see I knew him better than anyone. I knew him better than he knew himself.

[*She blows out the candle, and the bell rings. Music begins as she walks back to her costume stand, removes her costume, and proceeds to take the position of* NARRATOR-GUIDE. *She begins to sing but is interrupted by* CARLOTTA. *She dashes over to* CARLOTTA'*s chair as if pulled by her force and puts on her hat and boa still draped over her chair.*]

CARLOTTA [*Unmasked. Turning to the man in the lighting booth.*] No, no, darling, I have something very important to say.... Excuse me, playwright, darling, I do hate to pop up at such an inopportune time, dear, but why did you put that woman on the same stage as I? My agent warned me about being in this little potboiler, but I had no idea that I would be subjected to such humiliation, such degradation in front of all these charming little academicians.

[*She sits.*]

I suppose that Agnes deserves *some* credit, poor thing, should be given some credit for bearing his children, but so what! Anyone can do that! Besides I am the true nurturer of his real children, the children that matter, his plays, his plays, surely that is not too difficult for you to understand, is it?

[*Bell rings.*]

Oh, I see, think you can just dismiss me, do you?! Well, let me remind you that I am participating in this little fiasco of my own free will, and I can leave anytime I choose. It is my opinion that you are biting off far more than you can chew, sweetheart! My life with Eugene O'Neill would have made an epic in and of itself. If you were any sort of mediocre playwright, you would know that, darling.

[*Bell rings emphatically.*]

Very well, but I warn you I am growing weary of this whole affair!

[*Bell rings.* CARLOTTA *removes her hat and boa. Transformed into the* NARRATOR-GUIDE, *who again takes his/her position in the spotlight.*]

scene three

NARRATOR-GUIDE   [S*ings a capella with* SARA SANDY *in mind.*]

A dottering old Carli came over the lee
Aha, but I would not ha' him
He comes or' the lee, and to court me
With his grey beard newly shaven

My mother she tell to me to give him a drink
Aha, but I would not ha' him
I give him a drink, and he begins to wink
With his grey beard newly shaven.
My mother she tell to me to give him a kiss
Aha, but I would not ha' him
If ye like him so well, you can kiss him yourself
With his grey beard newly shaven![11]

"THE OTHER"   [*Speaks through the poetry of Eugene O'Neill as O'Neill.*]

If you'll remember
A silly soothsayer once said to me
I'd be stabbed in the back
So I put mirrors on every wall
And nobody came behind me
That I couldn't see.[12]

---

[11] A Scottish ballad of unknown origin.
[12] A Scottish ballad of unknown origin.

"THE LOVER"

> When our dreams come true,
> As we hope they may;
> When the skies are blue,
> And the clouds astray,
> We shall laugh and play God's children do;
> Put the world away,
> Just I and you.[13]

[*The musicians play a jig-polka (note D, flute and bodhran) as the* NARRATOR-GUIDE, *suddenly caught up in the music, dances a jig about the stage, then proceeds to costume as the nanny.*]

SARAH SANDY (EUGENE O'NEILL'S NANNY)   [*Masked.*] "I hope I know him better than you ... sleepin' like a baby—so innocent-looking. You'd think butter wouldn't melt in his mouth. It all goes to show—you never can tell by appearances."[14]

[*Bell rings; her mask is removed.* SARA SANDY *is a tight, compact, little woman in her early 60s. When he was a small boy, she was hired to serve as O'Neill's nanny. Her outward appearance is one of a jovial, friendly, little elderly woman ravaged by hard times in her youth, but her words reveal a frustrated, confused, dualistic, and manipulative alcoholic whose twisted sense of humor indicates an abusive behavior directed towards herself and others.*]

SARAH SAND   [*Unmasked.*] Now you're goin' to hear it from the horse's mouth; and any one who knows me can tell ye, I'm not one to exaggerate. Master Gene was the dearest, sweetest little boy that ever a nanny could love. I used to call him me little sailor lad, that's cause he loved the sea, see.

[*Opens a small flask of brandy, pours some into the cap.*]

Oh, he loved the sea, he did ... loved the sea. Must a'been the Irish in him ... give 'em a little boat to bob about in, and they're as happy as clams!

[*Takes a discreet sip from the cap, then screws it back on the bottle.*]

---

[13] Written January 11, 1915, and sent to Beatrice Ashe, Berg Collection of the New York Public Library, Yale Univeristy Press, *Poems of O'Neill*, 59.

[14] Mrs. Miller, from Eugene O'Neill's play, *Ah Wilderness!* Bogard, Later Plays, 99.

Now that I have your undivided attention, I'm goin' to set an ugly rumor straight once and for all. Contrary to what you may have heard, I did not scare the livin' bejesus' out of him with horror stories. I did not. I told him little fairy tales as any good nanny would. Ah, sure, you don't think I'd frighten the lad, do ye? And even if I did, wasn't I there to comfort him? That's more than I can say for his family. Now take his mother... there was a tragic hoot. Missed her callin' to be a nun, no doubt o' that. And she be weepin' and wailin' about her lot in life... blamin' her husband and the like. And sure, why not? Father and sons alike drinkin' and shoutin' night and day, why it'd be enough to drive a saint mad. Then again, who wouldn't be driven to drink with a spook of a mother like that? Now I'm not sayin' that Gene didn't do his share of drinkin' and shoutin' when he was a man, but when he was a boy, he was the dearest sweetest little boy, you'd ever want to know. Why, I remember one day he comes up to me, couldn't a' been more than that high...

[*Indicates height.*].

...he comes up to me, the tears rollin' down his cheeks, and he says to me, he says, "Nanny Sarie...," that's what he used to call me see, Nanny, or Sarie, or Nanny Sarie... he comes up to me and he says, "Nanny Sarie, I seen dead seagull on the beach." "Did ye now," says I, "well, we'll just have to go and take a look at it, then won't we." And so off we did trot through the sand, until we come upon a dead seagull, and sure enough it was dead... as dead as dead as ever I'd seen dead. And it'd been dead for some time, no doubt o' that. "Yes, Master Gene," says I, "that is indeed a dead seagull." And then he says to me, "Nanny Sarie, will the seagull go to heaven?" "Of course, my little lad, the seagull will go to heaven. It will go to seagull heaven."

[*Directed to the audience.*]

Now I wasn't sure about that, mind ye', but I'm thinkin' to meself, where the hell else would a seagull go? "Yes. my lad, the seagull will go to seagull heaven." "Should we give it a Christian burial then?" A Christian burial for a seagull? A seagull is no Christian! Now I don't know much about much, but I do know that much! "No, Master Gene, a seagull should be buried out to sea . . . like one o' them heathen vikings and the like, see . . . and when the tide comes up, a great wave will roll over the little seagull, and gently carry its body out into the deep blue sea . . . and there it will be rocked to and fro, to and fro, to sleep in peace for ever more. But if it's not been a good little seagull, the sharks will tear it to pieces bit by bit!"

[*She laughs gleefully.*]

Well, he seemed quite content with that answer.

[*Bell rings.*]

Oh, there's the bell, ringy dingy dingy, how time goes by when you're havin' fun! I just want to pay me last respects to Master Gene. . . . Master Gene darlin', you know your Nanny loved you best, she did. She loved ye loved ye loved ye to death, she did!

[*The bell rings again.*]

Alright, alright! I'm leavin' for Christ's sakes!

[*She extinguishes her candle, and the bell rings. The musicians play a polka as the nanny removes her costume and, as if possessed, dashes over to CARLOTTA's chair and puts on her hat and boa. CARLOTTA stops the music.*]

CARLOTTA   [*Speaks to the "playwright" in the lighting booth.*] Stop this Irish rabble rousing!

[*Music stops.*]

Playwright dear, I could not hold my tongue any longer. Why in God's name would you include an inebriated servant in your repertory? Surely you must realize they came to hear my story, my life with Eugene O'Neill they are most curious about? And I am sure someone more clever than yourself is writing the script even as we speak.

[*Sits. To the audience.*]

My dear friends, our playwright, I'm afraid, is something of an amateur, and so explains this unfortunate miscarriage of art. Why she has subjected us all to the diatribe of a drunken nanny is beyond me. Rumor has it, as ugly as it may be, that she was once a nanny herself! How else can we account for this ghastly choice of characters?

[*The bell rings.*]

You know, I am really fed up with this ringing and dinging routine. I am resigning. I am no longer participating in this crude little farce. I am leaving for good. If you have a problem with that, my dear, you can speak to my agent!

[*An aside to audience.*]

Oh, I have always wanted to say that!

[*Bell rings emphatically again.* CARLOTTA *exits by removing hat and boa and becoming the* NARRATOR-GUIDE, *who returns to the spotlight.*]

scene four

NARRATOR-GUIDE   [*Sings a capella with* Ella O'Neill *in mind.*]
Here I sit on yonder hill
and who should blame me cry my fill,
And every tear would turn a mill
Escode a mauverin slan
Shul shul shul aroon
Shul a sacir, shul akuin
Shul agas, agas ale gloom
Escodee to a mauvrin slan
I'll dye my petti coats
I'll dye them red
And round the world I'll beg for bread
Until my parents shall wish me dead
Escode a mauverin slan
Shul shul shul aroon
Shul a socir, shul a cuin
Shul agas, agas ale gloo
Escodee to a mauverin slan.[15]

---

[15] Irish lament of unknown origin. Two hundred years of American singing has altered the original Gaelic into gibberish. This version comes from West Virginia.

"THE OTHER"   [*Speaking through the poetry of Eugene O'Neill, as O'Neill.*]
>Silence,
>Pale, ivory-skinned,
>A naked nun
>With a rosary of great black pearls between her breasts—
>Silence
>With cool lips kisses me,
>And gives me her rosary
>Of dead centuries to play with.[16]

"THE LOVER"
>I remember a sweet strange girl,
>With affectionate, bewildered eyes,
>As if God had locked her in a dark closet
>Without any explanation.[17]

[*The musicians play "Endearing Young Charms," (chord E♭, note G, 1 verse + 2nd B) as the character of* ELLA *costumes.*]

ELLA (EUGENE O'NEILL'S MOTHER)   [*Masked as Mary in Long Day's Journey into Night.*] "It's not the fog I mind. I love the fog. It hides you from the world and the world from you. No one can see you or touch you any more."[18]

[*The bell rings, and the mask is removed. A small, delicate woman stands before the audience.* ELLA *is dressed in a black Victorian bonnet and cape. She is the mother of Eugene O'Neill. Her twisted arthritic hands are hidden under white gloves. She is frail and frightened, and in a state of inner anxiety. Her nervous energy is frenetic and agitated. All her concentration is focused on staying in control. Her thoughts are scattered and fragmented. She seems to have dual personalities. One, a good little girl, obedient*

---

[16] Printed from the typed copy, made probably about 1940 from the original autographed manuscript, extensively revised, dated July 9, 1916. Among O'Neill's papers (Yale University Press, *Poems of O'Neill*, 79).

[17] From Eugene O'Neill's *The Great God Brown:* The character Dion Anthony reminisces about his mother (modeled after Ella) (Sheaffer, *Playwright*, 102).

[18] "I remember a sweet strange girl...." Dion reminiscing about his mother in O'Neill's *The Great God Brown*. "It wasn't the fog I minded, Cathleen...," says Mary, from O'Neill's *Long Day's Journey into Night*. The fog in which the action takes place is the same fog of ignorance and fear that surrounds his characters in the play (Falk, 19).

and self-effacing. The other, a raging fury, angry at her lot in life. She is the pure embodiment of 'lover' and 'other,' and represents the dualism between the real self and the socially inherited feminine gender mystique. She has been a morphine addict for many years, and although her unbalanced state of mind can be attributed to this addiction, her agony in not being a whole and independent human being, began manifesting long before.]

ELLA [*Unmasked.*] Eugene was my very special boy; my gift from God. I so wanted him to join the priesthood . . . he was so delicate and frail. He would have been safe there, you see. He would have been my gift to God, my salvation for all the sins I have committed. Perhaps if I had told him that heaven was the sea and the holy ghost, a free flying gull, perhaps then I should have persuaded him.

[She hesitates, not knowing where to go or what to do, like an actor who has forgotten her lines and is struck with stage fright. CARLOTTA takes over her body and speaks to her.]

CARLOTTA [*The voice of CARLOTTA spoken through ELLA.*] Oh, sit down, for God's sake, we don't have all night!

ELLA [*She looks about to see who has spoken, and then sees and addresses the audience.*] Oh, yes! Of course, thank you.

[*She arranges herself primly in her chair, the one closest to O'Neill. Suddenly with childish glee.*]

I think he takes after his father, James! James O'Neill, the great, handsome actor who swept me away, and beguiled me into marriage when I was just a girl. Oh, how I loved him so! . . . as he loves me, as he loves me . . .

[ELLA *transforms from the sweet, shy, and retiring little girl to a bitter woman, betrayed by life. Her voice deepens.*]

It's not my fault, you know, the way the boys turned out, all that drinking and carousing. They have their father to blame for that. I come from a respectable family, not James. What is he anyway . . . just a two-bit matinee idol, dragging his family from theater to theater, living out of suitcases, hotel rooms and staring at barroom floors. If the boys had been raised in a proper home, everything would have been different. That's all I ever wanted, you know, was a real home...a home of my own, with friends and neighbors to talk to. No, I never should have married so young. I never, never, never...

[*Her voice grows louder and more desperate. She claps her gloved hands over her mouth to regain composure. She enters a morphine induced "other world"...a dream state. She speaks in the plaintive voice of a lost child.*]

I wonder what it would have been like if I had never, never married. Perhaps I should have devoted my life to God. Oh yes, I should have been happy then. Or perhaps I should have been a great musician. Everyone said I played the piano beautifully.

[*She begins to play the imaginary keys of a piano while humming "Gene O'Dreams."*]

La la la la la la la la la la.

[*Upon seeing her own deformed hands, she quickly draws them to her breast, and with obvious embarrassment, hides them in her lap. Gaining composure, she begins to speak in a controlled monotone, as if reciting a mantra.*]

"You can't undo the past. What's done is done. Things are as they are, and will end as they must."

[*She regains her composure and resumes speaking with child-like enthusiasm.*]

We were not expecting Eugene to come along. That is why he is my special boy, my gift from God. My husband James always wanted a large family...a great theatrical family, he used to say, like the Booths or the Jeffersons. My husband James, loved children...as I loved him...as he loved me...as I loved him...

[*Her voice lowers as the bitter woman emerges.*]

I never should have had another child. My health was never the same after Eugene was born. I suffered. The doctors gave me morphine for the pain....

[*Looks at her crippled hands.*]

I still take my cure for the pain. No I never should have had another child. I didn't want another child. I tried very hard not to have another child.... No, I never, never, never should have had another....

[*Morphine-induced trance, the plaintive voice of the lost child.*]

I wonder what it would have been like if I had never, never.... Perhaps I should have been ...

[*She begins to play the imaginary piano as the flute plays the melody. ELLA repeats (la la la) the first few bars over and over, while the flute continues on with full melody. The noisy discord that results is a metaphor for the confusion taking place in ELLA's mind. She dances in circles like a little girl as she makes her way over to the candles, snuffs out her own, and walks over to her chair still "lalala"-ing the tune, still in discord with the flute accompaniment. With her back to the audience she stretches out her arms straight as in the form of a crucifixion. The rosary is still swaying from her left arm in a slow dance as she injects her right arm with the morphine needle; it jerks up, and with that sudden movement, the noisy discord of "la la la" and flute music stops abruptly. With arms again stretched out, she recites the "Hail Mary."*]

Hail Mary full of grace, the lord is with thee. Blessed art thou among women ...

[*She laughs incredulously.*]

Blessed art thou among women? Blessed art thou among women?

[*She laughs hysterically and then collapses to her knees and, weeping, buries her head in the seat of her chair.*]

Oh, please, God, take me home. Oh, please take me home.

[CARLOTTA's *stronger personality enters the crippled body, the empty shell of* ELLA, *and symbolically takes over the role of "Mother." ELLA is transformed into* CARLOTTA.]

CARLOTTA [*Unmasked. As she pulls off the mother's garments, her back still to the audience.*] Oh my God! This has gone on long enough. I have never witnessed such a travesty. What melodrama!

[*The figure of* ELLA *with the voice of* CARLOTTA, *removes her gloves, hat, cape, and piles them next to her chair. Only her rosary beads remain on the seat of the chair. She rises and returns to* CARLOTTA's *chair; putting on* CARLOTTA's *hat and boa, she now has completely transformed into* CARLOTTA. CARLOTTA *turns to the audience and speaks.*]

What a charade! Well, I did warn you, didn't I? So we might end our mutual suffering, I shall tell you everything you need to know about Eugene O'Neill, then we can bring to a close this pathetic little evening at the theater. Do all you little scholars have your pen in hand? Good. We can begin.

[*She sits in her own chair, changes her mind, and sits in the mother's chair.*]

Eugene O'Neill...

[*There is a pause as she realizes that she is sitting on something very uncomfortable. She looks to find the large black pearl rosary that she pulls out from beneath her, and disdainfully drops it onto the pile of garments once worn by* ELLA. *She begins again.*]

Eugene O'Neill could have been a great actor. Oh, he appears demure, shy, and civilized, but there lurked a pagan underneath that coat and tie, a rough, tough black Irishman who would have much preferred to paint his naked body blue and run screaming into battle than to kneel before a priest with "Father forgive me for I have sinned." He was as selfish and as stubborn as a spoiled child... but he could also be as gentle and as wise as an old sage. I can't say I understood him altogether. I do know that he loved me... if indeed he loved anyone, if he loved himself. Oh, he loved the image of himself, the image, the image he projected... like the wailing child who stops abruptly before the mirror to inspect his own tears, and then proceeds to wail on. He spent his entire life observing humanity, searching for a key, a password, a formula for how to belong, how to love. He never did find the answer, and therein lies the tragedy of Eugene O'Neill... my Gene. Well, he certainly was a genius in his search, wasn't he? And I knew a genius when I saw one. I sacrificed everything for that man. I was his nursemaid, his secretary, his lover, his mother; why, if it hadn't been for me, Eugene O'Neill would be just another name in the telephone directory! Oh, you think that presumptuous of me, do you? Well, I don't care what you think. There. That is all you shall get from me. So you can pack up and go home to your dull little lives. Genie and I prefer our privacy.

[*Walking over to his portrait.*]

And however volatile or unorthodox our lives together may have been, it is after all, in the end, none of your business. Why, you wouldn't know a genius if he bit you in the behind!

[*Turns to O'Neill's photo.*]

Oh, you liked that, did you, Gene? I knew you would, darling.

[*The bell rings.* CARLOTTA *removes her costume and walks to the one remaining candle lit for O'Neill. The musicians whisper in choral and the* NARRATOR-GUIDE *joins in.*]

NARRATOR-GUIDE   [*Chanting with voices from the band and with Eugene O'Neill in mind.*]

It's home again to the sea, my brother

Home again to the sea.

Where the seagulls cry and the land lights die

It's home again to the sea.

[*Sings a capella as he/she slowly lifts up the remaining candle in homage.*]

When sleep comes

And dreams come running clear

The Hawks of Morning

Cannot find you hear.

Home is the rover

Your journey's over

[*Blows out the candle. Black out.*]

• • •

III

Joe Salvatore

Joe Salvatore

Joe Salvatore is a director and playwright based in New York City. His original plays and performance pieces include *Open Heart*, *The Class Project*, *III* (Overall Excellence Award, Outstanding Play, NYC Fringe 2008), *You Know*, *"Someone's in the Kitchen with Dinah,"* *Homage to Edvard Munch*, *NSA*, *Transfigured* (with Julie Marie Myatt), *That's Not How You Do It*, *Full of Grace* . . . (James Baldwin Playwriting Award), *Empty*, *Fag/Hag* (with Kate Nugent), and *At Wit's End: You Are Here*. Recent directing projects include *Medea Redux*, *The Tempest*, *Twelfth Night*, and *Polaroid Stories*. Additional directing work has been seen at the Lincoln Center Director's Lab, LAByrinth Theater Company's Barn Series, Brooklyn Arts Exchange, New WORLD Theater, the Del Corazon Festival, INROADS: The Americas, Jump-Start Performance Space, Santa Fe Stages, New York University, and the University of Massachusetts at Amherst. Salvatore teaches in the Program in Educational Theatre at New York University. He has a MFA in theater (dramaturgy/directing) from the University of Massachusetts at Amherst and a BA in history from the University of Delaware. He is a member of the Lincoln Center Directors Lab. For more information, visit www.joesalvatore.com.

···author's note···

The events surrounding the 15-year ménage between Glenway Wescott, Monroe Wheeler, and George Platt Lynes depicted in this play are based on historical research that I conducted using a number of primary and secondary sources. Some of the language of the play, particularly (but not exclusively) those moments where the characters are reciting letters to one another, is taken directly from the letters that the three men exchanged. Also, other scenes and monologues draw their inspiration from moments described in letters, personal journals, and personal accounts retold in secondary sources. Therefore, all productions of the play must acknowledge the source material in a program note, which I provide below.

The play also uses projections to identify time period, geographical location, and some material that is quoted, like Wescott's fiction or poetry. These projections are clearly marked in the stage directions and must be honored. Where particular images are mentioned in a projection, I would encourage directors and designers to explore George Platt Lynes's photography, and then create original photographs that emulate the poses and the style of his work.

To be included in the program of all productions:

> From the playwright:
>
> The spoken text and the circumstances in this play come from three sources: the collected letters and journals of Glenway Wescott, Monroe Wheeler, and George Platt Lynes; descriptions provided in secondary source materials; and of course my imagination. I am greatly indebted to the following sources and their editors, curators, and authors for inspiration and historical accounts:
>
> Glenway Wescott Papers, Yale Collection of American Literature, Beinecke Rare Bookand Manuscript Library, Yale University.
>
> *George Platt Lynes, 1907–1955* by David Leddick.
>
> *Intimate Companions: A Triography of George Platt Lynes, Paul Cadmus, Lincoln Kirstein, and Their Circle* by David Leddick.
>
> *Continual Lessons: The Journals of Glenway Wescott, 1937–1955* edited by Robert Phelps with Jerry Rosco.
>
> *When We Were Three: The Travel Albums of George Platt Lynes, Monroe Wheeler, and Glenway Wescott, 1925–1935* by Anatole Pohorilenko and James Crump.
>
> *Glenway Wescott Personally: A Biography* by Jerry Rosco.
>
> *The Moon Is Down* by John Steinbeck.
>
> *The Bitterns* by Glenway Wescott.
>
> *The Apple of the Eye* by Glenway Wescott.

The playwright wishes to thank Anatole Pohorilenko for his guidance and support throughout the creation of *III*.

This play was developed with the support of a 2007 New York University Steinhardt Faculty Research Challenge Grant in the Arts and Culture category.

III (pronounced "three") was presented in August 2008 at the Cherry Lane Theater, New York City, as part of the 2008 New York International Fringe Festival, a production of The Present Company. The play was directed by Joe Salvatore; Ryan Weible served as the assistant director and stage manager; set design by Troy Hourie; lighting and projection design by Emily Stork; costume design by Traci DiGesu; sound design by Benjamin Johnson; and company management by Derek Travis Collard. The cast was as follows:

GLENWAY WESCOTT	Joe Salvatore
MONROE WHEELER	John Del Vecchio
GEORGE PLATT LYNES	Daryl Embry

III received the 2008 New York International Fringe Festival's Overall Excellence Award for Outstanding Play, an honor selected by an independent panel of over fifty theater professionals.

• • •

[*The playing space resembles an artist's studio. It contains a period camera, a desk with a chair and a typewriter, a bench, and a small round table with three chairs. All of the pieces are covered with drop cloths spattered with paint. As the action of the play unfolds, these pieces of furniture are revealed and used by the actors as needed. Upstage is an 8 ft. x 10 ft. flat that appears to be a painting canvas turned backwards. It will be used as a projection screen throughout the performance. As the audience enters, the screen contains images of* GLENWAY WESCOTT, MONROE WHEELER, *and* GEORGE PLATT LYNES, *as well as the title of the play. Projection:* III *and images.*]

[*Lights go to half and then out. In the darkness, the audience hears the opening notes of "Pace, pace, mio dolce tesoro" from Mozart's* The Marriage of Figaro. *As the song plays, the three images and the title fade away. They are replaced by the next projection:* Poetry Club, University of Chicago, 1919.]

[*When the lights come up, we find* GLENWAY WESCOTT *sitting on the revealed bench writing in a notebook.* MONROE WHEELER *enters, sees* GLENWAY *writing, becomes interested, looks to see if anyone else is around, and then approaches.*]

MONROE   [*Flirtatious, but subtle.*] Excuse me. Do you know where the club is meeting today?

GLENWAY   [*Ignores him.*] I think it's in Room 333.

MONROE   2:00 p.m., yes?

GLENWAY   [*Exasperated, looks up; interested.*] Yes, 2:00 p.m.

MONROE   You know, I'm a big fan of yours. Of your poetry, I mean.

GLENWAY   [*Embarrassed.*] Thank you. I've seen you before at the meetings. You're always with—

MONROE   Faith. Yes, we've been friends for a long time.

GLENWAY   Friends?

MONROE   Friends. She's a dear friend.

GLENWAY   [*Relieved.*] That's good.

MONROE   Pardon?

GLENWAY [*Begins to pack his things.*] Nothing, I mean, uh, that's very nice. It's important to have good friends. I should be going.

MONROE Wait! No! Your poetry is very powerful. It speaks to me.

GLENWAY Really?

MONROE Yes, I understand what you're saying. Who you're writing for.

[*Awkward pause.*]

It's quite good. Dangerous.

[*He extends his hand.*]

Monroe Wheeler. From Evanston.

GLENWAY Glenway. Glenway Wescott.

MONROE From?

GLENWAY Oh, from Wisconsin.

MONROE Milwaukee?

GLENWAY No, uh, Washington County.

MONROE Ah.

GLENWAY [*More embarrassed.*] Ah, yes.

[*Apologetic shrug.*]

Just a farm boy.

[*Awkward pause again.*]

You mentioned that my poetry was dangerous. Do you like danger?

MONROE I've been known to dabble.

[*Silence.*]

Are you a writer?

GLENWAY I don't know. Maybe . . .

MONROE Jack of all trades?

GLENWAY [*Flirting.*] Jack maybe.

MONROE You should think about it.

GLENWAY About what?

MONROE Becoming a writer. Your poetry is quite beautiful.

GLENWAY Thank you. I have more if you'd like to see.

MONROE Maybe some other time. Have to get to the meeting. See you there.

[MONROE *walks away, leaving* GLENWAY *completely befuddled.* GLENWAY *slumps on the bench, and recites the following poem. Projection:* Black Art.]

GLENWAY You did not know how brave you were,
　　　　And I, like a starving wolf,
　　　　Followed the shadow of your fire,
　　　　Sorted your secrets from the dust
　　　　To satisfy my hunger.

　　　　You did not know,
　　　　I was a coward . . .
　　　　Now we can shift the skies.
　　　　We can endure
　　　　The hoof-beats of the wind upon our heads.
　　　　Why, we would dare to climb
　　　　Out of a withering world
　　　　Into a new star!

　　　　But let us laugh carelessly like other men.
　　　　Let us be timid, even among fools.
　　　　Let us knot silence round our throats.
　　　　For they would surely kill us.

[*Sound cue to indicate the progression of time. Lights find* MONROE *and* GLENWAY *together again on a bench.* GLENWAY *is writing in his notebook, struggling with a new poem.*]

MONROE It would do you well to change the imagery from the sky to a road.

　　　　[GLENWAY *looks up, back down to the notebook, and begins to erase furiously.*]
　　　　[*Laughing.*]
　　　　You don't have to take my word. You're the writer.

GLENWAY   No, no, I think it's good.

[GLENWAY *writes in the notebook again.* MONROE *enjoys the sun.* GLENWAY *stops to survey the words.* MONROE *notices it over his shoulder. He smiles.*]

MONROE   Read it to me.

GLENWAY   [*Moving closer.*] Why don't you read it to me? It helps me to hear it out loud.

[*Projection:* The Bitterns—I, in My Pitiful Flesh.]

MONROE   [*Reads aloud.*]
    I, in my pitiful flesh
    Transfigured, have woven
    Music of wilderness.

    And now that my old fear is flung
    Aside, I will hold
    In my hands what hunger has sung.

    From all the roads where I go
    Shame like a red mist vanishes.
    On, oh . . .

    The desert is shaken with cries:
    "Come, and I will be kind."
    I am the lover with the frightened eyes.

    [GLENWAY *is a bit self-conscious about this reading, as he's written this for and about* MONROE.]

    It's good.

GLENWAY   You're just saying that.

MONROE   No really, it's great. I think I'd like to publish it. Make a chapbook of all your poems.

GLENWAY   Really?

MONROE   I have some spare time at the advertising agency. No one will know.

GLENWAY   [*Making an advance.*] Would you like to have a cup of coffee?

MONROE   [*Retreating.*] I'd love to but I have to meet another friend. She's waiting for me. Maybe some other time?

GLENWAY   [*Repelled, awkward.*] Oh. Alright. Sure.

MONROE   [*As he is exiting.*] Nice work today, Wescott.

[GLENWAY *is left watching* MONROE *leave yet again. Music comes up. Sound indicates the passage of time.*]

[MONROE *is sitting and* GLENWAY *is standing.* MONROE *is reading from a manuscript. Projection:* The Apple of the Eye.]

MONROE   Book Three. Dan Alone.

The earth lay dead in its grave-cloths. Some women—minute black figures—went weeping from a poor house, following a corpse. Clouds mourned from horizon to horizon. Over the rough marble fields the sun rose between sun-dogs. The excrement of the cattle fell steaming on the frozen clods, and melted the ice to a crystal network. The barns and houses lay in the drifts like seeds. A dead stillness endured for months.

[MONROE *looks up from the manuscript at* GLENWAY.]

Glen, what's wrong?

GLENWAY   What? What do you mean what's wrong?

MONROE   This is just so ... depressing.

GLENWAY   And?

MONROE   It's just that I'm not sure it's your best work. Where's the hopefulness? Where's the sense of light? There's no beauty in this at all.

GLENWAY   Monroe, I always write from this same place.

MONROE   I know, but—

GLENWAY   You've never had any trouble with it before. You've always praised it as truthful and honest. What's changed?

MONROE   Nothing. I just—

GLENWAY   You just what?

MONROE   I just don't see "you" in here. There's no transformation. No hope.

GLENWAY   Well, I'm not feeling very hopeful about anything. I have no job, no future...

MONROE   You have me.

GLENWAY   I'm not so sure.

MONROE   What?

GLENWAY   You're very confusing to me, Monroe.

MONROE   In what way?

GLENWAY   I'm confused about your other "friends."

MONROE   [*Understanding that this means his female "friends."*] Oh. I see.
[*Pause, no reaction from* GLENWAY*;* MONROE *reaches for his hand,* GLENWAY *pulls away.*]
You know I'm not going to leave you.

GLENWAY   [*Bitterly.*] Why would you want to stay around? People find me difficult and strange and—

MONROE   [*Trying to face* GLENWAY.] I don't know how I know this, but I feel very strongly about it. In the American culture artists have privileges. Most artists are eccentric and difficult and strange. Be a poet, Glenway. Make your life as a writer. Then people will leave you alone. Think about it.

[MONROE *exits, leaving* GLENWAY *to think about this statement. Music begins to play and* GLENWAY *unveils the typewriter. He recites the following excerpt from* The Apple of the Eye *with growing conviction.*]

GLENWAY   Then February, like the architecture of a tomb, melted from sight. The cakes of ice broke, and trembled, and flowed off in lumpy currents. The drifts grew ghostly. Jets of water came up out of soiled springs. The dawn rose each day from its bed with an imperceptibly clearer lustre.

[MONROE *enters with a series of clippings that he is reading.*]

MONROE   Sinclair Lewis says, "I have finished with the greatest delight *The Apple of the Eye*. It seems to me that it has something curiously like genius." *Vanity Fair*: "Wescott has perfected a prose of extraordinary suppleness, strength, and beauty." *The Brooklyn Eagle*: "There is nothing in recent novel writing so poignant as Dan Strane's struggles. It is moving and grips the imagination."

[GLENWAY *is slightly embarrassed by all the fuss, but he is happy for the attention from* MONROE. *There is a pause, eye contact, and suddenly* MONROE *kisses* GLENWAY, *who backs away from the kiss and looks alarmed.* MONROE *won't let him out of his grasp.*]

You're an artist now. They'll leave you alone.

[*The two men share a kiss.* GEORGE LYNES *enters with a pen and paper and begins to compose a letter. He starts over several times. At the top of the second attempt,* MONROE *leaves the stage with the clippings. Projection:* January 1927.]

GEORGE   Dear Mr. Wescott, our dear mutual friend, the beautiful and intelligent Bernadine Szold sends her regards and requests that you and I should make each other's acquaintance. You see, I am an aspiring writer…No, that's not right.

[*He crumples the letter and begins again.*]

Dear Mr. Wescott, my name is George Lynes, and I'm writing at the suggestion of our dear mutual friend Miss Bernadine Szold. She has said that I should meet you as I am an aspiring writer and publisher…

[*He stops, re-reads to himself, crumples, and begins again, this time with a resolve to sound more confident.*]

Dear Mr. Wescott, I am writing at the encouragement of our mutual friend Ms. Bernadine Szold. I have a small publishing enterprise called AS Stable Publications based in Englewood, New Jersey, and I am interested in beginning a writing career of my own. I have had the very distinct pleasure of publishing Gertrude Stein's pamphlet "Descriptions of Literature," featuring the artwork of Pavel Tchelitchew, René Crevel's "1830," and Ernest Hemingway's "Today Is Friday" with artwork by Jean Cocteau. I have enclosed copies for your review.

I understand that you are currently in New York at the Hotel Lafayette. Perhaps I could pay you a visit, as I would be most grateful for any suggestions you might have about my future as a writer and publisher of great works. Your recent story, *The Apple of the Eye*, seems to indicate that you are one of the *great writers of our time*, so it would be an honor to hear your thoughts. I hope to make your acquaintance in person. Very truly yours, George Lynes, AS Stable Publications

[GEORGE *quickly scans the letter, places it in an envelope, seals it, and exits.* GLENWAY *sits down to the typewriter and composes his response.*]

GLENWAY   Dear Mr. Lynes, if you are ever in New York, I should like very much to see you. I have a large number or rather a large quantity of greetings to convey to you, and of course our friends have made me look forward eagerly to making your acquaintance. I delight in the pamphlets. Yours, G. Wescott

[*There's a knock at the door.* GLENWAY *goes to open it. There stands* GEORGE LYNES.]

Mr. Lynes.

GEORGE   [*Star-struck.*] Glenway Wescott . . . How are you?

GLENWAY   I'm well and very pleased to meet you. Won't you come in?

[GEORGE *enters the room.*]

Have a seat.

GEORGE   [*A bit overwhelmed.*] This is very nice.

GLENWAY   Yes, we're—I mean, I'm staying here briefly until I return to Paris.

GEORGE   Bernadine said I should send you some of my pamphlets.

GLENWAY   [*Picking up some pamphlets from his desk.*] Yes, I received them. I have some thoughts if you'd like to hear them.

GEORGE   That's why I'm here.

GLENWAY   First, I must say, Mr. Lynes, you're very talented. I think you show quite a lot of promise. Your words far exceed your age in wisdom. And Gertrude Stein's piece is beautifully produced.

GEORGE   Think so?

GLENWAY   Yes, I do. I think all of your pieces are remarkably beautiful.

GEORGE   You're just saying that . . .

GLENWAY   No, no! Beautiful people make beautiful things.

GEORGE   [*Embarrassed.*] Yes, well, your writing is something to aspire to when it comes to beauty.

GLENWAY   Thank you, Mr. Lynes. That's very kind.

GEORGE   Well, it's the truth. *The Apple of the Eye* is one of my—

GLENWAY   As you said in your letter.

GEORGE   Yes. I guess I did say that already . . .

GLENWAY   Yes.

[GLENWAY *is touching* GEORGE*'s face and playing with his hair, moving in to try and kiss him. Projection:* Photo of Monroe Wheeler. *Then* GEORGE *notices* MONROE*'s picture on* GLENWAY*'s desk.*]

GEORGE   Who is that?

GLENWAY   What?

GEORGE   Who is that? In that picture?

GLENWAY   [*Looking.*] Oh. That's Mr. Wheeler. Monroe Wheeler.

GEORGE   Monroe Wheeler.

[GEORGE *gets up to move to the picture.*]

GLENWAY   He is my traveling companion.

GEORGE   [*He whistles.*] Oh really. Is he a writer?

GLENWAY   No, no, a publisher and he's quite good.

GEORGE   I'm sure he is.

GLENWAY   [*Standing in between* GEORGE *and the photo.*] So let's continue on about your writing.

GEORGE   When I'm writing and I actually finish a book and I think it's ready for publication, who would I speak with?

GLENWAY   [*With flirtation.*] Well, that depends on the kind of book you're writing. Do you have a part of it with you to share with me? Maybe we could sit on the couch and you could read it to me?

GEORGE   Yes, and who would I see about the publishing part? Who would I meet with when it gets to that stage?

GLENWAY   But you aren't really at that point, are you? I thought you wanted to develop your writing a bit more and then publish something new.

GEORGE   Well, yes, that's true but I—

GLENWAY   But what?

GEORGE   What kind of a publisher is Mr. Wheeler? He's the one for me.

GLENWAY   Mr. Wheeler focuses on specialty publications. You're publishing is already quite similar to his.

GEORGE   And how old is he? Late 20s?

GLENWAY   Ahh, 27. What does that have to do with his publishing?

GEORGE   Will he be here later?

GLENWAY   Actually we have a dinner engagement but I can—

GEORGE   How about tomorrow afternoon?

GLENWAY   Well, he'll be here but I'll be meeting with my publisher to discuss my new book, *The Grandmothers*.

GEORGE   Oh, so you're not monogamous with your publisher?

[*They both laugh, but* GLENWAY*'s is a bit forced.*]

GLENWAY   You know I'm just remembering that Mr. Wheeler may join me for my meeting with the publisher. He might not even be here tomorrow.

GEORGE   Well, perhaps he will be here, so I'll just stop by anyway. We can just stay here for however long and talk?

GLENWAY   Yes, well, sometimes my meetings are very short and then I just come right back to the hotel.

GEORGE   Then maybe I'll see you too. I'll plan to stop by tomorrow afternoon at 1 o'clock. Thank you.

[GEORGE *exits.*]

[GLENWAY *watches him leave.*]

[*There is music here to help with the transition to an outdoor location where* MONROE *and* GLENWAY *are sitting on a bench,* GLENWAY *with head buried in a book and* MONROE *looking out to the park.* MONROE *finds something interesting to look at, presumably a man. He nudges* GLENWAY. GLENWAY *looks up, does not look at* MONROE, *not interested. Same sequence.* GLENWAY *looks up from book, looks, looks at* MONROE, *and goes back to book. Sequence repeats, and on the third time,* GEORGE PLATT LYNES *appears.* GLENWAY *looks up. He whistles "Pace, pace, mio dolce tesoro."* MONROE *stands up from the bench and is smitten with* GEORGE. *He turns to speak to the audience. As he does,* GLENWAY *spends more time in his book, and then eventually also speaks to the audience.*]

MONROE   Glen and I, we have an understanding.

GLENWAY   An understanding.

MONROE   We've made some decisions together.

GLENWAY   Decisions.

MONROE   If, and when, we meet another individual that we find attractive—

GLENWAY   Someone else.

MONROE   And we decide that we want to pursue that individual—

GLENWAY   The other whistles.

MONROE   The other whistles.

GLENWAY   It's a code.

MONROE   That gives the other permission to pursue.

GLENWAY It's a peace offering.

MONROE A rather simple tune.

GLENWAY Compensation in a difficult moment.

MONROE It goes like this.

> [GLENWAY *whistles a line from Mozart's "Pace, Pace."*]
> Mozart's "Pace, pace, mio dolce tesoro."

GLENWAY From *Le Nozze di Figaro*.

MONROE [*Pauses and looks at* GEORGE.] Lovely isn't it?

GLENWAY Lovely.

[GLENWAY *shuts his book brusquely and exits, leaving* MONROE *and* GEORGE *alone on stage.*]

MONROE Mr. Lynes.

GEORGE Mr. Wheeler.

[*They look at each other and* GEORGE *smiles. Takes a step forward.*]

MONROE Mr. Wescott told me that you paid him a visit. That you liked my picture.

GEORGE Ah, yes... I did. I mean—uh, paid a visit. I was interested in hearing more about writing and publishing and—

MONROE He said that you whistled and said, "He's the one for me." Is that true?

GEORGE Well, um, I, well, I just thought—

MONROE How old are you, Mr. Lynes?

GEORGE I'm 20, but—

MONROE And where do you live?

GEORGE Englewood, New Jersey.

MONROE With?

GEORGE My parents.

MONROE On a farm?

GEORGE   In a rectory.

MONROE   [*Surprised chuckling.*] A rectory.

GEORGE   My father is a minister.

MONROE   The son of a minister.

[*George takes another step forward.*]

GEORGE   What's wrong with that?

MONROE   Nothing, Mr. Lynes. Nothing at all. Well, it's been a pleasure.

[MONROE *turns to go.*]

GEORGE   I may be twenty, but I've lived in Paris, I have my own publishing company with some friends, and I know what I want.

MONROE   [*Turning back to him.*] Really?

GEORGE   Really.

MONROE   And that would be?

GEORGE   You.

[MONROE *smiles to himself.*]

MONROE   How can you be so sure?

GEORGE   The dust you raised here will not settle. You're the one for me.

[GEORGE *moves in closer to* MONROE. *The tension increases.*]

MONROE   I see. Well, I have a dinner engagement uptown. Would you like to join me? Then we can see if you're the one for me.

GEORGE   I'm confident you won't be disappointed.

[*They look at each other for a moment.*]

MONROE   After you.

[GEORGE *smiles and exits.* MONROE *begins to exit, looks back, goes to typewriter, and leaves a note for* GLENWAY. *Sound and lights move forward in time.* GLENWAY *enters with a manuscript, looking for* MONROE.]

GLENWAY   Monroe?!

> [*Listening for him.*]
>
> Are you here?
>
> [GLENWAY *goes to his typewriter, sits down. There's a note there from* MONROE *saying he is out with* GEORGE. *He crumples the note then loads a piece of paper and stares at it for a moment. Nothing comes. He turns out to deliver a letter to* GEORGE. *As he begins the letter,* GEORGE *and* MONROE *enter the playing space upstage of* GLENWAY. *They share a gentle but passionate kiss.*]
>
> My dear boy, I'm glad that you have found Monroe's company so enjoyable. It has been a fine distraction for him as I race to meet my deadline before we sail back to France. Monroe loves the opera, but he hates to go alone, and I, in my nervousness to finish, am in no shape to accompany him. You have done us a great service, Boy New York.

[GLENWAY *stops and returns to type, very slowly. When the typing begins,* GEORGE *exits. Not much comes out on the paper.* MONROE *enters with a spring in his step. He sees* GLENWAY *and becomes slightly cautious.*]

MONROE   [*Testing the waters.*] Hello. How's the writing?

GLENWAY   [*Not looking up.*] How was dinner?

MONROE   Good

GLENWAY   I got your note.

MONROE   Written much?

GLENWAY   [*Looks up at* MONROE.] Not enough.

MONROE   Good night, Glen . . .

[MONROE *begins to exit.*]

GLENWAY   I think he should come visit us in France.

> [MONROE *stops and whistles "Pace, Pace" then exits, leaving* GLENWAY *to try and resume working. The typing sounds are simple finger pecks. Nothing sustained. He stops and looks up again to finish the letter to* GEORGE.]
>
> I do wish you would find it in your heart to pay me another visit, George. Had I accomplished what I longed to do the first time we

were acquainted, we both might have been closer. I to my
deadline and you to me. Tout Coeur, Glenway.

[*Lights and sound indicate moving forward in time.* GLENWAY *exits with his
manuscript.* MONROE *enters carrying a suitcase.* GEORGE *follows with a stack of
clothes. The two men are playing a flirtatious game with flowery prose that they make
up as they go along.*]

GEORGE   And you must write me and very often. Or else I won't sleep
at all. I'm afraid that too much of your absence will leave me cold.

[GEORGE *places the clothes down on a chair and hovers around* MONROE.
MONROE *places the suitcase on a chair, opens it, and begins to pack.*
GEORGE *tries to hand him things, and* MONROE *prefers to do his own
packing.*]

I think I sufficiently warned you. You run me off the chart of all
language.

[MONROE *continues to pack. Finally, he speaks to* GEORGE.]

MONROE   Tell me, Gio, when did you become aware of your mad love
for me?

GEORGE   The day that my heart grew rich with desires, size, and
suffering, and when my eyes filled with tears and my throat with
weeping.

MONROE   What did love bring you?

GEORGE   The fine features of my beloved's face, and comprehension of
his worth, and his omnipotence.

MONROE   And how did that come to you?

GEORGE   On the wings of my thoughts and memories.

MONROE   How did he receive them?

GEORGE   With charity and hope.

MONROE   How did you keep them?

GEORGE   [GEORGE *moves in for a kiss here, but* MONROE *stops him.*] With
justice, prudence, strength—

MONROE   [*Stopping the game.*] And moderation.

[MONROE *closes the suitcase and begins to exit.* GEORGE *stops him.*]

GEORGE   There's nothing left to say. You've made me so happy. I won't forget now. I will always be waiting for you.

MONROE   Narcisse.

[MONROE *continues to exit.* GEORGE *cries after him.*]

GEORGE   Never forget me, darling; think of me!

> [MONROE *turns and waves one more time. Then he exits.* GEORGE *lets him go and then yells after him again.*]
>
> Monie, please come back!
>
> [*There is no response.* GEORGE *is distraught. He throws himself across the room to a writing desk and chair and begins to write frantically. He writes a line, posts an envelope, rests for a moment, and then grows agitated again and repeats the whole process.*]
>
> February 18, 1927, 2:30 p.m. Monie darling: I cannot write a letter now. You are too immediate, too close, the break of your departure is too sudden.
>
> [GEORGE *starts another letter.*]
>
> 6:40. I cannot tell you, though you will guess, how horrible, how painful, it is going to be waiting for all the months between now and November.
>
> [GEORGE *starts another letter.*]
>
> 11:10. I cannot give you up. I will not give you up. And yet this distance between us is so appalling.
>
> [*And another.*]
>
> February 19, 4:25 a.m. I think that I shall never again know the joy and the unhappiness that I have known this last week before you left.
>
> [*And another.*]
>
> 11:35. I think that I shall never again experience the thrill of eyes I felt when you looked at me.
>
> [*And another.*]
>
> 3:55. I will write letters when I am calmer. Always adoring you, George.

[GEORGE *posts the last letter and seals it. The stage can be littered with these letters.* MONROE *and* GLENWAY *have appeared together on the other side of the stage.* GEORGE *grabs another piece of paper and begins to compose a poem.* GLENWAY *watches* MONROE *open the letter as this is happening, and* GEORGE *is speaking the poem out loud as he writes.* MONROE *is reading the poem. The two worlds are bleeding together.*]

breathing against his mouth
so firm under the sun

under the shadow
of identity
this boy playing
and shadows
showing no moon and no mouth
bitter

MONROE   Your Giorgio

[MONROE *looks at* GLENWAY *who has been reading over his shoulder.* GLENWAY *looks up at* MONROE.]

GLENWAY   Bitter?

[MONROE *shrugs his shoulders. There's a pause.*]

MONROE   I think our young George needs a hobby.

[GLENWAY *snickers and moves, leaving* MONROE *standing alone with the poem.* MONROE *delivers a letter to* GEORGE, *and during this,* GEORGE *exits.*]

My Gio, Glenway and I are anxious for you arrival here in Paris. I think it's better that you not stay with us at the beginning. I adore you and can't wait to wrap my arms around your beautiful waist. Glenway is writing and looks forward to conversations about your newest project. We will meet you at the train station on the day of your ship's arrival. Wire us when you know. My love, Monroe.

[*There is the sound of a ship whistle and French music from the period plays to announce* GEORGE's *arrival.* GLENWAY *and* MONROE *stand together and* GEORGE *enters with two suitcases. There's a pause, and* GLENWAY *moves forward to greet him.*]

GLENWAY   George!

[*The two move together and kiss each other on both cheeks, and then* GEORGE *breezes by, leaving* GLENWAY *with the suitcases.* GEORGE *and* MONROE *embrace and share a passionate kiss.* GLENWAY *is uncomfortable and moves to pick up the bags.*]

MONROE   Let's take George to lunch at our favorite café.

GLENWAY   George must be tired, Monroe. Maybe he'd like to rest.

GEORGE   Oh no, I'm actually quite hungry. Lunch would be wonderful.

MONROE   Put those bags down and join us.

GLENWAY   I should get back to my writing and—

MONROE   Stop it and come along.

GLENWAY   No, really I—

GEORGE   Please join us, Glen.

[*Pause.* GLENWAY *looks at* GEORGE *and then puts down the bags to join them. The three move together to the edge of the stage.*]

GLENWAY   How was the crossing, George?

GEORGE   Fine. A bit rough in the first part, but the seas calmed, and it was smoother for the second half of the journey.

MONROE   Calm seas. We appreciate calm seas.

GLENWAY   Yes, we do.

GEORGE   I'm glad for that.

[GEORGE *and* MONROE *smile at each other in a knowing way. The three then break off into separate positions that face the audience.*]

MONROE   George arrived today.

GLENWAY   We met George at the station today.

GEORGE   I arrived in Paris today!

MONROE   He looked radiant as he stepped on to the platform.

GLENWAY   His greeting was unexpected.

GEORGE   It was wonderful to see Glenway and Monroe.

MONROE   Our kiss was something that I'll always remember.

GLENWAY   His kiss with Monroe was unforgettable.

GEORGE   The feel of Monroe's lips on mine will never leave me.

GLENWAY   When we returned home, George insisted that I read his writing.

GEORGE   Glenway insisted that he wanted to see my writing as soon as we arrived back at the apartment.

MONROE   He has great talent this one, just like Glenway.

GLENWAY   I'm having some trouble with my writing.

MONROE   And he has a charming personality that all our friends adore.

GEORGE   Gertrude Stein told me that Glenway has a certain syrup, but it does not pour.

MONROE   George can be a bit of a gossip.

GLENWAY   Gertrude Stein is an ass.

GEORGE   Monroe always wants to discuss my future.

GLENWAY   Monroe seems preoccupied.

MONROE   How can I help him?

GEORGE   What will I do to make my mark?

GLENWAY   George's writing has not gotten any better.

MONROE   I must convince Glenway to help him.

GLENWAY   His writing lacks focus.

GEORGE   I'm writing each day that I'm here.

MONROE   He's having trouble concentrating.

GLENWAY   His ideas are never fully realized.

GEORGE   I like some of the new ideas I've started.

GLENWAY   George doesn't seem to be able to finish anything that he starts.

MONROE He needs help.

GEORGE But most of it feels forced.

MONROE Maybe our Giorgio needs a hobby.

GLENWAY I don't think he's a writer.

GEORGE I think I just need more time.

[GEORGE *and* MONROE *exit, leaving* GLENWAY *alone.*]

GLENWAY Dear Gio, You better learn to write. I mean—you'd better learn how to sit down and write a "piece." You astonish me with your knowledge of the language. Furthermore, you have profited by admiring Miss Gertrude Stein more than anyone else. If you could admire your own thought in that way, simply, doggedly, and without too much conceit, you would be a fine writer.

[*Lights shift to a moment outside the Villefranche flat.* MONROE *is enjoying the sunlight again.* GLENWAY *turns to face* MONROE *who is on the bench, and* GEORGE *crosses with a satchel that contains a camera and some photos.*]

GEORGE Afternoon, gentlemen.

MONROE Hello, Giorgio.

GLENWAY Where are you off to?

GEORGE For a walk.

GLENWAY Is everything alright?

GEORGE I just can't focus on the writing, so I'm going to—

GLENWAY We talked about setting aside the time to write, George.

GEORGE Three hours at a time is a long time.

GLENWAY Do you have anything new that you'd like to share with us?

GEORGE I sat for two and a half hours. Of course I have something.

MONROE Let's hear it.

GEORGE No.

MONROE George?

GLENWAY   George, please?

MONROE   Read it to us, Gio.

GEORGE   [*Still hesitant, taking a folded piece of paper from his satchel.*] No judging.

GLENWAY   [*Playfully.*] Yes, Monie, no judging.

GEORGE   This is from a book that I started last week. The lover is writing to his love and he's—

[GLENWAY *stops him and gestures for him to just read.*]

It is more than affection that makes me want for you, and rather more particularly for myself, all the quality, the sureness and inquietude, the farewell kiss and future blessing, of our brotherhood—

GLENWAY   It's not bad, George.

GEORGE   [*A bit defensive.*] In context it's not bad at all.

MONROE   Maybe if someone else read it for you?

GLENWAY   "Inquietude" is a great word!

MONROE   George, come here and sit down.

GEORGE   I want to go take pictures before the light changes. This is the best time of day to get—

MONROE   George?

GEORGE   [*Takes out some pictures and hands them to* MONROE.] Look, if I take pictures at this time of day, they turn out so well. I want to get down to the café. The sunlight is—

GLENWAY   George, how do you ever expect to improve if you don't keep writing? Gertrude writes four hours a day and—

MONROE   These are very good, George. How long has this been going on?

[GLENWAY *moves over to see the photos.* MONROE *hands them to him.*]

GEORGE   Well, I've been trying off and on for a couple of months now. It's not easy, but I—

GLENWAY   This one is beautiful. When did you take it?

GEORGE   Right about this time a week ago. See? That's why I want to go now.

[MONROE *lays the photos out before them.*]

MONROE   What do you see in this photo?

GEORGE   A sailor.

GLENWAY   [*Suddenly more interested in the sailor.*] Could I see that one?

MONROE   [*Slapping away* GLENWAY's *hand.*] And this one?

GEORGE   A tree?

MONROE   What else do you see?

GEORGE   A field. Flowers.

MONROE   How does the photo make you feel?

GEORGE   What do you mean?

MONROE   How does it make you feel?

GEORGE   Calm?

MONROE   How did you feel when you were in the field?

GEORGE   Calm.

[GLENWAY *smiles. He knows what* MONROE *is doing because it's been done to him.*]

MONROE   Yes. Calm. What does that tell you then about this photo?

GEORGE   [*Confused.*] It's a calm picture?

MONROE   Why did you take pictures of this sailor?

GEORGE   [*Still not getting it.*] Because he was interesting.

MONROE   [*Slightly frustrated.*] George . . . What makes the sailor interesting? Be more specific.

GEORGE   [*Looking at the photo.*] He's beautiful. And more than anything else, beauty is what makes things interesting.

[MONROE *smiles and looks at* GLENWAY, *who smiles back.*]

MONROE   Gio, have you thought about taking up photography?

GEORGE   Well, I already do.

GLENWAY   I think Monroe means in a more focused way.

GEORGE   Why?

MONROE   Because you have an eye for it. For the beauty that you can capture with it.

GEORGE   But I don't have the equipment.

MONROE   We'll find you the equipment.

GLENWAY   I'm sure Barbara can help fund this little project.

GEORGE   Who's Barbara?

MONROE   Excellent idea. Barbara Harrison, my publishing partner, has plenty of resources. She will help you with the start-up costs.

GLENWAY   And she has friends and we have friends that will sit for you and pay for your photos.

GEORGE   [*Protesting.*] But it's just a hobby.

[MONROE *grows silent. He does not like to be questioned like this.*]

MONROE   It would be a shame to waste this talent, George. Think about it.

[MONROE *exits.*]

GLENWAY   He's right, George. He knows what he's talking about. You don't want to disappoint him.

[GLENWAY *exits.*]

[GEORGE *sits staring at the photos on the ground and slowly begins to gather them as the lights shift. Sound of the boat steam whistle again, as* GEORGE *walks to the camera and removes the drop cloth. He also puts his signature work coveralls on over his other clothing. Projection:* New York City.]

GEORGE   Dearest Monie, Photography is interesting. I have taken dozens of pictures of which three were presentable, one above average. Portraits of socialites and dancers. Some of those were nudes and near nudes. I dislike the acid under my fingernails, enough to be unwilling to go on doing shop work forever, but hope for better days is still too strong in me to doubt the end of it all. I really believe I am working more for the perfection of our relationship than for any other single thing. It all requires much patience, and I have not a patient nature. I adore you more each day. Your Giorgio.

[GLENWAY *enters. Projection:* France.]

GLENWAY   Monroe still urges me to write about myself. I'm not sure that the old stimulus of wishing to please him will have an effect, but it may deter some of his little comments about my failure. In the old days, when he hurt me, I usually tried twice as hard. Now I react less well.

[*A duet from* Le Nozze Di Figaro *begins to play: "Via Resti Servita, Madama Brillanter."* GLENWAY *is at his typewriter,* GEORGE *is with his camera, and* MONROE *stands in between them.* GLENWAY *begins to type at breakneck speed, and* MONROE *is drawn over to him.* GLENWAY *stops to survey what he has written, and* GEORGE *takes a photo.* MONROE *is drawn over to him.* GLENWAY *looks up and sees that* MONROE *is gone. Looks down at typewriter and begins to type furiously.* MONROE *is drawn away from* GEORGE *and back to* GLENWAY. GLENWAY *slows down again, and with a flourish* GEORGE *takes another photo.* MONROE *is drawn back to* GEORGE. GLENWAY *picks up typing again, but it is weaker.* MONROE *begins back to him, but* GEORGE *snaps another photo before he can get to* GLENWAY. MONROE *turns.* GEORGE *snaps another photo. And another, and another, and another. Each time* GEORGE *takes a photo, a new projected image appears.* GLENWAY'*s typing turns into hunt and peck. Very slow, single-finger typing.* GEORGE'*s photos have filled the projection screen. Projections:* George's Photos. GEORGE *produces a photo to show to* MONROE, *which prompts a passionate kiss between the two.* MONROE *then moves away to center between* GEORGE *and* GLENWAY.]

GEORGE   Dearest Monie, I miss you. And I love you. Yet the price of loving you is always the fear that I will lose you. Never, dearest, has separation been so intimate and melancholy. My desire is intellectual, and I am doubly astonished that all the beautiful people, clothed and unclothed, I have photographed have affected me no more than if they did not exist. When I dream at all it is of you. Your loving, Giorgio.

MONROE My dearest Gio, my St. Sebastian, your observation about your relationship to your subjects interests me. Except when there is a basis of absolute intimacy one never does know "where one stands," and that intimacy cannot be arrived at without a certain amount of love, and one hasn't time or heart enough to love more than two people. You have changed in so many ways that please me and make me love you more. I am proud of you and your new career. I love you, Monie. PS: Barbara has hinted that she would like to marry me. I'm not sure what to do with this tempting proposal. Our impending trip to Shang Hai grows in importance.

[MONROE *moves up the projection screen. Projection:* Photo of Barbara Harrison. *The sound of a boat steam whistle.*]

GEORGE My dear Glen, I want to begin by telling you what I feel about Monroe. I have loved Monroe from the moment I first saw him; I have never loved anyone else. I have not been unfaithful to him, and will not be unfaithful to him, and seriously doubt if I should be capable of it. Yet suddenly there is the understanding that, if it seems possible (for I gather it seems desirable), Monroe might marry Barbara! And that has not been pleasant to contemplate. My imagination is not good enough for me to be able to come to any conclusions about a happy ménage à quatre; moreover, I have felt Monroe has his hands full enough with you and me.

GLENWAY Gio, I think I know, dear, how difficult this is for you. You'll have to trust your future (our future, if that sounds more substantial). Barbara Harrison is Monroe's business partner. If they deem it necessary that a marriage seals the deal, then so be it. They are in China, I am here in Paris, you in New Jersey. You've got to be heroic in order tọ *be* at all.

[MONROE *stands beside the projected image of* BARBARA.]

GEORGE Mon, my love, I have tried to rid myself of the seed you planted, but I can't destroy the weeds of my thoughts. It has been the bitterest of pills. Will you marry Barbara? Have you married Barbara? What will become of me? I have given up trying to cross that bridge before coming to it. But don't you see, my sweet, that I am frantic with wanting to know?

MONROE My Gio, How sorry I am to have alarmed you about the marriage thing—it is quite out of the question. I see now, as I should have seen then.

[*The sound of boat steam whistle again.* GEORGE *collapses with relief and* GLENWAY *smiles a knowing smile.*]

[*Wedding bells begin to play, and we see projected on the screen an image of* BARBARA HARRISON *and* LLOYD WESCOTT. MONROE *removes the drop cloth from the table and three chairs while* GLENWAY *speaks.*]

GLENWAY April 8. Barbara Harrison, daughter of Virginia Crocker of the banking and railroad Crockers of California, and of Francis Burton Harrison, former United States congressman, marries Lloyd Wescott, son of Josephine and Bruce Wescott of Wisconsin and brother of novelist Glenway Wescott. The happy couple intends to honeymoon in Italy after a visit to the Wisconsin farm where Lloyd grew up.

[*Projection:* Apartment at 48 East 89th Street, New York City. *Lights come up to find* MONROE *entering the apartment from the direction of the master bedroom. He looks around and establishes the living room of the apartment for the audience.* GLENWAY *enters, sees* MONROE, *and looks at him looking at the apartment.*]

MONROE This is a lovely place, Glen.

GLENWAY I thought so. I'm glad you—

[GEORGE *enters abruptly with suitcases.*]

GEORGE Gentlemen!

MONROE Giorgio!

GLENWAY [*Overlapping.*] Hello, George.

GEORGE [*Taking in the apartment.*] What a delightful apartment for us. Excellent job, Glen.

GLENWAY Living room, kitchen, and dining room off to the left, master bedroom and bath back down this hall, and second bedroom and bath down this hall to the right. I thought this would be a nice space for you, George. The view could be great inspiration for your photography.

GEORGE Wonderful!

[*Handing* MONROE *a suitcase.*]

Would you put this in the bedroom, please?

[MONROE *exits in the direction of the master bedroom.* GEORGE *moves towards the second bedroom to take a look.*]

So where is the third bedroom?

GLENWAY There are only two bedrooms.

GEORGE Oh. Well, where will you stay?

GLENWAY Monie and I will stay in the master bedroom, and you will have this room.

GEORGE Oh no, Glen. I have my huge studio on East 58th. I've got plenty of room. You should have the privacy for your writing. Monie and I will be fine together.

GLENWAY No, I think—

GEORGE No, no, no, Glen, it's fine.

GLENWAY But the cost will—

GEORGE With all of my photography assignments—

GLENWAY [*Overlapping.*] Monie—

GEORGE from *Harpers, Town and Country*—

GLENWAY [*Overlapping.*] Monroe—

GEORGE and *Vogue*, I'll be able to keep that studio for quite a while. No need for space here.

[MONROE *returns to hear the end of* GEORGE*'s line.* GEORGE *moves to the master bedroom.* MONROE *crosses to* GLENWAY.]

MONROE   I thought we discussed this.

GLENWAY   You think we "discuss" a lot of things when it comes to George.

GEORGE   [*Coming back in from the bedroom.*] Monie, do you think we can fit an armoire in here?

MONROE   [*Not really looking. To* GEORGE.] Sure.

[*To* GLENWAY.]

You agreed to this arrangement.

GEORGE   Will there be enough room for both of us or will we need two?

MONROE   [*Turning to face* GEORGE.]

I think one will be enough, Gio.

[GEORGE *smiles and exits to bedroom.* MONROE *turns back to* GLENWAY. *There's an awkward silence.*]

GLENWAY   Fine.

[GLENWAY *exits to the guest room, leaving* MONROE *alone onstage.*]

MONROE   [*Loudly, so both men will hear.*] This is going to work out well, I think. Yes. Great.

[MONROE *looks after both men, lights shift, and he speaks a letter.*]

Dear Barbara, Glenway found us a lovely apartment just a block and a half from Central Park. It's a beautiful two bedroom, just enough for the three of us. George and I share one room, Glenway has the other room for his writing. He and I haven't been intimate in over four years, so it just made sense. So much of this simply makes sense. The feelings that we share for one another are difficult to describe, and I wonder what you and Lloyd must think. We are determined to make our complex ménage thrive. We are a family.

[*Lights shift and music begins Beethoven's "Sonata Pathetique" as played by Elly Ney.* MONROE *moves to the table and* GEORGE *enters with a deck of cards. He hands them to* MONROE, *who begins to shuffle the cards.* GLENWAY *enters.* MONROE *sees* GLENWAY *and motions to the empty chair.* GLENWAY *hesitates, looks at* GEORGE, *who smiles, and then looks at* MONROE. GLENWAY *decides to take the seat and begin a hand.* MONROE *deals him in. The three play a hand of rummy, and* GLENWAY *is very protective of his cards. He sees this as a chance to win at something, to beat* GEORGE. GEORGE *finds his determination amusing, and* MONROE *is actually oblivious to the competition. In fact, he is rather bored with the game. After three plays, he begins to build a house of cards. The scene shifts into slow motion at this point.* GEORGE *and* GLENWAY *continue to play the hand, and* GEORGE *eventually puts his cards down: he's won. He smiles at* MONROE, GLENWAY *looks and tosses his cards on the table.* GEORGE *begins to build with* MONROE, *and* GLENWAY *sulks over his loss.* MONROE *eventually hands* GLENWAY *a card, as if to invite him to participate.* GLENWAY *takes the card from* MONROE, *and he adds it to the house. The three continue to build the house of cards, as a cooperative family. There is a lightness among them, a compromise, until* GEORGE *gets up to go and motions for* MONROE *to join him. The two exit as if they are going to have an intimate moment, leaving* GLENWAY *at the table alone. He looks at the home, looks after* MONROE *and* GEORGE, *and then decides to move back to his typewriter, slowly. He is in place when the song ends.*]

[GLENWAY *is at his typewriter, trying to write, and it's not happening. He is upset and frustrated. He re-reads what he's written and it's not very good. He tears the sheet out of the typewriter, crumples it, and throws it on the floor. He loads another sheet into the typewriter and begins typing. He stops, reads again.* GEORGE *enters while he is reading. He has three photos in his hands. He enters as* GLENWAY *says.*]

GLENWAY   Merde!

GEORGE   [*Taken aback.*] Glen? Are you alright?

GLENWAY   I'm fine.

[GEORGE *looks at* GLENWAY *for a long moment.* GLENWAY *looks up at him.*]

GEORGE   [*Smiling.*] You don't sound fine.

GLENWAY   Is there something that you need, George? Because if not, I'm trying to work, and you're distracting me.

GEORGE   [*Going to him.*] Oh, I'm sorry. How's it coming?

GLENWAY   Not very well, which is why I asked you—

GEORGE   Why? Is there something I can do?

GLENWAY   No, George, I just need to concentrate. I'm trying to write and—

GEORGE   [*Not leaving, still looking at* GLENWAY.] Yes. I know. What are you working on?

GLENWAY   Just another aborted project.

GEORGE   What about the story that you started about Alwyn and the hawk?

GLENWAY   How do you know about that?

GEORGE   I read it. Monie left some of the pages on his nightstand. So I read them. It's quite good.

GLENWAY   Yes, well, the characters just aren't speaking to me anymore . . .

[*Awkward silence.*]

[GLENWAY *looks at* GEORGE, *getting a bit more frustrated.*] What do you want?

GEORGE   What do you mean?

GLENWAY   Why are you in here? You haven't come in here in months.

GEORGE   [*Sheepishly.*] Well, I actually need your help. I need an opinion about these photos and—

GLENWAY   And since Monie is away, now you're going to ask me? How quaint.

GEORGE   Glenway, that's not fair. I always ask your opinion about my photographs. And you always give me the best advice.

GLENWAY   I'm sure.

GEORGE   You have a very keen eye.

GLENWAY   Yes, well—

GEORGE   So will you take a look?

GLENWAY   I'm trying to write, George. Can't you see that?

GEORGE   Please? It will only take a minute.

[*A moment passes.* GLENWAY *looks at the typewriter and the papers on the floor, then to* GEORGE.]

GLENWAY   Alright.

GEORGE   [*Lays out the photos for* GLENWAY.] I've got three prints of the same sitting, but I experimented with the lighting in each one, and I'm trying to decide which one to show the client.

[*Projection:* Ballet photo, Orpheus and Eurydice.]

GLENWAY   [*Looking at the photos but aware of* GEORGE's *presence.*] Who's the client?

GEORGE   Balanchine

GLENWAY   Who?

GEORGE   [*Smiling, almost flirtatious.*] George Balanchine.

GLENWAY   Lincoln Kirstein's friend? The choreographer?

GEORGE   Yes.

GLENWAY   [*Looking at the photos.*] Uh-huh. And these are of?

GEORGE   American Ballet Company. *Orpheus and Eurydice.*

GLENWAY   Yes…

GEORGE   What do you think?

GLENWAY   Well, I think they're all beautiful, as your photographs usually are.

GEORGE   But?

GLENWAY   [*Pointing to the center photo.*] But I think that this one captures something about the story for me.

GEORGE   [*Pointing across* GLENWAY *to a photo.*] Really? I was actually leaning toward this one. I think the lighting is stronger.

[GEORGE *looks intently at* GLENWAY, *not breaking the eye contact.* GLENWAY *looks back, not breaking the gaze.*]

GLENWAY [*With some flirtation.*] Well, you're the photographer, not me.

GEORGE [*Moving in closer.*] Yes, I guess I am.

[GEORGE *touches* GLENWAY *again.* GEORGE *kisses* GLENWAY. GLENWAY *responds and the two begin to kiss. There's a passion between them in this moment that's not been seen.*]

GLENWAY [*Coming to his senses; trying to break the embrace.*] What are you doing?

GEORGE What do you mean what am I doing? I'm asking your opinion, Glen.

GLENWAY I think you're asking for a bit more than my opinion.

[*The two continue kissing, unbuttoning clothing,* GEORGE *takes the top of his coveralls down.*]

GLENWAY [*Stopping the process.*] You stopped this months ago.

GEORGE [*Stops and looks at him.*] Glen, can't you just—

GLENWAY No, I can't. What's going on, George?

[*There is silence between them.*]

GEORGE Well, I've been a little lonely without Monie. I thought maybe we could, you know, like before.

GLENWAY Like before?

GEORGE You know. Like before. We've had some nice times together, Glen.

GLENWAY [*Dawning on him, re-adjusting his clothes.*] Uh-huh, I see. I think I should get back to work, George.

GEORGE Glen, I didn't really—

GLENWAY Enough.

GEORGE mean to, you know—

GLENWAY Just stop it! This is difficult enough watching you with Monie, seeing how happy you are.

GEORGE   But you're a part of that, Glenway.

GLENWAY   Yes, of course, George. A second bedroom part.

[GEORGE *can't really respond.* GLENWAY *moves away from him.*]

GEORGE   Glen, I wish that you could be happier. Happy in this family.

GLENWAY   It's alright, George. Love with lust may be divine, but love without lust is the noblest part of mature human behavior.

[GEORGE *nods and the two look at each other for a long time.*]

I should really get back to work.

GEORGE   Yes, and I need to see Mr. Balanchine.

[*He goes to exit but turns around for one last time.*]

Write about the hawk.

[*There is another look here.* GEORGE *exits.* GLENWAY *looks at his typewriter, and then back to where* GEORGE *has exited.* GLENWAY *begins to type in a very methodical, rhythmic manner, not frantic. Some music to indicate the passage of time.* GEORGE *re-enters with his camera and begins to set his lights for a photo.* MONROE *enters center and speaks this letter over the work of* GLENWAY *and* GEORGE. *Projection:* Paris.]

MONROE   Dear Gio, I met with Matisse today, Chagall tomorrow. Matisse agrees to the museum's request. The painting will accompany me back to New York. I hope to secure the acquisitions from Chagall as well. He is a tougher nut in the very best sense. MoMA trusts me with these men because of my years here. Our years here. Such happy days together, at the beginning of our family. When I walk down the Boulevard St. Michel before or after dinner, I think of you. That boulevard is the essence of centuries, the effervescent blood of centuries of artists, and builders and lovers. Everything is rather sober here without you. My chief joy is thinking of you, my sweet. Je t'aime. Monie

[*As* MONROE's *speech ends, we hear a series of snapshots and a few of* GEORGE's *photos come up on the projection screen. Projections:* More of George's photos. *The typing stops.* MONROE, GEORGE, *and* GLENWAY *loosen their shirts, and move into position inspired by Cadmus's drawing of the three men called "Conversation Piece."*]

They are outside. Projection: Hampton, New Jersey. The country home, Stone-blossom. GLENWAY *is looking down at* GEORGE, *then looks off into the distance.* GEORGE *and* MONROE *enjoy the sun.*]

MONROE   I love the first weekend out of the city after a long winter.

GEORGE   Hhhmmm.

MONROE   Barbara and Lloyd were so kind to give us this home in the country.

GEORGE   Hhhhmm.

GLENWAY   They certainly have enough money to spare, with her fortune and now the farm and the horses...

[*Silence. All are enjoying the quiet.*]

GEORGE   When are we going back?

GLENWAY   Never.

MONROE   Sunday.

GLENWAY   Evening.

MONROE   Yes. Evening.

GEORGE   I think I'll stay in the city next weekend.

MONROE   Why?

[*Pause.*]

GEORGE   To get things done.

MONROE   Glen?

GLENWAY   Yes?

MONROE   Someone named Matthew called. Who is Matthew?

GLENWAY   Michael?

MONROE   Yes, Michael. I knew it started with an "M."

GLENWAY   Michael Lansdale. He called?

MONROE   Yes.

GLENWAY   When?

MONROE   Yesterday afternoon.

> [*Pause.*]

> You've never mentioned him before.

GEORGE   Who is he?

GLENWAY   [*Getting up to look closer at something in the distance.*] No need to.

MONROE   Why not?

GEORGE   [*Sitting up.*] Who is he?

GLENWAY   He's just a writer.

GEORGE   That sounds familiar.

GLENWAY   He's a reporter for *Newsweek*. He interviewed me for a story he was doing about—

MONROE   Am I going to meet him?

GLENWAY   [GLENWAY *lays back down.*] Not this time.

[*A collective chuckle amongst the three.*]

MONROE   Has he been helpful?

GLENWAY   In what way?

GEORGE   Is he helping you with that new book?

GLENWAY   He's a friend now.

MONROE   Is he helping you?

GLENWAY   Helping me how?

MONROE and **GEORGE**   With your book!

GLENWAY   Well, I haven't finished it yet.

GEORGE   Glen? Are you smitten?

GLENWAY   God...No.

MONROE   That's very sweet.

[GLENWAY *sits up and faces away from them, staring out into the distance. Silence.* GEORGE *gets up.*]

GEORGE   I'm going in.

GLENWAY   Could you put some tea on, George?

GEORGE   Earl Grey?

GLENWAY   Fine.

GEORGE   [*To* MONROE.] Need anything?

[MONROE *shakes his head and* GEORGE *exits. More silence.* MONROE *slides down next to* GLENWAY.]

MONROE   It's alright, you know.

GLENWAY   What's alright?

MONROE   Michael.

GLENWAY   What's there to be alright about, Monie?

MONROE   It's alright if you want a muse.

GLENWAY   A muse?

MONROE   Michael amuses you. You should let him.

GLENWAY   I don't need amusement, Monroe. I need to finish my book.

MONROE   If he helps you finish your book, so be it. That's fine too.

    [GLENWAY *does not respond.* MONROE *looks away. Then looks back at him.*]

    I'm sorry I haven't been helpful.

GLENWAY   It's not that you aren't helpful. It's just hard. Sharing.

MONROE   Do you like him? Michael?

GLENWAY   Sure.

MONROE   Then you should use him. Use him and write about your life.

[GLENWAY *and* MONROE *kiss and then* MONROE *exits. As he goes, he whistles "Pace, Pace."* GLENWAY *exhales loudly and lies back on the ground. Then sound to indicate the passage of time. As the sound continues,* GLENWAY *moves from the ground to his writing desk and picks up a series of newspapers and magazines. He reads them aloud and as finishes, he tosses them to the ground in a stack. Projection: The Pilgrim Hawk.]*

GLENWAY [*Enjoying these reviews.*] *The New York Herald Tribune:* "Brilliant. . . . The writing is beautiful, cut to the bare bones."

[*Drops this one to the ground.*]

Chicago News: "Glenway Wescott's short novel is the sort Henry James would have written, if he had that much talent."

[*Drops this one to the ground.*]

Kenyon Review: "*The Pilgrim Hawk* is at least as special in its point of view as *The Turn of the Screw*, but it is not ambiguous."

[*Drops this one to the ground.*]

The New York Times: "The product of an intensely individual mind."

[GLENWAY *looks at this and repeats it.*]

"The product of an intensely individual mind."

[*He looks up, looks around and sees that he's alone, no one is there to share it with him. Sadness.*]

Sometimes I feel as if I live with a couple of blind men.

[GLENWAY *exits and* MONROE *enters. Something is wrong. He carries a battered, worn chapbook,* The Bitterns. *He opens the book, finds a passage, and reads.*]

MONROE "Let us laugh carelessly like other men. Let us be timid even among fools. Let us knot silence round our throats, for they would surely kill us."

[MONROE *closes the book and returns it to his suit pocket. Beat and shift.*]

Dear Barbara, I'm sorry for my recent extended absence from Stone-blossom. I miss conversations with you and Lloyd and the simplicity of the country. The work of the museum keeps me very busy. More exhibits to oversee means more publications to supervise. The trustees say they appreciate many things about my work: my attention to detail, my understanding of aesthetics, my "brilliant diplomacy," as they like to call it. I only wish they could live up to their own notions of modernity. But I'm being trivial.

Maybe it is the tiredness that makes me more sensitive than usual.
I shall write again before the week's out with a much finer
disposition. Forgive me. Monroe.

[*Projection:* Museum of Modern Art, *followed by a painting by Matisse.
The men are in a museum. There's a murmur of a crowd underneath as if it's
an opening.* GLENWAY *and* GEORGE *enter facing the audience, admiring
the painting that is projected. They stand close together.* MONROE *enters
and gives a bit of a lesson to* GEORGE *and* GLENWAY.]

If you look closely you can see that he's using a number of
different brush strokes to achieve this effect.

GLENWAY   Yes.

MONROE   And the imagined light source adds to the texture of the
image.

GEORGE   It's a shocking piece of work.

[MONROE *puts his arm around* GEORGE.]

MONROE   What do you see in the painting, George?

GLENWAY   Please, Monie, these questions are so—

MONROE   George, what do you see? In this painting?

GEORGE   What do *you* see, Monie?

GLENWAY   Touché...

[MONROE *puts his arm around* GLENWAY *and the three stand this way for a
moment, admiring the painting. After a moment, the murmuring crowd turns to
snickering and laughing.* MONROE *looks over his shoulder, realizes where they are
and that they are being watched, and moves away from* GEORGE *and* GLENWAY.
They continue to look at the painting and ask questions. The laughing continues.]

GEORGE   How did you convince him to give it to you, Monroe?

MONROE   [*Distracted, looking for an exit.*] Oh, it was nothing special.
Could we maybe—

GLENWAY   Now, Monie, don't be modest. You told me the other night
that this was one of your most difficult acquisitions.

MONROE   I know, but maybe we could talk about this somewhere else. Let's go home.

GEORGE   Why? The reception's just started.

MONROE   [*More agitated.*] Because I'm tired.

GLENWAY   [*Going to him, touches his forehead.*] Are you alright? You look a little pale.

MONROE   [*Exploding, batting* GLENWAY's *hand away.*] I'm fine! I'm just tired. Could we please go?

[MONROE *exits.* GLENWAY *and* GEORGE *look at each and* GEORGE *exits after him.* GLENWAY *turns to address the audience. Projection:* September 1942.]

GLENWAY   In this time, perhaps any war time, no one can do anything by himself or for himself; one is *in things* with others, one has to yield to the collectivity and trust it. If the "we" is good enough, it will come out all right after a while, and the "I" can have its turn again. The "I" just now is a hopeless delusion.

[*Lights change to the living room at Stone-blossom.* GEORGE *is in a chair doing needlepoint,* MONROE *sits in a chair reviewing some of* GEORGE's *photos, and* GLENWAY *reads to* MONROE *from a book. Projection: The Moon Is Down* by John Steinbeck.]

"On this Sunday morning the postman and the policeman had gone fishing in the boat of Mr. Corell, the popular storekeeper. He had lent them his trim sailboat for the day. The postman and the policeman were several miles at sea when they saw the small, dark transport, loaded with soldiers, go quietly past them. As officials of the town, this was definitely their business, and these two put about, but of course the battalion was in possession by the time they could make port. The policeman and the postman could not even get into their own office in the Town Hall, and when they insisted on their rights they were taken prisoners of war and locked up in the town jail."

[GLENWAY *closes the book.*]

Mr. Steinbeck is at it again.

MONROE   Giorgio?

GEORGE   Hmm?

MONROE   These photos are striking.

GEORGE   Which ones?

MONROE   All of these. This young man. Blonde hair, tall.

[*Projection:* Photo of Jonathan Tichenor.]

GLENWAY   He looks familiar, George.

GEORGE   He's my studio assistant.

GLENWAY   Ahh. Jonathan. Yes.

MONROE   I didn't know you had made him your subject.

GEORGE   Can you blame me?

GLENWAY   I saw him first, but obviously that didn't work out.

MONROE   How long has he been your assistant?

GEORGE   Three or four months.

MONROE   Four months. Is he a good assistant?

GEORGE   Yes, he's excellent. Very thorough. He photographs very well.

GLENWAY   Evidently.

GEORGE   I mean, he takes good photos. I'm taking him under my wing. Very eager to learn.

MONROE   I know the sort.

GLENWAY   Hmm.

MONROE   This is remarkable. This is some of your most . . .

GEORGE   Inspired. I don't know what it is. He makes me feel . . . artistic.

MONROE   Yes.
  [*He recognizes that something much deeper is happening here.*]
  I'm happy for you.

[GLENWAY *discovers a note in the book he has been reading. He picks it up and opens it.*]

GLENWAY   What's this?

MONROE   I don't know.

GLENWAY   It's a note to you, Monroe.

GEORGE   Fan mail, I'm sure.

GLENWAY   I don't think so.

> [*He begins to read the note aloud.*]
>
> "Dear Monroe, it has come to my attention that Conger Goodyear is calling for your resignation to clear the name of the Museum."

MONROE   Glen. Glen, could I have that, please.

[*He goes to take the note from* GLENWAY, *but* GLENWAY *dodges and continues to read.*]

GLENWAY   "He has called for a meeting of the Executive Committee to go into the matter. We could refute these attacks, even counter them with our own, but your 89th Street home-life is difficult to defend."

MONROE   Glen, give me the note, please.

GEORGE   Home-life?

GLENWAY   "While Goodyear is a lone voice at this time, and we have refused his demands, he is gathering some support amongst the trustees."

> [GLENWAY *reads silently to the end of the letter.*]
>
> This is from the director of the museum.

MONROE   It's nothing.

GLENWAY   Nothing?

GEORGE   What's happening?

GLENWAY   They're trying to fire you.

GEORGE   What? Why?

GLENWAY   [*To* GEORGE.] Because of you.

MONROE   Glenway...!

GEORGE   What do you mean me?

GLENWAY   Alright. Us. Because of us. Is that better?

MONROE   You're overreacting.

GLENWAY   Overreacting? You could have discussed it with us.

MONROE   It doesn't concern you.

GEORGE   How does this not concern us?

MONROE   I spoke with Jim about this yesterday. There's nothing new here. This gossip has been going on for a long time about "the nudes on our apartment walls." Goodyear and his cronies are using it down in Washington against Nelson and—

GLENWAY   They're involving Nelson Rockefeller?

MONROE   and because Nelson's an army colonel and the chairman of the Exhibitions Committee for the museum he feels like he's involved. I've decided to lie low and just let it all blow over.

GLENWAY   Of course you have, Monroe.

[*Long pause.*]

I think that you need to—

MONROE   [*Ending the discussion.*] I don't care what you think. They aren't going to break up the family.

GLENWAY   That's not very diplomatic of you, Monroe. "We" are the family. Not just you.

[GLENWAY *crumples the note and exits.*]

GEORGE   Monie, I think—

MONROE   The discussion is over. I should have burned it.

[*Pause and then a shift back to normalcy for him.*]

Some of your best work, Gio. You should be proud of yourself. Seems like the family is expanding.

[*As* MONROE *exits, he swats at the house of cards, which crumbles.*]

[*Lights and sound shift with a Projection:* Parkers Ferry, South Carolina. Home of W. Somerset Maugham. February 1943. GEORGE *alone with the photos;* GLENWAY *enters in another location.*]

GLENWAY   Giorgio mio, all is well here in Parker's Ferry. Willie sends his greetings to you and Monie. Please tell him we look forward to his arrival, as I know the museum question has made him distracted and irritable. The thought of his coming down here naturally makes me lonesome for you; and concerned for you. Your affair with Jonathan has created a tension in our family, one that Monroe and I suffer with, but we are willing to bear because we love you. You have to decide what pattern of life is best. If you don't want to live *á trios* any more, that's that, and you must strike out on your own in search of a suitable *deuxieme*. I don't want you to feel that in our extraordinary love for you we are ganging up on you, to boss you into a way of life that is not for you. I do wish you could come down here. Your Glenway.

[GLENWAY *exits.* GEORGE *is still in the same place, now doing needlepoint.* MONROE *enters with a suitcase. There is tension.*]

MONROE   I'm all packed.

GEORGE   When's your train?

MONROE   5:25. Sure I can't convince you to come?

GEORGE   No, no, I have too much work.

MONROE   You can't bring it with you?

GEORGE   Studio's here.

MONROE   And so is Jonathan.

GEORGE   So is Jonathan.

MONROE   That's what I thought.

GEORGE   What are you going to do about the museum?

MONROE   Their lies are preposterous and lurid. They will evaporate and everything will be fine. I'm not going to quit. Glen thinks I should take an apartment on my own, but he's not sure whether he can live with you after all that's happened. And I'm not sure how to live without you.

GEORGE   Whatever you decide I'll back you up with all my heart.

MONROE   Is that the truth?

GEORGE   Of course.

MONROE   You sound a little detached.

GEORGE   I don't want to think about what change you'll choose.

MONROE   I love you as much as I always have.

GEORGE   I know.

MONROE   Although it all might be easier if I didn't.

GEORGE   I know.

[GEORGE *goes to* MONROE *as he would when they first met, with passion and abandon, but instead of a full kiss, he kisses* MONROE *lightly on the forehead.*]

Have a safe trip.

[MONROE *looks at him, realizes the difference, and exits.* GEORGE *looks after him as he goes. Lights and sound indicate a passage of time.* GEORGE *then moves to a new location and begins his letter.*]

Dearest Mon. I've been trying and trying to think, and the more I try the deeper the confusion becomes. But I am sure of one thing and *that* is that I am not going to be able to get the child out of my head, not for a long time; I suppose that means I cannot try with a whole heart to pick up the pieces of our life, to start over, to be nineteen again. If Jonathan will ever be a comfort to me I cannot guess. You have been hurt so much and I've been hurt too and I feel I cannot face any more of my own double-dealing and you shouldn't have to. It's so hellish because I'll never love anybody as I've loved you, perhaps not as much as I love you still, hard as you'll find that to believe. But I've got to get my life simplified, even for the worse, heart-breaking as it is, sick as it makes me to write it.

[GLENWAY *and* MONROE *enter into their location;* MONROE *seated and* GLENWAY *standing.*]

GLENWAY   Dear George, It seems almost presumptuous of me to be writing you this morning while Monroe is doing so too.

GEORGE   Nobody knows better than I what I'm giving up, and yet I cannot believe it will necessarily be for the worse. I think I agree, without considering your museum complications, that we shouldn't live together in the circumstances. And it would be terribly hard for Glen and me to live together, at any rate for the time being. It takes courage to write now. But maybe it will make a man of me. Do you want me and my things out of 89th Street before you return?

GLENWAY   I will return with Monroe a week from Monday, the seventh, and set about the business of subletting our East 89th Street home and establishing him in a little apartment of his own at once. It was wise and kind of you to suggest moving out and taking your things away before we get back.

GEORGE   I hope you understand. Our life was so wonderful before and I cannot face the half-measures and the probability of making you unhappy in countless little ways.

GLENWAY   What a blessing to have this happen while Monroe was down here with me in South Carolina. Probably you thought of that, dear good Giorgio.

GEORGE   Please believe I had no such resolution when you left, when I said that anything you decided would be okay by me.

GLENWAY   Now, as you have been my best friend so many years, I may say just a little more, without pretentiousness or indignity. I believe that I understand you, in this hard change, as well as any man can understand another about such things. I am glad of your decision, especially for your sake. I understand about loving Monroe: the fact that you have not ceased loving him, and the fact that you cannot love him in the old way. Your love of Jonathan is stronger, though perhaps lesser, which is perfectly simple, and cannot be helped.

GEORGE   This is a bad rambling miserable letter but how could it be otherwise. I haven't cried as I wrote since the first years I knew you, and it's horrible. I pray you are as strong as you say. I'm going to be stronger than I've ever been before. I'll wait for your response with my fingers crossed and my heart in my throat. Give my love to Glen. Bless you, Gio

GLENWAY   There is only this: you have a long habit of a certain family life, in fact you yourself set it up for us, for the most part; and you may sometimes feel an awful loneliness, which will be something of a temptation. But you must not be too much discouraged by that; it will pass after a while. Monroe must have simplicity now; peace of some sort. He has had almost more trouble than he can bear. He loves me, and that will serve for the present. He will be happy again in due time. My constant, though strange, devotion to you continues. Yours always, Glenway

GEORGE   Mon dearest. It is six hours after I wrote you that first letter. God knows what I've done to you. And now it's too late for me to take any of it back. I'll have to let it stand. But try to forgive me just once more. I've done you so much harm and you have been so good. The thing I cannot understand, the thing I've been asking myself all afternoon, is how I, who have loved you so much, could have behaved so abominably and so brutally. I've done something to myself I'll never get over. I wish to God I could know that you will be alright. Geo

MONROE   Dearest Giorgio – Thank you for your letter, so clear and unmistakable as to your desires. I know what it cost you to write it, and I understand and appreciate it. It is obvious that you cannot be the kind of man you want to be in the old way; therefore I think your decision must be the wise one. As regards 89th Street, it is a good plan as you suggest to accomplish the moving while I am away and not to see each other for a while. All the rest you know without my telling you. Monie.

[*As* MONROE *finishes,* GEORGE *fades away.*]

GLENWAY   Monroe...?

MONROE   I'm well, Glenway.

GLENWAY   I don't believe you.

MONROE   You should. You know I'm only heartbroken. Not angry at all.

GLENWAY   You've got that starry-eyed look, that brilliance mixed with humility that I've grown to love.

MONROE   You know me better than anyone ever will. For the rest of my life.

GLENWAY   I've been prepared to play my part, Monroe, because we've had an understanding.

MONROE   An understanding.

GLENWAY   We've made some decisions together.

MONROE   Decisions.

GLENWAY   If, and when, we meet another individual that we find attractive—

MONROE   Someone else.

GLENWAY   And we decide that we want to pursue that individual—

MONROE   The other whistles.

GLENWAY   The other whistles. It's a peace offering.

[GEORGE *fades back in.*]

MONROE   Compensation in a difficult moment.

[GEORGE *whistles the melody from Mozart's "Pace, Pace." There's a pause as* GEORGE *and the audience take in what they've witnessed.*]

GEORGE   Lovely, isn't it?

[*All three men smile, remembering the very best times together. The lights fade on them, and an image of the three together comes up on the projection screen. Projection:* Image of Glenway Wescott, Monroe Wheeler, and George Platt Lynes together. *Hold the image as the three men turn to look at the image. Then fade to black.*]

• • •

Pete and Joe at the Dew Drop Inn

Lewis Gardner

Lewis Gardner

Lewis Gardner's plays have been presented by the APA-Phoenix Theater, Aspen Playwrights Conference, Cherry Lane Theater, Greenwich House Theater, Lee Stasberg Institute, Miniature Theater of Chester, New York Avant Garde Festival, Theater Off Park, the Village Gate, and at theaters in other countries and throughout the US. His autobiographical play *Tales of the Middlesex Canal* has been widely performed. He has worked with directors Peter Bennett, Susan Einhorn, and Stuart Vaughan and with actors Kim Hunter, Danny Goldman, Stephen Lang, and Lee Wilkof. He has written musicals with Oscar Brand and Daniel Paget and has acted onstage and in film. A number of his one-act plays have been published by One Act Play Depot (oneactplays.net). In addition, more than sixty of his poems and light-vere pieces have appeared in the *New York Times*.

time

The present.

characters

PETE could be in his late twenties or thirties.

JOE is five to ten years older.

• • •

[*For most of the action they sit at a bar, facing the audience. They are drinking beer, which has its effect on them.*]

[*Ambient sound: voices, music, laughter.*]

scene one

JOE   Got time for another?

PETE   [*Shrugging.*] I'm not goin' anywhere.

JOE   No one is.

PETE   No . . . Yeah . . . Hey, it isn't our fault . . .

JOE   I'll drink to that.

PETE   Yeah . . . When you were growing up, did you have a hero?

JOE   Well, yeah, there was a radio show . . .

PETE   About a hero?

JOE   Sure. A dog.

PETE   You mean, a talking dog, like Goofy?

JOE   Goofy's a *dog*?—No, this one didn't speak English.

PETE   He spoke *dog*? He barked? How can you have a radio show about a dog? He *barked* for half an hour? Ru—ru—ru—ru—ruff . . . Ru—ru—ru—ru—ruff . . . The story was told in *barking*?

JOE   [*As if to a small child.*] No, Pete, it was about his *master*. His *master* solved crimes in the Yukon.

[*Remembering the name.*]

Sergeant Preston.

[*Music: The Sergeant Preston radio theme—from the "Donna Diana Overture" by Reznicek. He stops to listen in memory, enjoying it greatly.*]

I guess the dog was a supporting character. The star would've been Sergeant Preston. *He* was a human, although Canadian. But I identified with the dog.

[*Smiling as he remembers.*]

What a dog!

PETE   What kind of a dog?

JOE   Come on—you couldn't *see* him. It was the *radio.*—A husky, maybe.

PETE   That was your hero?

JOE   Yeah. Didn't *you* ever have an—oh—an unconventional hero?

PETE   Well, to be honest? I used to want to be Mr. Clean. You know, all those muscles...helping housewives who relied on him in their domestic work...no intellect to get in the way...

[*Notices that* JOE *is staring at him.*]

What? What?

JOE   Wow. Takes all kinds, doesn't it?

[*Lights fade to half, then rise on the next scene.*]

scene two

PETE   I have to tell you, Joe: we've been married four months now, and I never imagined anything could be so good. We spend all our time together. If she gets home first, she starts supper. If I'm home first, I cook something; then we spend the evening together. I can't believe how lucky I am. She can't stand if I leave for an hour—she'll come with me to buy some beers or the paper. She hates if I stay on the phone with my buddies, and I don't make plans to see anyone for bowling or fishing or watchin' a game. I find ways to do those things with her.

JOE You're off the leash tonight...?

PETE She went with her friends to a male stripper show.

JOE Yeah?

PETE It's a rare occurrence, though. It's flattering as hell, how she can't stand if I'm away for my job or my folks, or we see an old girlfriend of mine at the mall or even a friend of hers, she'll get all jealous—and angry—sayin' the woman was comin' on to me— and that's so cute, I can die.—Do you think it'll stay this way forever?

JOE [*Under his breath.*] Sure it will...

[*Aloud.*]

Tell me about it in a couple of months. I can't wait.

[*Lights fade to half, then rise.*]

scene three

JOE Have you noticed how the world has changed? All the things you can't do anymore?

PETE You mean, like smoke in here? Or flirt with a woman who works for you?

JOE Or stand outside a schoolyard and show the children tricks with a Duncan yo-yo...

[PETE *gives* JOE *a look.*]

PETE Or tell jokes about dumb blondes...

JOE Disabled people...

PETE Members of any ethnic group except white Anglo-Saxon Protestants...

JOE People who have sex with farm animals...

[PETE *gives* JOE *another look.*]

Or make jokes to a flight attendant about havin' a bomb in your carry-on luggage...

[*Laughs at the idea.*]

PETE [*Looking closely at* JOE.] Innocent fun, right? Right, Joe?

JOE Did I tell you the one about—?

PETE Don't!

[*Lights fade to half, then rise.*]

scene four

PETE You know...I've been havin' trouble with my wife.

JOE [*Not surprised.*] You're kiddin'...

PETE No, really. We have arguments.

JOE That happens...

PETE It's bad.

JOE Okay, tell me.

PETE Well, pretend you're her. Okay?

JOE What?

PETE That way I can show you.

JOE [*Shrugging.*] Okay.

PETE You've been havin' trouble with your boss. He's too critical.—Go ahead. Pretend.

[JOE *is tentative at first. Then he gets into it, although he does not use a "feminine" voice.*]

JOE *You know, I've been havin' trouble with my boss. He's too critical.*—How was that?

PETE Good.—*Well, why don't you tell him you'll be a better member of the team if he isn't so critical?*

JOE *Okay, I'll do that. Thanks for your help.* —Hey, that was pretty easy. Cool.

PETE   It doesn't work that way.

JOE   Why not?

PETE   I'll show you: ask me why I look miserable tonight.

JOE   *Why do you look miserable tonight? Want me to massage your feet?*

PETE   Nice ad-lib.

JOE   Thanks.

PETE   *I've been having trouble with my boss. He's too critical.*

JOE   *Well, why don't you tell him you'll be a better member of the team if he isn't so critical?*

PETE   *Look, I'm not asking you to solve my problem. I just need you to be supportive.*

JOE   *How the hell can I be supportive if I'm not givin' you a solution?!*

PETE   *That isn't what I need! When you try to solve my problems, you're not showing you're on my side or that you acknowledge my feelings. You're trying to be Mr. Strong Fix-It Man. I resent that. It's demeaning, and it really turns me off.*

JOE   [*After thinking about it.*] That's fuckin' crazy.

PETE   No, it's what she says.

JOE   How long you been married?

PETE   Six months.

JOE   That's too soon to get a divorce…

PETE   I don't want a divorce. I want it to work out.

JOE   I hear you, pal. You must feel really frustrated. Hey, it's tough, isn't it? I wish I could help you…But hey…

PETE   No, it's okay. Thanks for understanding.

[*Hugs him. Lights dim, then rise.*]

scene five

[They are facing the back wall, a few feet from each other, as if at non-adjacent urinals. They turn their heads towards each other to speak.]

JOE   I saw somethin' in a catalog. They have these T-shirts that say, "The Dicky-Do Club: My gut hangs out more than my dicky do."

PETE   What is it? *"My gut hangs out more than my dicky do"?* That's pretty lame if it's a joke.

JOE   Yeah, but that's not what sparks my curiosity. My question is: Who's gonna buy one? Who's gonna brag about a big gut and a small— you know…

PETE   Someone who's in denial?

JOE   You'd pick up great babes, advertisin' like that…

PETE   Maybe some women prefer big guts and small *you-knows.* Or maybe it's a gift item.

JOE   Like for Father's Day? Or your anniversary? A way a woman can show her love for her husband?

PETE   Is this a hint, Joe? You want me to get the T-shirt for you?

JOE   *[Staring straight ahead—dryly.]* You're a real pal.

[They zip up. Lights fade to half, then rise.]

scene six

[They are sitting at the bar.]

PETE   I get tired of all the bullshit. My boss wants me to say his ideas are brilliant, my wife can't take an honest opinion. No one wants the truth about anything.

JOE   Pete, don't be naïve. That's what makes human society possible. Bullshit is the oil in the wheels.

PETE   What wheels?

JOE   Bullshit greases the wheels of communication. Bullshit is the mother's milk of human interaction. Bullshit makes civilization go round. You know the first thing every child should learn before he goes to school?

PETE   [*Doubtful.*] Bullshit?

JOE   No, it's self-respect.

PETE   Oh.

JOE   The *second* thing is bullshit.

[*Pause.*]

PETE   Joe, I think I'm wasting my life.

JOE   Yeah?

PETE   I mean, comin' to this place.

JOE   Yeah?

PETE   I mean, I'm glad to see my friends.

JOE   Yeah?

PETE   We can talk about everything under the sun.

JOE   Yeah.

PETE   Yeah.

JOE   Yeah. You know what your problem is?

PETE   No.

JOE   You think too much.

PETE   Yeah?

JOE   Yeah... Did you see the game last night?

PETE   I guess I did. Yeah.

JOE   Yeah?

PETE   Listen, maybe I won't come here so much. I'm gonna miss talkin' to you, but it's becoming too much of a habit. Maybe I'll see you around. So long.

[*Goes.* JOE *stares straight ahead. Lights dim out, then rise.*]

scene seven

[PETE *is sitting next to* JOE. *They have gotten pretty drunk.*]

PETE   There's something new goin' around with women.

JOE   They didn't get it from *me*.

PETE   It's not a disease. It's psychology.

JOE   Great—there's psychology goin' on, and I'm still tryin' to figure out PMS.

PETE   This woman wrote a book about how she'd rather eat chocolate than have sex.

JOE   I think I know her.

PETE   She says women have this low sex drive, while men are horny most of the time.

JOE   I *told* you I know her!

PETE   At the same time—get this: women expect their husbands to be monagamous.

JOE   Mo*na*gamous? Isn't it mo*nog*amous?

PETE   Not if they *nag* about it.

[*Laughs at his joke.*]

JOE   This is great: I don't just have to understand their feelings—I have to compete with *chocolate*?

PETE   You can dress up like a Milky Way or a Three Musketeers.

JOE   Or a Hershey bar.
[*Pleased with his joke.*]
With nuts.

PETE   This is serious. This could mean the end of life as we know it.

JOE   Shit, you're right.—Wait a minute—Josie, the one who tends bar Saturday night—*she'll* never give up sex.

PETE   True, but would you want *her* to be the mother of the human race?

JOE   That's depressing. Jeez...

PETE   Yeah. We have to do something drastic.

JOE   I know: give 'em what they want—listen to them, understand their feelings, buy them candles that smell like flowers...

PETE   That'll be tough...

JOE   Buyin' candles?

PETE   No, the rest of it.

JOE   The human race is dependin' on us.

PETE   Yeah. Think that'll do it?

JOE   What else have we got?

[*Starts to get up.*]

PETE   Where you goin'?

JOE   The store across the street. They sell those fancy candles.

PETE   [*Not getting up.*] I'll go with you. Maybe there's one that smells like chocolate.

JOE   On second thought, I should finish this beer.

[*Settles back on his bar stool.*]

PETE   Maybe they're not open. You wouldn't know their hours?

JOE   We can go there tomorrow.

PETE   We got plenty of time.

JOE   Sure we do.

[*Lights fade.*]

• • •

Decades Apart: Reflections of Three Gay Men

Rick Pulos

Rick Pulos

Rick Pulos is a published playwright, experienced theater producer, multimedia artist, performer, and educator. He studied film and theater at Yale University and film at the University of Southern California. He has performed in Brooklyn, Long Island, and Manhattan. *Decades Apart* opened the first ever Long Island Fringe Festival in fall 2009 to a reaction none of the producers could predict: homophobic outbursts and downright disgust at the material. *Decades Apart* was not written to incite audience members to hate, but to lead them toward compassion. The stories are very candid and are for mature audiences only. *Decades Apart* was first produced by the Ryan Repertory Company, Inc., at the Harry Warren Theatre in fall 2009 and had a successful run in spring 2010 at the famed Nuyorican Poets Café in Manhattan's Lower East Side.

characters

BOB, a carefree soul living it up in 1970s San Francisco, thirties

PATRICK, a gay Republican retreating from the gay scene in 1980s New York City, late twenties

DANNY, a club kid dancing his life away in 1990s Los Angeles, early twenties

note

A single actor may be used to play all characters.

note on media

Decades Apart was envisioned as a multimedia performance that utilizes projections onto various surfaces. LCD or other screen technology (new or old) may also be used. Much of the media is described in a general way to ensure that the creative team working on the media will have a great deal of creative license. Future media designers of *Decades Apart* may need to augment media to ensure a true reflection of current issues. Interpretations without media (or limited media) are certainly possible. Media is often used as subtextual commentary, as well as introductions to each character's return to the stage.

> *Be who you are and say what you feel, because those who mind don't matter and those who matter don't mind.* —Dr. Seuss

• • •

prologue

[*Lightning and thunder burst from ominous clouds as superimposed video imagery of the male body (preferably the characters' bodies) shift around: legs, eyes, nose, lips, mouth, etc. . . .*]

[*The following text slowly crawls across the screen: FAG, NIGGER, KIKE, CHINK, WET-BACK*]

[*The calm sound of rain as the images fade.*]

spoken live by the actor(s) onstage

These are the stories of men past and present that were shaped and sculpted from

love,
fear,
death,
pain,
pleasure,
happiness,
loneliness,
addiction,
and illness.

Their stories are your stories.
Your kid's stories.
Your grandkid's stories.
They are your brothers.
They are God's children.

They are individuals.
They are Americans.
They are beautiful.
They are you.
They are gay.

Bob

(1979, San Francisco)

[*Media: Imagery that recalls 1970s San Francisco, with music that clearly defines the disco mood of the time and place.*]

[BOB *sits in a yoga position and breathes heavily.*]

I never knew Harvey.

[*Media: Harvey Milk.*]

I only knew of him. I mean it was news

[*Media: News reports of Mayor Moscone and Harvey Milk's assassination.*]

and I slightly paid attention. I know I walked down Castro Street one day and wandered into that camera shop and bought something. Something. I met him in person. I'm sure I flirted with him. But I didn't vote for him. I didn't vote for anyone.

I did walk with the others in the vigil, though.

[*Media: Candlelight vigil.*]

I was so stoned, though. And there were so many hot men. Who could tell who was straight or gay? Nobody seemed to care. You can be a drag queen and nobody cares. All kinds of people will come to see you. You can have an Afro—even if it's gone out of style—and nobody cares.

These are good times, even in the face of tragedy. Everyone seems to be on our side. Finally, oh man, it's so good to be in touch with yourself and the city you love. I feel so much love. Jesus, I've had more sex in the '70s than most people have in their lifetimes. And all of it felt good.

[*Media: Images of Castro Street.*]

I never felt bad or guilty or dirty or sad or lonely.
I feel fine.
I feel love everywhere.
For the first time in my life, I really feel good.

Patrick

(1985, New York City)

[*Media: Imagery that recalls 1980s New York City, with music that defines the coke sniffing, AIDS fearing, greediness of the time and place. Useful images might include Nancy Reagan, subway trains overrun with graffiti, and executives in suits crowding NYC streets.*]

I voted for Reagan. Twice!

[*Media: Ronald Regan with an American flag proudly in the background.*]

I'm not ashamed to say it. Why should I be? It feels like every single fag in New York City hates me for my political views, but they have no problem fucking each other to death. I'm protecting myself and this body. This is all I have. It's gotten to a point where all I see are sick faces. Even the healthy ones look like death to me. Too much decadence and overindulgence has run amuck in the city.

I used to see sexy bodies and transcending smiles, but now the bodies seem emaciated and teeth are falling to the floor everywhere.

[*Media: Rock Hudson turning from gorgeous to a skeleton.*]

Well, I'm not bending down to pick those teeth up. I'm not getting my hands dirty for people that take unforgivable risks. I'm not waking up one morning and looking in the mirror to see the back of my mouth when I smile—it's not happening to me!

I spend a lot of nights at home.

[*Media: a map of America engulfed in flames.*]

I spend a lot of days at funerals. Men I loved and men I've made love to. So I can't put myself out there and maybe that's made me cold and maybe that's made me smart.

Maybe being cold and smart is the only defense against all this suffering.

Danny

(1990s, Los Angeles)

[*Media: Imagery that recalls 1990s Los Angeles, with music that defines the crystal meth club kid craze that swept the gay scene (then and now). Useful images might include Bill Clinton and Monica Lewinsky, fabulously decadent outfits, and anything with Matthew Shepard.*]

I take this pill and everything is fine. Just fine.

[*Media: Pills tumbling out of bottles.*]

I am invincible. I will live forever. I take them down with a cocktail in hand.

[*He swallows.*]

Just like that! And I am ready to go all night up and down Santa Monica Boulevard.

I walk into the club with my entourage in toe and all eyes fall on me. I glimmer in the club lights. My face is alive. I know my life is fierce. No one doubts that.

And I have no fear.
No inhibitions.
No limitations.

People might think I live recklessly, but I don't care. I'm like a 1990s James Dean.

[*Media: James Dean.*]

I'm a fucking rock star!

I'm out living and breathing. One day, I might be too skinny to walk or dance and even too out of it to talk, but no matter what happens to me, I'm having my fun now, tonight. I'm no scarecrow in a field with blood running down my face.

[*Media: Matthew Shepard.*]

I'm not letting anyone fuck with me.

You might not like the way I live, but you're gonna let me live. Because I'm not ready to die. I'd rather see *you* rot in hell before I let you get your hands on me and take any of this away.

So back the hell up, step aside and let me move forward.

Patrick

(1980s, a Record Store, New York City)

[*Media: Images of a distorted yet bustling and hurried NYC. Images might include packed sidewalks or NYC transportation hubs or piles of trash on street corners in the city.*]

I see so much greed and so much gluttony. I see people with a hand out while they hold a crack pipe in the other. I've become totally immune. Most of the time these dumb-ass Democrats are standing up at the podium, their pants wide open while some hooker blows them underneath, and preaches how you and I need to fix all this. *We* must help those who can't help themselves.

I'm tired of hearing about it all. How about I help myself and the ones I love? How about that?

All of sudden in this great city, in this grand country, the glue is a mix of dirty money, cocaine, and Aquanet. What happened here?

Walking down these vast city streets, I see the heat burning through Hefty bags left out on the curb too long. I smell the stench of all these filthy bastards. They're taking their time, digging their heels in and fortifying trenches, and they are slowly tearing the heart and soul of this great nation to bits. One fix at a time.

The more I think about it, the more I feel sick inside.

Just to get away from it all, I walk into my favorite record store, a small dopey place I'd been going to for years in the West Village. A hole in the wall with a decent selection. You know the kind, where people let you do your thing and don't mess with you. Nobody raises an eyebrow if you ask about some offbeat composer no one has ever heard.

I go all the way in the back of the store, past the rock, the gospel, the country section, right into the classical music—an oasis, of course stuck right next to the very gay Broadway show section. Why these record stores have this kind of odd organization, I could never understand. It's like putting filet mignon next to beef jerky.

Anyways, I'm minding my own business, flipping through the newest editions, when he turns to me and says:

"You hear anything about this new show on the West End, *Phantom of the Opera?*"

And I say, very shortly, "No," without even taking one glance. I simply continue flipping through the records at a much more fierce pace. Why is this guy bothering me anyways?

But he doesn't stop. He's persistent.

"I've heard it is absolutely amazing. I mean, Webber's done some amazing work and they're all saying this beats anything he's ever done. That certainly says something."

And then I make my first mistake—I look at him. I barely manage to say, with such despise and attitude, "Sorry, I don't follow *musicals*."

And he smiles.

You ever choke on a smile?

He's perfect. He's gorgeous. His eyes, even his teeth. Why is he even talking to me?

And then it happened.

It's so depressing when you give into your heart. The only power you have over anything else is your self-control. But infatuation is the most incurable infection. And once it has a grip, you don't.

I could rub myself this way or that way, I could start a fire in my imagination that would satisfy my every sexual whim.

But a single stroke, a delicate touch, a foul-mouthed breath, anywhere on my skin by him and I was like an AIDS article, stuck 10 pages deep in a newspaper, so far away from the front page of myself that I was unrecognizable to myself.

I turned my back on so many things so many times that when this sweet creature came along, I was lost. Hopelessly lost.

I felt protected by him. I was safe. I was comfortable. Suddenly, I wasn't angry anymore.

Most of you have been there and some of you have been back again. This was not like some crazy trumped-up crush. This was it. It.

Relationships are exactly like a Rubik's Cube.

[*Media: The Rubik's Cube.*]

There are many faces, many colors, everything gets mixed up, and one wrong move can send you further and further away from the goal.

Which is, as far as I can tell, growing old together while facing the decades in our past.

That's all I could think about.

Imagine the poppy field in the *Wizard of Oz*. He's my poppy field.

That stench, that contempt I had been seeing all around this city, my clenched fists, gone. Blood returned to my knuckles for the first time in years, my hair felt like it was growing again and not falling out strand by strand. I was afraid, for the first time in my life, I was afraid. I was afraid because I felt responsible for someone other than myself.

Danny

(1999, West Hollywood and Beverly Hills)

[*Media: Any imagery or lighting that allows* DANNY *to be beautiful in the club lights. Also, any imagery that might recall the advent of the Internet.*]

[DANNY *dances almost as if he were a go-go boy, then the lights come up as if the club night has ended.*]

So, I'll admit this, only to you.

[*Whispering.*]

This life is not so fabulous. Don't let anyone else know; I'll fuck you all up if you do.

Some of us need to do things that others would find appalling. I find them amusing. Yes, amusing.

Maybe I've always hustled in one way or another. But all these other more descriptive terms with dirty underlying meanings suddenly popped into my mind, like escort, male prostitute, and whore.

Don't get me wrong, I asked to be called a whore many times, with many men, in many beds.

But knowing that money would change hands made it feel so dirty and so sexually exciting. Which was the absolute last thing I ever thought would get me going on this planet.

Okay. So the Internet was like this web of communication. Ultra-technology or some bullshit like that, so *they* say. Send. Receive. Send receive. Little balls of energy squirting across the planet in the blink of an eye. All types of people entangled in a web of fascination *and* flirting with their darker anonymous sides.

Me? I used it. For my benefit. Maybe you did too. And maybe, it used me. It's so hard to tell. But Goddamn it, it got me through some of the hardest weeks.

So I found my "John" on gay.com, aka the men's network, or as I call it, the men's warehouse, suits optional. On gay.com I could say what I wanted, how I wanted, and act as dumb as a hooker or dealer at the hottest street corner in town. And nobody was paying attention.

His "profile"—Ed, that's the name he gave me—seemed fine. Not f-i-n-e fine but just fine. I negotiated for about five minutes. Yep, that's all it took. I had what he wanted and he had what I needed.

I immediately hopped into my super-compact Geo Metro convertible, top down, and pushed my right foot down so hard on that damn accelerator that it was like I was instantly in overdrive. The smog-infused Los Angeles air whipped by me whistling Dixie.

[*Media: Los Angeles traffic.*]

Now, any right-minded person would have asked me *right* then: what is going through your fucking mind?

Rent, bills, cigarettes, booze, drugs. No. Wrong.

I was hungry; desperately hungry after a long night of dancing and partying. I wanted a fucking Grand Slam Breakfast from Denny's.

[*Media: A Denny's sign rises into clouds like a soul to heaven.*]

Warm fucking eggs, some goddamn flapjacks, and some seriously processed sausage links. I didn't care that the maple syrup would be fake.

In my mind, all I could hear was:

Sausages. Pancakes, *mmmmm*. Warm eggs.

[*Media: Sausages, pancakes, and eggs in various states and, if possible, with the human body.*]

Maybe that was in my stomach. *Whatever.*

So, yes, I was driving like a motherfucker. I mean, like a bat outta hell, and all these assholes were flipping me off, calling me names (even worse than a fucking whore), and I just turned the radio up louder and louder and louder to drown out all those dumb asses.

I was weaving down Wiltshire Boulevard.

In and out.
In and out.
In and out.

I was in high pursuit of a Grand Slam Breakfast. And nothing was stopping me.

Sausages. Pancakes, *mmmmm*. Warm eggs.

[*Media: Sausages, pancakes, and eggs in various states and, if possible, with the human body.*]

Now, I was approaching Beverly Hills, where this guy's place of business was located. Where we planned our little rendezvous. This was not some silly 90210 surprise for me—the more high class, the more ass... they like.

I passed by security like smog through a crack. And for a second I thought, he's looking at me funny. *That* dumb ass in the rent-a-cop outfit *is looking at me funny.*

And immediately my arrogance was like some sort of streak of anger that flashed through me instantly, and I darted him a look that reduced him to some kind of ant, a peon, a cockroach.

Yep, in the wake of me becoming some kind of prostitute for processed pork, I had some balls to judge someone else making an honest living.

Who the fuck was I?

[*Beat.*]

I was the hottest motherfucker to ever grace that Bev Hills office building. I walked in as if I were headed for an interview to take over the CEO position at Coca-Cola or GE. I was all attitude.

Sausages. Pancakes, *mmmmm*. Warm eggs.

[*Media: Sausages, pancakes, and eggs in various states and, if possible, with the human body.*]

And then... I met Ed. Fat ass, not so bad in the face, slightly balding... Ed. What a dumb motherfucker. He bullshit-talked me about his PR job and his asshole co-workers, pointing things out on the way to his private office like the *lovely* plants at the receptionists desk and the very expensive furniture in the high-tech conference room. Was this guy for real?

Sausages. Pancakes, *mmmmm*. Warm eggs.

[*Media: Sausages, pancakes, and eggs in various states and, if possible, with the human body.*]

Finally, we were in his private zone. And as soon as he closed that door and he rubbed his wedding ring apprehensively, I got so fucking horny, I thought I'd blow a load right there. I don't know why.

But I held it all together for the money shot. You know what I mean?

The concept of a condom never came up in our chat on gay.com. I don't even know if that conversation happened for most of us who were bouncing around that Web site. We all seemed so fearless with the new technology. Fearless and fabulous.

Sausages. Pancakes, *mmmmm*. Warm eggs.

[Media: Sausages, pancakes, and eggs in various states and, if possible, with the human body.]

I was so horny at this point. Hungry and horny. Not the best combo, in my opinion.

So while I was pulling down my pants and bending over his neatly organized desk—a desk littered with paperweights, probably gifts from his wife or kids, from various tropical and cultural destinations—I just begged for it. I couldn't help it. And that got him going like some animal in the wild.

And I gritted my teeth:

Sausages. Pancakes, *mmmmm*. Warm eggs.

[Media: Sausages, pancakes, and eggs in various states and, if possible, with the human body.]

And I swear to God I saw a memo on his desk from some fuck-face executive at Denny's. Maybe it was IHOP or the Waffle House—it was there, IT WAS THERE! I swear.

Sausages. Pancakes, *mmmmm*. Warm eggs.
[Media: Sausages, pancakes, and eggs in various states and, if possible, with the human body.]

[Breathing heavily.]

And it was over like that. Like a gay.com chat gone wrong, where the guy just shuts down all his windows and disappears and never chats you up again.

He started counting under his heavy breathing. 20, 40, 60, 80. He was counting so fast that I could barely hear myself thinking:

Sausages. Pancakes, *mmmmm*. Warm eggs.

[*Media: Money.*]

Bob

(1970s, a Bathhouse in San Francisco)

[*Media: Disco music mashed-up with images of men at bathhouses.*]

[BOB *has a simple white towel wrapped around his waist. He is bouncing around a seedy bathhouse or, for those of you who do not see seediness, a funhouse for gays.*]

Love is like God. You know what I mean.

You've heard this before: I can't see God but I knew he exists.

Or what about that one when some try to explain all this mystery to you: you can't see the wind but you know it's there because you can feel it.

Personally, I think God is a menopausal whacked-out woman.

You know the type, comes after you with a quick wit and sharp tongue. Slices you to pieces by seeing right through you. Points out all your faults and highlights all the things you desperately try to hide from the light.

Thunder's like that heat that won't stop. Floods are like the floods that won't stop. And men are always doing stupid things that annoy you. That's who God is. This is *her* wrath.

Now I'm not trying to make enemies of any of you religious folk. Far from it.

You see, I pray.

Hell, I've been to Vegas and I've prayed for the big one. I've been to all the bathhouses, and I prayed for the big one. And I've been to the confessional, and I prayed that the priest would take me in his arms and love me like he loves his God.

But what I realized is all that praying is like scratching that space between your neck and your ass crack; it's like you're constantly reaching for something, *something*. But you can't quite ever satisfy that itch.

We've all been there.

The first time I heard "I love you" was the first time a boy unzipped his pants while I was kneeling on the ground.

[*He kneels down.*]

Dear God,

Please tell me this will last forever.
This feeling.
This love, it makes me feel so special.
Wanted.
Unique.
Alive.

Don't take this from me.

[*He stands.*]

Love is also punishment. At least, that's what I found out that day. I remember my mother slapping my face: "You don't do that. That's disgusting."

What did I do? I prayed! I was praying.

When you get this. All this foolishness we call life. When someone like you or me understands this much. Too much . . . We should be dead. But that bitch, that beautiful bitch, God, she wants us to suffer on and on. And we linger in this world, looking right through it as if through a crystal ball.

Maybe she wants us to see more to learn more, I'm not sure.

But I'm not afraid.

Hell. I walk the halls of the bathhouse cruising for love in every backroom, dark and dank. The odor is delicious: unwashed socks, boxers stuffed in little lockers—lockers never cleaned, at least, that's what I imagine.

There's this guy or that guy or, damn it, any guy.

Here's the one reason I love God more than anything: she knows how to have a good laugh. She can make a man . . . and she can make a woman . . . and she can make a man that acts like a woman and vice versa.

This is some serious comedy.

302 • Rick Pulos

Think about it.

But like a sundae, she tops it off with a bright delicious cherry, neither you nor me could ever have dreamed of: fetishes.

I don't know why people are so embarrassed by them. We all have them. Look, you can act like you don't but I know you do.

[*Pointing to audience members.*]

That one likes his nipples gently touched, oh, and she's a real beggar for her hair being pulled, you know, just so . . . oh, and most of us love dirty filthy sex talk.

It's true. And you know what you like.

So I never blink when this one or that one asks for whatever's gonna get him going. I mean, all of us have our limits, but sometimes you stretch because it's the only thing you can do when he's all you have going at four in the morning.

So out of the blue—and I mean this one was a bit out there—this guy asks me, "Got a Kleenex?"

This guy wanted me to sneeze. Sneeze on him?

I've heard it all now!

People always get so stressed when you're learning the behavior of new people, but I truly think even the weirdest shit is fascinating. I mean, everywhere I go, from the Castro to the Haight to the Pacific Ocean, even inside the walls of these saunas, I'm like living inside one of those nature film documentaries, you know, on PBS, where they study the lives of lions and tigers in their own natural habitat, in the wild. In my head, I'm always hearing that narrator, "The mating practices of the homosexual are fascinating. Let's watch as the top male approaches the bottom male aggressively, by participating in the tradition of cruising. The top male will look seductively at the bottom male for many moments, often walking by him and then walking by again. There is rarely talking. They will both look for any signs that will initiate the act of coitus."

Anyone can choose to look away or run and hide. But that doesn't mean what exists is itself going to evaporate into some mystical wind that no one can truly see:

There's always a path and *sometimes* a choice and hope is deceptively wrapped up in the "sometimes" and not even I can believe that it's just confusion or anxiety or injury that makes sense of any path to anything if anything is something anyone would ever want.

Danny

(1990s, West Hollywood)

[*Media: Religious imagery set against a Los Angeles background.*]

[*He is dressing for a night on the town.*]

You ever see these people out on the street passing out Bibles? What are they trying to do? I mean, I always pass by them as if they are handing out flyers to some seedy straight strip club. Somehow, all the street peddlers seem the same to me, whether they're asking for a dime or trying to hand me a Bible.

And it's always all sorts of people doing this. White, black, old, young, ugly, cute. God, the variety of Jesus freaks is frightening!

As usual, I'm on my way to a fabulous night out, right. What's left but to have me a good time?

When this little punk starts to flirt with me, right. What a great gimmick he had going in West Hollywood.

Instead of handing me a Bible, he hands me a card. He says that I can get help. That he used to be like me. That there are others who have broken through the sin. That all I needed was a clear path to God. That it wasn't too late.

Now you gotta understand something: I was curious, no doubt. I mean, a bunch of reformed fags—probably cute and straight-laced, all nice and cleaned up—sitting around in a circle trying to avoid that quick glance at the package or a quick peak at an ass while getting coffee on a break.

Of course I just looked him up and down. His smile disgusted me and yet turned me on too. What's up with that?

And I said bluntly, "Honey, all paths lead to God. They curve and shift like light refracting. There is no straight path." I bounced away so fast, but he was quick too. As I careened forward towards my perfect night out, I could hear him in the distance reciting the scripture.

And God blessed them, and God said unto them,
Be fruitful, and multiply, and replenish the earth, and subdue it:
and have dominion over the fish of the sea,
and over the fowl of the air,
and over every living thing
that moveth upon the earth.

Patrick

(Fall 1986, His Apartment, New York City)

[*Media: Imagery that recalls autumn in New York City.*]

[*He wears a brilliantly white robe.*]

It all gets complicated. That's the way autonomy ends. Or perceived autonomy, if you will.

And suddenly you magically realize that there's something more to living than the life you've been leading.

And therein lies the problem.

Why must I be the one wrapped in a blanket of guilt? Why must I be the one to recognize my limitations just because he loves me so? Why must I see myself when all I want to see is beyond me?

Fact.

I am not in love nor have I ever been in love.

Fact.

He turned to me one night with the seriousness of a politician and said bluntly, "I am addicted to you."

That's not my problem, I thought. That's not my problem, *no way*.

[*Beat*]

I thought.

Fact.

There is something special about feeling special. My veins worked overtime around him, pumping karma through my heart with a vigor unlike any I ever knew. I saw colors in the stars no one should ever see. Red, white, blue.

Fact.

I was a slave to my own fears. He had a power over me that made me feel desperate for a longer life. A life I spent uncountable hours trying to escape.

Fact.

I knew I would lose myself to him as soon as he recovered from his addiction.

Fact.

The people closest to you never recover from the things you wish they could.

Fact.

He did not die of AIDS or some mysterious pneumonia.

Fact.

His brain swelled like a balloon and it impaired his vision and his ability to interpret reality.

Fact.

He died April 5, 1986, under a blanket of mystery. Actually, under a sheet that depicted the bizarrely happy world of the Smurfs. He loved the Smurfs. He died gasping for more life while I prayed for a swift end.

Fact.

I looked at the recognizable image of Smurfette on that sheet and slowly began to take my clothes off. Not that I was retreating to some freaky heterosexuality, some oddball fetish that not even my childhood could explain. I wanted so much to just have an ounce of the love he had for me.

[*He takes off his robe and kneels down to touch the body.*]

Fact.

He was still warm.

Fact.

I felt cold everywhere.

[*He puts his robe back on.*]

What is this thing? What is this disappointment? Is this what everyone should expect from living? From the first breath to the last.

Is this what we have to look forward to?

They took him away on a dirty, used stretcher. I swear it was still warm from the last one they carted out, from wherever, to wherever. It looked like it was stained with sweat or feces, I don't know what. I couldn't even think about who or what was there before.

He was out of my house and out of my life as fast as he came in. And nothing about it was delicate or beautiful or smart. It was . . . indescribable.

[*Media: Thunder, lightning, and then silence.*]

I didn't even send flowers. I DIDN'T SEND A GODDAMN SINGLE FLOWER! There was no one to send a simple condolence to. There was nothing to say, to anyone.

So I said nothing. NOTHING!

How can a man feel this much and say absolutely nothing?

His mother claimed the body. She had already told me I was "uninvited."

My friends, oh, the poor bastards, called on me to say this and that, but most of them were so tired of death, it was like they were reading from index cards. It wasn't their fault.

And I thought about that word a lot. *Fault.* You know, like a lawyer. I thought about that word, about that language, that term. And I thought . . . I thought about a lot of people that I knew and I was hoping to know better.

And I thought about the significance of one man, one woman, one child. I thought about all those memories, washed away too soon. Lost.

And I thought about God. Because God was the *only man* I ever knew that ever knew me. And he knew me in my faults and my follies. Whatever any of that meant.

And of course I tried to feel so much for those who had suffered and those who were suffering but I was so chained to my misery that I could hardly care.

I'm not a crier. My mother taught me to never ever let anyone see me cry. So I never cry. *Even before God.*

But she never told me not to think. To think about why, *why* any of this is the way it is.

In the dark. In the corners of our houses, our apartments, our minds, whatever you feel comfortable calling it, in those spaces, you and me see ourselves and we know who we are. We have dreams beyond those walls, but prisoners have dreams beyond theirs. And so?

And so, the chore, I feel, that you and I have, as residents of these spaces, is simple: figure out more. Figure out more about yourself.

When he left my house. He left a scent.

But more importantly. He left a thought.

And as I go through the daily grind, brushing away the filth from my teeth, looking in that mirror, I can't help but ask myself, I can't help but taking a silly little pulse to find some kind of vital sign, in all this, in all that has happened to me, in all that has happened to my friends, in all that has ever happened, I *must* ask: Who am I? Who *am I?*

Bob

(New Years Eve, 1979, Castro District, San Francisco)

[*Media: The ball dropping, showing the start of the 1980s, punctuated by wild fireworks that recall the birth of a new decade.*]

Anyone could have guessed disco would die. Please, that was a given. I mean, we all hoped Anita Bryant would, but that was just wishful thinking. And we all loved screwdrivers too much to stay off that juice for too long. I mean, I guess we made our statement but who did it really change?

There was this euphoria out on the Castro in December 1979. There was this I can do what I want attitude. It was sexy and empowering. Guys were sleazy and it was cute. Girls were out mouthing off against the men and that was totally necessary. There was a sense of community and communication. Sure some guys and gals were still hidden from view, but people kept getting braver and braver by the minute. Time and virtue seemed to be on our side. And it felt like a lot of people were coming around to support us.

So as the ball dropped in New York City and the balls came out on the Castro, the 1980s looked to be one of the best decades for my sisters and brothers.

I could feel it all over, everywhere. Things can only get better from here.

Danny

(Fall 1999, Los Angeles)

[*Media: A vicious gay bashing mixed in with images of* DANNY *bruised and beaten. Any news media that reports a hate crime.*]

[DANNY *speaks over the media offstage.*]

The things I've done to my body. The constant abuse that I mistook for pleasure. Sometimes if you're one of the lucky ones, there appears a moment of clarity, or oxygen magically materializes while you're drowning in a sea of murkiness in a horrid, real-feeling dream.

My oxygen, my clarity, surfaced as a fractured cheek bone, several cracked ribs, a displaced shoulder, scrapes, bruises, even partial loss of vision in one eye.

[*He enters, moving slowly, using a cane.*]

I'll never dance the same. But that is very insignificant.

What happened to me could happen to any of you. I was truly minding my own business.

I remember leaving the club. I had had some drinks but nothing to write home about.

I never saw any of them coming.

I lied in the hospital bed, I could barely see through all the bandages, and I tried to piece it all together.

Cops, nurses, doctors, all swarmed around me like flies to shit. A few people, I'd only call acquaintances now, came in quick, going through the motions, and looked down at me like I was some kind of freak. I didn't want visitors, I didn't want that pity, I never wanted to see that face—that telling face—by some people who in that fucked-up way were trying to tell me somehow that all of this was my fault. That I'd asked for it and that they had always warned me I was heading for trouble.

I could barely mumble, my lips were so swollen. So I pretended I couldn't talk at all.

It was better that way.

I had all these feelings suddenly.

They weren't exactly feelings. It was actually one immense crude sensation: rage.

And I thought: I want a gun. I *need* a fucking gun. I want to shoot every motherfucker that fucks with me. I mean, this is what I'm thinking in that hospital bed. I want to wipe out all the idiots in the world. You know the type, department store clerks that act like you're going to steal something, losers that can't get an order right at McDonald's, DMV clerks looking up goddamn who knows what on their little computer screens with such contempt and mightiness.

Am I really just a number? Reduced to this old address or that old car?

It's amazing when you become a headline. All of a sudden, you realize you're not a number. What happened to me wasn't front-page news, but it was bigger than three lines in the police blotter.

"GAY MAN BEATEN BY TWO TEENAGERS"
"TEENS GONE WILD ON HOMOSEXUAL IN WEST HOLLYWOOD"

I never remembered these guys' faces. I remember the soles of their boots. I remember numbness in my head. I remember the taste of blood and concrete. I remember wanting to laugh at it all. Even while it was happening.

When I went to court and looked at them, I felt a new sensation.

A difficult feeling.

More complex than love or hate or disgust or respect.

I felt compassion.

It did not help that they were kind of attractive all dressed up in suits and ties, I'm not going to lie about that...

But I felt deeply: they were wrong and they should be punished, but something seems off in all this. Don't I have a responsibility to try to understand whatever it is that set them into motion? Don't I have a responsibility as a human being to be compassionate and learn from everything that led these boys to that moment?

Was it their parents, their culture, their rage, our country's temperament, their testosterone...what the fuck was it?!

And suddenly, I cried on the stand like some goddamn sissy-boy. Jesus, that really did them in for the trial and the sentencing.

That was not my intention.

What I found out was that I had a job. That I was needed for something other than to be the life of the party. That I had responsibilities.

And maybe, just maybe, I could raise a mirror to some other kid somewhere else and stop this from happening to someone else...

I'm not excusing this. Any of this hatred. I just want to learn more.

But. And I say this without hesitation.

Maybe our differences, our fears, these things we all pile up behind our eyes, are just little nuggets of light waiting to be seen. If there's a chance we could see them before they turn into fists full of fears, each and everyone one of us should take that chance, open that door, and walk through it with a single intention: to better understand each other.

And the only way any of us can be understood is for each of us, in our own way, to stand up and be seen even in all our ugliness because there is beauty in ugliness. Drag it all out into the streets, shine a light right on each and every face here and out there and take a moment to see what's really going on. This next millennium, this new millennium, we must all stand in the light and bee seen.

[*Media: Useful media here would be a current hot issue from LGBT community regarding human rights issues, whether from America or abroad.*]

epilogue
(performed either live or through media)

I am not a single reflection.
I am light refracting.
I am many parts.
I am not the sum.
I am moving through life.
Life is moving through me.
I am who I am in a single moment.
I will never be perfect.
And I wouldn't want to be.

[Media: This has happened. This is happening now.]

• • •

508

Amy Herzog

Amy Herzog

Amy Herzog received the 2008 Helen Merrill Award for Aspiring Playwrights. Her plays have been produced at Ensemble Studio Theater, American Conservatory Theater in San Francisco, The Williamstown Theater Festival, The Actors Theatre of Louisville, and the Yale School of Drama; she has had readings and workshops at Manhattan Theater Club, New York Stage and Film, Arena Stage in Washington, D.C., The Black Dahlia in Los Angeles, and The Rattlestick Playwrights Theatre, among others. Herzog recently completed commissions for the Yale Repertory Theatre and the Williamstown Theatre Festival. Herzog is an alumna of Youngblood at Ensemble Studio Theater and a current member of Play Group at Ars Nova and the SoHo Rep Writer/Director Lab. She teaches playwriting at Bryn Mawr College and has a MFA in playwriting from the Yale School of Drama.

characters

LEO, mid- to late twenties
BRIDGET, mid- to late twenties

setting

Bridget's studio apartment in Manhattan. The present.

• • •

[*Lights rise on* BRIDGET *and* LEO. *He has a box in one hand and a CD in the other. The door is open.*]

LEO   This isn't mine.

BRIDGET   I gave it to you.

LEO   I never listened to it. You did.

BRIDGET   The rule is you keep gifts. I kept the tea set.

LEO   I thought you liked the tea set.

BRIDGET   Nope.

LEO   Oh. Still, you should—

BRIDGET   It's on my computer anyway, Leo, keep the stupid CD.

LEO   Okay.

[*He puts the CD back in the box.*]

BRIDGET   I think everything's in there. Do you want to look through, or—?

LEO   I trust you. Thanks for putting it together.

BRIDGET   Sorry it took a year.

LEO   Well.

BRIDGET   You want a glass of wine?

LEO   I should get home.

BRIDGET   One drink. You came all the way here.

LEO   Bridget—

BRIDGET   I already opened a bottle. It's "breathing."

LEO   One.

> [*She gets the wine and pours.*]
> It's so clean. Was it always this clean?

BRIDGET   No. Mrs. Housekeeper.

LEO   What?

BRIDGET   I pay someone to clean now. Mrs. Housekeeper.

LEO   I bet that's not her name.

BRIDGET   That's how she introduced herself.

LEO   What do you write on the checks?

BRIDGET   I pay her cash.

> [*He laughs.*]
> What?

LEO   How do you afford it?

BRIDGET   My parents. Don't make criticisms couched as questions.

LEO   It looks great.

BRIDGET   Well, I'm not picking up after anyone else now, it's easier.

LEO   Easier to pay Mrs. Housekeeper?

BRIDGET   Wow, fuck you. Here.

> [*She hands him a glass of wine. They insert their noses into the glass and sniff, like professionals. They drink.*]
> Not bad. Right?

LEO   Not bad at all.

BRIDGET   So! How is it? Married life?

LEO   It's great. No complaints.

BRIDGET   Good.

LEO   Have you met Anna?

BRIDGET   You know I haven't.

LEO   You'd like her.

BRIDGET   Great, let's have dinner. The three of us.

[*He laughs.*]

LEO   You know, when you make the right choices, it's obvious. Things just kind of line up for you. It's like rowing downstream.

BRIDGET   Doesn't sound like very good exercise.

LEO   That's because it's not exercise, it's life.

BRIDGET   Actually it's a metaphor. A shitty one.

LEO   I think you'd be a little less aggressive if you were a little happier.

BRIDGET   I think you should publish. Immediately.

LEO   Right. Thanks for the drink, Bridget.

BRIDGET   Oh, come on! This is fun. We're reminiscing. No one's taking anything seriously.
[*Pause.*]
Hey, how's your grandmother?

LEO   She died.

BRIDGET   Oh my God. When?

LEO   Two months ago.

BRIDGET   I'm so sorry.

LEO   Thanks.

BRIDGET   At least she got to see your wedding. Shit.

LEO   What?

BRIDGET   I meant to write her a letter.

LEO   Why?

BRIDGET   To thank her. She always made me feel so welcome in your family. I never got to say good-bye.

LEO   She wouldn't have opened it.

BRIDGET   What?

LEO   She wouldn't have opened a letter from you.

BRIDGET   Of course she would have.

LEO   She told me she wouldn't.

BRIDGET   This came up?

LEO   She just volunteered it one day. I don't remember why.

BRIDGET   You're lying.

LEO   I wouldn't lie about my dead grandmother.

BRIDGET   Then she just said that to support you. She would have read my letter.

LEO   I don't think so, Bridge. I think she meant what she said.

BRIDGET   Well, she once told me she had no idea what I was doing with you but she hoped I'd never see the light. Which I bring up only to make the point that she sometimes said things she didn't mean, just to be nice, or flattering, or...

[LEO *drains his glass.*]

LEO   Thanks, but I should get going.

BRIDGET   Sit down, you can't leave after that, you have to give me a chance to not be an asshole. Sorry. She was a great lady.

[*Pause.*]

LEO   You repainted. I mean, *you* didn't. Someone did.

BRIDGET   I did. Actually.

[*He looks closer.*]

LEO   Oh yeah. You did.

BRIDGET   Shut up.

LEO   You didn't like the colors I picked?

BRIDGET   Um...*yeah*...

LEO   You were thrilled at the time.

BRIDGET   I was thrilled it was done. I was so tired of those tarps. Do you remember the tarps?

LEO   Not really.

BRIDGET   I still have dreams about tarp. Endless tarp.
[*Musing.*]
Tarp. Trap.

LEO   Part.

BRIDGET   Hm.

LEO   How's 508?

BRIDGET   What?

LEO   Your friend in the 508 area code.

BRIDGET   What do you mean?

LEO   It took a while to cancel our family plan, remember? I received your cell phone bills. You made a lot of calls to a number with a 508 area code for a few months after we broke up. And about a month before, for the folks at home counting.

BRIDGET   Oh.

LEO   So...?

BRIDGET   508...is eighty-sixed.

LEO   Oh.

BRIDGET   He eighty-sixed me.

LEO   Sorry to hear that.

BRIDGET   Yeah, thanks.

LEO   You'll find the right one. When it's right, you know. It's like nothing you've ever felt.

BRIDGET   Do I owe you money?

LEO   For what?

BRIDGET   The phone bills.

LEO   Oh, don't sweat it. 508 is in our network.

BRIDGET   Really.

LEO   That made me feel even closer to him. There was so much we shared.

BRIDGET   Is there something you want to ask me, Leo?

LEO   Ask you? No. I think it's pretty clear what happened.

BRIDGET   Whatever you're imagining is probably much more interesting than the truth.

LEO   It's not very *interesting*, Bridge, you fucked another guy while we were still together.

BRIDGET   I didn't fuck him while we were still together.

LEO   So you, what, shared a milk shake?

BRIDGET   Do you want to know?

LEO   Sure. No. No, I don't want to know.
[*Pause.*]
Are you happy?

BRIDGET   What? Of course not. The only happy people I know are under three.

LEO   That attitude is really going to hold you back.

BRIDGET   OH MY GOD! STOP! Two seconds ago you were prepared to hear what I did in bed with another guy while we were still together, this Zen shit is so obviously bogus, do you think I'm retarded? I know you're not over me.

LEO   Oh real—

BRIDGET   And this is a one-hundred-dollar bottle of wine, which we bought on our first anniversary to be consumed on our fifth, which would have been tonight, I know you know this, you picked the date to pick up the box, so let's cut the crap. Okay?

LEO   Everything doesn't always have to mean something, Bridget. It was a convenient time for me.

BRIDGET   You forgot what day it was.

LEO   I guess I didn't think it was important.

BRIDGET   Right. Well, I guess I didn't think it was important that you were receiving my cell phone bills.

[*Off his look.*]

We make choices. I'm sorry I hurt you. I'm glad you're here.

[*She reaches to touch him. His phone rings. He looks at it, silences it.*]

LEO   Thanks for the drink.

BRIDGET   One more.

LEO   I can't.

BRIDGET   Come on!

LEO   Bridge. No.

[*An awkward pause. He reaches out to shake her hand. In disbelief, she takes it and shakes it. He picks up the box. He takes the CD out of it again.*]

I really won't listen to this.

[*Lights.*]

• • •

Naked Old Man

Murray Schisgal

Murray Schisgal

Murray Schisgal has an extensive career spanning plays, screenplays, fiction anthologies, and as a producer of five feature films. His Broadway plays include *Luv* (Tony nominated), *Jimmy Shine*, *All Over Town* (Drama Desk Award, Outstanding New Play), *The Chinese and Doctor Fish*, *Twice Around the Park*, and *An American Millionaire*. His films include *Tootsie* (Oscar nominated), *The Tiger Makes Out*, and *Luv* (based on the play).

Schisgal's Off-Broadway plays include *The Typists and the Tiger* (Vernon Rice Award, Outer Circle Award, Saturday Review Critics Poll Award), *Fragment*, *The Basement*, *The Flatulist*, *Walter*, *The Pushcart Peddlers*, *Sexaholics*, *Extensions*, *Road Show*, *Jealousy*, *Circus Life*, and *Angel Wings* (Off-Off-Broadway Award for Excellence).

Published works include *Days and Nights of a French Horn Player* (novel), *Luv and Other Plays* (collection), The Best American Short Plays (twelve short plays over a number of years, published by Applause Books) and *Great American One-Act Plays*.

···production note···

The cast of characters is to be published as a program note.

cast of characters

JOSEPH HELLER, novelist, *Catch-22*, etcetera; 1923–1999

ROBERT ALAN AURTHUR, sole producer, co-screenwriter of *All That Jazz*, etcetera; 1922–1978

ARTHUR KUGELMAN, creative director at advertising agency; 1928–1999

MURRAY SCHISGAL, playwright, *Luv*, etcetera; 1926–

···

scene

set

A seven-room apartment on Central Park West. A dining area adjoining the kitchen: a glossy, square, mahogany table, four matching, square, ladder-back chairs.

Upstage a long, rectangular, serving table on which we see the following: center, a bowl of fruit; to the right, on a silver tray, two or three large bottles of mineral water and glasses; to the left, several framed family photographs.

time

Spring, early evening, 2009.

[*Lights: Rise and gradually change from natural lighting to artificial lighting. Sound: Softly, Berlioz's "Requiem."*]

[*Offstage, in the foyer, we hear* MURRAY SCHISGAL *speaking in a didactic voice to his wife,* REENE (*pronounced Renee*), *who is getting ready to leave the apartment.*]

MURRAY   [*Offstage.*] Go slow. Take your time. There's no hurry. Don't rush. Be careful. Look where you're walking, especially on the corner of 86th Street. Make sure you look first to the left, then to the right, don't trust the lights, those cars come at you from every direction. And watch where you walk. The sidewalks and gutters are often in disrepair, cracked, caved in. You don't want to trip. You don't want to fall. You don't want to fracture your wrist or your fingers again. Please. Do it for me. And if the bus doesn't come in five minutes, grab a cab. Use your cell phone if you're having any problems. I'll be here. I'll be home. I'll be waiting up for you.

[*Sound: We hear the entrance door open and slam shut. Lights: Rise on dining area as . . . Sound: Berlioz's "Requiem" fades out.*]

[MURRAY *enters: his hair (possibly a beard) is disheveled. He wears bruised sneakers, khaki trousers, an open-necked, faded, denim shirt, and a maroon cardigan sweater, unbuttoned.*]

[*When seated, he will be at the head of the table, center. Seated from his right to his left are the specters of his grievously missed friends:* ROBERT ALAN AURTHUR, JOSEPH HELLER, *and* ARTHUR KUGELMAN (*aka* BUNNY). *They exist and speak only in* MURRAY's *imagination (no problem for a playwright).*]

Sorry I'm late. My apologies. Reene usually leaves earlier. But tonight she's having dinner with her friends at Calle Ocho, a South American restaurant on Columbus Avenue. She doesn't have that far to travel. I'm somewhat discombobulated now that you're all here; apprehensive is probably the preferable word. I was afraid you'd think me presumptuous, if not paranoid, in asking you to come visit with me this evening. By the way, if I can get you fellows, anything, please speak up.

[*At the serving table,* MURRAY *unscrews the cap and pours himself a glass of mineral water.* JOE *speaks.*]

How many friends is Reene having dinner with? Is that what you asked, Joe?

[*He waits for* JOE's *assent.*]

Six of them. They play bridge at a midtown club, three, four times a week. It's been terrific for Reene, a lifesaver. It gets her out of the house, keeps her busy, mentally challenged, and happy. I can't tell you how grateful I am to those six women. Not only do they play bridge together, three, four times a week, they also call each other almost every day, meet for lunch, dinner, go shopping, go to Weight Watchers, go to bridge classes, go to the playground to watch their grandkids on the swings and monkey bars until the cows come home.

[*He wipes his brow with a handkerchief.*]

I'll give it to you straight, fellows, I'm envious of Reene for having these six friends. And here's the irony of it.

[*Heatedly.*]

Years ago, I... *I was the one* who had the friends. She didn't have any friends. The friends she had were *my* friends, not her friends. They were all *my* friends. If I wasn't hanging out with you fellows, I was hanging out with friends on whatever play or film I was working on, with friends from Commedie Productions, where, as you know, I was consultant and producer for eighteen years; I also had friends from high school, college, law school, friends from the Actors Studio, the Ensemble Studio, the Writers Guild, the Dramatists Guild, and the Academy of Motion Picture Arts and Sciences!

[*A change of tone.*]

Hey, gimme a break, will you? I had friends up the gazoo. I'm not exaggerating. I had friends I didn't even like, but they were *my* friends nonetheless. I'd estimate I must have had literally hundreds of friends during my lifetime. And they were close friends, not mere acquaintances. We hung out together, spent weekends together, boat trips, vacations... You name it, we did it. But don't ask me what happened to them. I looked around one day and they were gone, disappeared, popped into thin air like bubbles from a bottle of seltzer.

[BOB *speaks.*]

Are you serious, Bob?

[*Laughing.*]

You're asking me how it feels to be an old man?

[BOB *speaks.*]

No, no, I'm not offended. Frankly, I approve your choice of words. I am an old man. You were never one to soft-pedal it. I do miss you. Enormously.

[BOB *speaks*.]

I know where you're coming from, you don't have to apologize. You left us early, at fifty-six, if memory serves.

[BOB *speaks*.]

No, no, it's no imposition. You can't imagine how much I appreciate you fellows coming here this evening.

[*Musingly*.]

Well, let's see, how does it feel to be an old man? To start off with, you wake up one day and you realize that there are countless worlds out there that you somehow missed the first time around.

[*Emphasizing each phrase*.]

Worlds to see . . . to taste . . . to touch . . . to study . . . to reflect on, to gorge yourself on. I'll paraphrase Tolstoy: Being old is the most adventuresome part of your life. The great man knew of which he spoke, more so than did poor, sad Jacques who described old age as "sans teeth, sans eyes, sans taste, sans everything." Certainly in the early seventeenth century that must have been the case, but certainly not in the early twenty-first century. Frankly, knock wood . . .

[*He does so*.]

I don't know what it would be like being old without good health. In that regard I've been lucky. A West Coast friend got me started decades ago on a Pritikin diet and a Pilates fitness program. You can't beat the West Coast when it comes to setting the standards for us East Coast slackers; that goes for health, style, cosmetic surgery, and a penchant for multiple liaisons.

[*He drinks, thirstily*.]

After good health, I'd list the necessity to keep busy. Busy with career, with avocation, with hobby, craft, chess, tennis, golf, gardening, with whatever activity engages you, brings a rush of gratification. So far that hasn't been a problem for me. I work every day, seven days a week, writing plays, exclusively. For me, there's nothing more challenging, particularly when writing a play I choose to write, of my own volition, and not for monetary gain. I believe it was Samuel Johnson who said, "No man but a blockhead wrote, except for money." Considering his time and circumstances, I wouldn't argue the point. But writing what one chooses to write? What an exhilarating thought that is. And yet, along with it, a negative thought immediately follows. I do worry about running out of ideas for future plays. When you've been at it for as many years as I have, there aren't that many new ideas loitering about in your imagination waiting for you to explore. Old age, apparently, is a period of reaping, not of planting. Recently, I was encouraged by reading a list of artists who continued to be prolific during their nineties and eighties. Here are a number of them.

[*He gropes through one, two, or three pockets of his cardigan sweater, pants pockets, and shirt pocket for the relevant piece of scrap paper or newspaper/magazine cutout he's searching for. Several pieces of scrap paper, stapled together, catch his eye.*]

This isn't what I was looking for, but I'd like you to hear it. In my opinion, it's the best brief definition of comedy ever written: "If nothing is serious, nothing is funny." That's from the inimitable Oscar Wilde.

[*Glances at the scrap paper behind it.*]

Ah, here's another. It's from Jonathan Swift: "Satire is a sort of glass, wherein beholders do generally discover everybody's face but their own." Not bad, huh?

[*Glances at the scrap paper behind it.*]

And one more: "Comedy is an escape, not from the truth, but from despair." Christopher Fry.

[*He returns stapled scrap papers to pocket, continues searching in his other pockets.*]

Now let me see, where did I put that list.... If I had half a brain, I'd file my scrap-paper notes and printed cutouts into the computer. But I'm so damned...Ah, here it is. I have it. On the list of artists continuing to be prolific during their nineties we have:

[*Reads from magazine cutout.*]

"Sophocles, Titian, Bernard Shaw, Somerset Maughm, Jean Sibelius, Frank Lloyd Wright, Louise Bourgeois, Knut Hamsun, P.G. Wodehouse, Oskar Kokoschka," etcetera, etcetera, etcetera. Prolific in their eighties we have: "Michelangelo, Goya, Tolstoy, Goethe, Wordsworth, Monet, Brancusi, Matisse, Stravinsky, O'Casey," etcetera, etcetera, etcetera.

[JOE *guffaws*. MURRAY *returns cutouts to pocket.*]

You may find it amusing, Joe, but I assure you, my best work lies ahead of me, of that I'm confident.

[JOE *speaks.*]

What was that?

[JOE *speaks.*]

Yes, Joe, I believe the improbable name of Murray Schisgal is right up there with the best of them. That may strike you as a classic case of megalomania, but I am firmly convinced that I have already written plays of lasting significance. Otherwise, I don't see how I could have survived as a writer this long.

[JOE *speaks.*]

[MURRAY *laughing.*]

What? You agree? You don't have to . . .

[MURRAY *laughing.*]

No, stop, I wasn't fishing for . . . You don't have to . . . Stop, that's enough already!

[JOE *speaks.*]

Thank you, Joe. Thank you. That's awfully kind.

[*Nodding.*]

I will. I am. I have no intention of quitting. You have my word on that.

[*He rises, paces around the table and chairs, hands clasped behind his back.*]

Now let's get back to answering your question, Bob: How does it feel to be an old man? Following the prerequisites of good health and keeping busy, I'll add having a few bucks in the bank. Poverty is demoralizing. This from growing up during the Depression. Success and wealth are the primary incentives for a satisfying creative life. This from the '60s, '70s and early '80s when everything I wrote was produced because of the early kudos I received from the New York critics. My professional decline began in the late '80s, after a few theatrical bombs and a number of perverse screenplays that never got made. I breezed along, nonetheless, primarily on the monies I earned at Commedie Productions as a consultant and producer. Of course, I continued to write plays, many of which were published and produced, both here and abroad; that brings us pretty much up to date.

[*He sits on the upstage rectory table.*]

So far we have good health, keeping busy, and an interest-bearing nest egg in the bank. And here I'm compelled to append a fourth essential ingredient to my recommendations for vigorous aging. Perhaps of even greater value than any of those I already mentioned is being fortunate enough to have at your side a wife, a devoted, affectionate wife-pal, if you will. That's how it goes, fellows. I don't make the rules. And here, once again, I've been a lucky man. It may have worked out in my favor because I married a younger woman.

[BOB *speaks.*]

[MURRAY *grinning.*]

You guessed correctly, Bob. She turned eighty in July. Since I'm eighty-two, she's, by definition, a younger woman. We recently celebrated our fiftieth wedding anniversary. I met Reene when I was twenty-seven and the strangest thing in the world happened when I met her. I felt, for the first time in my life, that I was loved, genuinely, unequivocally, and unconditionally loved. And once I felt that emotion coming from another human being, I was capable of loving another human being. This revelation brought home to me a reality that I had been totally ignorant of. I can only love when I feel I'm being loved. I'm incapable of initiating love. I can only respond to it.

[*He scrounges through his pockets for a handful of scrap paper.*]

I had a thought this morning, just before getting out of bed. That's become a bad habit of mine, jotting down every half-assed idea I have, first thing in the morning. One second.

[*He reads from scrap paper.*]

"Old age is an incomparable high, from which there is no coming down."

[*He looks at scrap paper stapled behind it, then the scrap paper behind that one.*]

By the way, anticipating your arrival, I filled my pockets with some personal notes I wrote on scrap paper and cutouts from newspapers and magazines I've collected these past few years. I thought they might be of interest to you. Listen to these.

[*Reads the first.*]

"Recently a man of ninety-five said to me, 'I've taken a vow of celibacy.'"

[*Waits in vain for a response.*]

Nothing? You don't find it amusing? Okay. Here's another one.

[*Reads the second.*]

"The eighty-one-year-old man shouted in my face: 'You will not rob me of my youth!'"

[*Waits in vain for a response.*]

Still nothing? Anyway, that's how I felt last year.

[*He returns scrap papers to his pocket.*]

Where was I? Oh, yes. I can say, without hesitation, I cherish every single day I'm with my wife. The simple truth of it is that I love her more today than I did yesterday. And I have no doubt I will love her more tomorrow than I do today. Talking about my wife brings to mind a grievance of mine, a decidedly unpleasant aspect of growing old. And for this inexcusable atrocity, I blame, in tandem, Almighty God and evolution. Both are guilty of imprinting, arbitrarily and senselessly, the male genome with the blight of senescent impotency.

[JOE *speaks.*]

You heard me right, Joe, senescent impotency, the inability of a healthy, physically-fit elderly man to have sex with his wife or his girlfriend or his boyfriend or with whomever else he damn pleases! You want to talk about insidious age discrimination, there you have it in a nutshell!

[JOE *speaks.*]

Never mind the argument that senescent impotency is initiated to prevent elderly men from conceiving offspring. I wholly disagree with . . .

[BOB *interrupts.*]

What was that, Bob? Because they won't be around long enough to raise and protect their offspring? That is such bullshit! How many teenage fathers or fly-by-night fathers are around to raise and protect their offspring? Google the figures and then we'll talk about it. Imagine what it's like living with a woman for fifty years and holding her, kissing her, fondling her, desiring her and . . . you can't, you're physically incapable of making love to her!

[BOB *speaks.*]

[MURRAY *angrily.*]

Yes, yes, at eighty-two, Bob; to a woman of eighty! Yes, yes, precisely! What is most hateful in all of this is to be forced to keep your hands off your own wife and pretend you're too tired or too old or too preoccupied watching television to indulge in that silly, infantile game of fornication. Bullshit! I'll offer you this platitude: neither Almighty God nor evolution ever had our best interests at heart. They've both proven themselves, again and again, insensitive, indecisive, and totally indifferent to the well-being and happiness of our species!

[*He sits in his chair at the head of the table, empties his glass.* JOE *and* BOB *protest.*]

[*Raising his hands in self-defense.*]

Okay. Okay. I'm sorry. I apologize. I shouldn't have raised my voice. I thought you might like to hear one of the negatives of reaching eighty-two. Let's drop it and get back to the positives. It helps, enormously, if you have devoted children, caring in-laws, and a gaggle of rambunctious grandkids. Granted all those ifs ands and buts . . . Growing old feels pretty damn good and being alive . . .

[*Grins.*]

feels even better. After much deliberation I've come to the conclusion that luck is a more valuable asset to possess in the long run than talent, wealth, intelligence, breeding, and the personal friendship of the Crown Prince of Saudi Arabia.

[JOE *speaks.*]

Who do I hang out with? That's an easy one to answer, Joe. As I said, except for you fellows, friends of mine are few and far between. Mobility and mortality have taken their toll. More than ever, I find myself hanging out with my wife. It's, frankly, embarrassing for me to always be waiting for her to come home from bridge or from lunch or dinner with her friends or...whatever. I was wondering. Could you fellows possibly come to visit with me once a week on a regular basis? Let's say every Tuesday at 6:30 p.m.?

[*Turns from one to the other.*]

Could you...arrange it? Same time, same place. You needn't stay for more than an hour. Is that possible?

[*He turns from one to the other, waits anxiously to hear a response. They respond positively. Excitedly, beaming, he bangs with fist on table.*]

You agree? It's unanimous? That's great, that is great! I sincerely appreciate it.

[*He rises to refill his glass at serving table.*]

How's it going, Bunny? How are you doing? You've been awfully quiet.

[BUNNY *speaks.*]

How stupid of me! I am sorry.

[*Turns to others.*]

Bob, Joe, my first cousin and my first and best friend of nearly eighty years, Arthur Emanuel Kugelman, better known as Bunny by members of our family. He retired as a creative director at Benton and Bowles a number of years before he...

[*Drops it; turns to* BUNNY.]

Don't be intimidated by these two. They come on like hard-asses, but they're quite harmless. Did you get to hear about Uncle Hymie? He died last year, one hundred years old. That's something, huh? I don't know if you've been counting, but we have three aunts left. Aunt Dora will be one hundred this year, Aunt Annie ninety-seven, and Aunt Rhoda eighty-eight. My mother died four years ago at ninety-nine. You have to admit we inherited a couple of good genes. Even you, in spite of smoking two packs of cigarettes a day since high school, lived for seventy-one years.

[*He returns to his chair at table.*]

I remember the day you came into my office at Commedia Productions. We planned to go out for lunch at Shun Lee West, chicken chow mein with plenty of crispy noodles, the way we liked it. I knew you had seen a neurologist that morning. He had completed a series of tests because you were having trouble reading. I asked you what he said. "You don't wanna know," you mumbled, turning away from me. "I do want to know," I said. And you said, turning toward me, your expression indecipherable. "I have lung cancer. It's metastasized to my brain." And then we both turned away from each other and said nothing . . . for a minute . . . for an hour . . . for an eternity.

[*A hesitant beat.*]

I was wondering, Bunny, what . . . what's it been like since you . . . ?

[BOB *interrupts.*]

[MURRAY *excitedly.*]

All right, all right, I heard you, Bob! What are you getting excited about? I was just going to ask him if . . . !

[JOE *interrupts.*]

I heard him, Joe. I'm not deaf. You don't have to repeat what Bob said. I get the message. Why are you . . . ? You want me to say it, I'll say it. I am not allowed to talk about what it's like . . . for the three of you: what you do, what you see, what you feel. It is not permissible.

[JOE *speaks.*]

Fine. Fine. But it seems grossly unfair to me that you can tell me what I can and cannot say when I place no restrictions on what you can or cannot say!

[JOE *speaks*.]

All right, all right, we'll drop it. End of discussion. I'm not wasting the time I have with you fellows on nit-picking technicalities. Now I'd like to tell you something that's totally unrelated to what I was going to ask Bunny. Since it happened to me and not to him, it is permissible. Those are the rules, am I right, Bob?

[*He waits for* BOB *to nod assent*.]

Thank you. We had services for Bunny at the Frank Campbell Funeral Chapel on Madison Avenue. That was in 1999, the same year you left us, Joe. Anyway, I was asked to say a few words. Fortunately, I kept a copy of what I said that morning.

[*Turns to* BUNNY.]

I'd like to read a part of it to you, Bunny. In case you missed it . . . the last time.

[*He rises, stands behind his chair as he removes a page from a pants pocket*.]

I highlighted what I wanted to read somewhere down at the . . . I have it.

[*After clearing his throat, he reads from near the bottom of the page*.]

"Bunny was the loudest and the happiest of us all. He loved his family and he loved being with his family. And as he grew older and matured and struggled to find his way, he carried with him a steadfast enthusiasm for family life. Eventually he found it in a second marriage and in fathering a pair of priceless daughters, Sarah, named after his mother, and Dana, named after his brother, David, who was killed on the Anzio Beach during the Second World War.

[*A beat*.]

"Bunny said two things to me toward the end of his life that haunt me to this day. He said that he was not afraid of death and he said what he resented most about dying was being pitied by others.

[*A beat*.]

"We are not here to pity him or to mourn for him. He lived a full, rich, and fulfilling life. He was and is a brave man; he was and is an irreplaceable friend and a revered member of our family.

[*A beat; without looking at page.*]

"It's not in bad taste to cry when you lose someone you love. If you forgive me my tears, I'll forgive you yours."

[*A beat to collect himself before he returns papers to his pocket and sits at table.*]

[*To* BUNNY.]

Wasn't it in the emergency room at Mount Sinai hospital you said that about dying to me?

[BUNNY *speaks.*]

I'm glad I didn't misquote you.

[*A beat.*]

That brings to mind the time I visited you at the Rusk Institute, Joe. Guillain-Barré syndrome brought you there. You couldn't move your legs, barely move your arms, and it wasn't easy understanding what you were saying. While we were talking, this tall, attractive nurse kept walking in and out of the room, wiping your perspiring face, lifting you up so you could sit properly in bed, taking your temperature and, overall, seeing to it that you were comfortable. None of that surprised me. What did surprise me, though, is when, responding to a gesture of yours, she lifted your body off the bed, seemingly without effort, and carried you to a wheelchair, cradled in her arms as if you weighed no more than a diapered baby.

[*Enjoys the telling of it.*]

And ... what was really a shocker, as she ... carried you ... you turned to me ... and you said to me, quite seriously ... in that slurry voice of yours: "I'm gonna marry this woman." And you did, you married your nurse, who, at the time, you only knew for a few weeks!

[MURRAY *spontaneously breaks out in laughter; quick to apologize.*]

No offense, Joe. She was a wonderful nurse and turned out to be a wonderful wife, I mean that.

[*Turns.*]

Bob, do you remember when Joe and I went to visit you at New York Hospital?

[BOB *speaks.*]

That's right. You were there for some tests. You thought you'd be getting out in forty-eight hours. Instead, you died before the week was over.

[BUNNY *speaks.*]

You guessed right, Bunny. The same, lung cancer. Kent for you, Lucky Strike for him.

[*A beat.*]

You probably had the easiest time of it, Joe. I heard you went to bed and never woke up from a heart attack. That was quite a memorial they had for you at Ethical Culture. There wasn't an empty seat in the house. Which reminds me, according to the public library, *Catch-22* sold, worldwide, over 10 million copies. It's listed as one of the largest-selling novels of all time. Having you visit with me tonight . . . It's a special treat for me. I thank you . . . dearly.

[*Looks to his right.*]

To bring you up to date, Bob . . . As the sole producer and co-writer with Fosse on *All That Jazz*, you might like to hear that the movie was released a year after you passed away. I know it wasn't anything near the kind of movie you wanted it to be. The good news is that it's become something of a cult favorite and your family probably made some money out of it. Bob Fosse didn't hang around much longer than you did.

[*He drinks some water.*]

But getting back to how it feels being an old man . . . It's odd, since childhood, I've been blessed and cursed with a rampant imagination. In spite of that, I rarely think about illness and decrepitude. It's as though I haven't the patience for idle speculation. Here's the payoff. Last year, a young woman on the cross-town bus offered me her seat. I was . . . What? Shocked? Mortified? Humiliated? Yes, all of the above and more. She actually asked *me* if I wanted *her* seat? Can you imagine that? Who . . . Who asked her to ask me? What provoked her? My demeanor? My posture? My body odor? I took a shower that morning, I shaved (trimmed my beard), I dressed neatly, smartly, I stood straight, shoulders back, chest out, chin tucked in. My mind was reeling. "Please sit down," she said a second time as she stood up. I was furious. I was beside myself. She couldn't possibly think I was incapable of standing on my own two feet! Didn't she realize everyone was staring at me, examining me for possible physical disabilities! I glared at her, venomously, as I shook my head, damning her to the ninth circle of hell for committing the most malicious sin of all: humiliating a...a...a senior citizen...humiliating him in front of a busload full of strangers!

[A beat to collect himself.]

I've reached the conclusion that being old can be defined as being naked. Every effort to conceal your aging from others has been in vain. Like King Lear, you're constrained to flaunt your naked self, your shriveled, desiccated, mortal self, so that you, too, can see with your eyes...what others see with their eyes...a poor, forked, naked old man as thou art.

[A beat.]

Friendship now requires that I introduce to you a dimension of my self that is *not* visible. I haven't told this to anyone, not even Reene. Frankly, I'm not even sure I'll ever tell her. I have no idea how she'll react, and I don't, above all else, I don't want to cause her any unnecessary heartache.

[He sits on serving table, clasping his hands on lap; ruminates.]

I was fifteen, employed as an after-school usher at the Loews Premier on Sutter Avenue, when I broke with my orthodox heritage. It was Passover and while at work, after much deliberation, I walked up to the candy counter and bought a Hershey bar with almonds. You should know, Bob, that during the Passover holiday you're only allowed to eat foods prepared for Passover on a separate set of dishes. Hershey bars with almonds were definitely forbidden. Nonetheless I ate the candy bar, seated in the last row of the balcony, watching a movie. Gradually I stopped going to religious services on a regular basis; from there on I was on the bumpy road to perdition. In spite of that, in times of dire stress, I prayed to God, asking for His help in solving one dilemma or another. I did see to it that my children were bar and bas mitzvahed and that my grandkids called me Zada. As a gesture of Jewish solidarity, I belonged to one synagogue or another, which I attended three times a year for the High Holy Days. Later on, much later on, when I was in my seventies, without any discernible cause except, perhaps, excessive anxiety, I started praying every morning, staring out of the living-room window as the sun rose in the east.

[*He rises, stands behind his chair, and prays, eyes closed, hands clasped, head bobbing back and forth, earnestly, quietly.*]

"Chamois Yisroale adonoi aliena, Adonei he Chad. Baruch hem recall melaena l'oilom voyed. Hear, oh, Israel, the Lord is my God, the Lord is one. Blessed be his glorious kingdom for ever and ever. You shall love the Lord your God with all your mind, with all your strength, with all your being. Set these words I command you this day upon your heart. Teach them faithfully to your children; speak of them in your home and on your way, when you lie down and when you rise up. Bind them as a sign upon your hand; let them be a symbol before your eyes; inscribe them on the doorposts of your house and on your gates. Be mindful of all my mitzvot and do them: so shall you consecrate yourselves to your God. I, the Lord, am your God, who led you out of Egypt to be your God; I, the Lord, am your God.

[*He opens his eyes, unclasps hands.*]

So I prayed, until recently, every morning at sunrise. I prayed for the recovery of people I loved who were dying. I prayed that the war in Israel would end. I prayed that the ice caps on the North Pole would stop melting. I prayed that a play of mine opening that evening would receive favorable reviews, etcetera, etcetera, etcetera. My naivety embarrasses me. I'm certain there's a simple theological explanation why my prayers went unanswered. But, obviously, throughout the millennia, billions of people have prayed billions of times, and if their prayers had been answered, there would have been and there would be today billions of healthy, wealthy, happy, peace-loving people. And we know none of that ever happened. We can logically assume, putting aside statistical probabilities, that their prayers went unanswered. And yet, by the billions, people continue to pray. Admittedly, there is in prayer itself an indefinable sense of consolation, of reassurance, of somebody up there really cares about me. So I, too, continued praying. I was touching all the bases and doing harm to no one. Pascal knew of what he spoke. There are no losses in the game of prayer.

[*Seated at table.*]

Once again, this was until recently. Now, I no longer get up to pray as the sun rises in the east. I no longer go to a synagogue three times a year for the High Holy Days. And, frankly, I feel better with myself for it, no more than that; I feel better with myself for it.

[*He scrounges through his pockets until he finds the cutout he's looking for.*]

Charles Kingsley, a nineteenth-century minister, wrote a letter to T. H. Huxley, offering his condolences on the sudden death of Huxley's four-year-old son. In his letter Kingsley stated that if Huxley would open his heart to God's promise of eternal life, he could look forward to meeting his son in heaven. This is Huxley's reply.

[*Reads.*]

"I cannot sufficiently thank you . . . My convictions . . . on all the matters of which you speak, are . . . firmly rooted. But the great blow which fell upon me seemed to stir them from their foundation, and had I lived a couple of centuries earlier I could have fancied a devil scoffing at me . . . and asking me what profit it was to have stripped myself of the hopes and consolations of the mass of mankind? To which my only reply was and is . . . Oh, devil! The truth is better than much profit. I have searched over the grounds of my belief and if wife and child and name and fame were all to be lost to me one after the other as the penalty, still I will not lie!"

[*He returns scrap paper to pocket.*]

Anyway, you may well ask: Why did I make the choice not to pray? Why recently? Why not sooner, earlier? Let me shed myself of all duplicity. At my age I refuse to speak to someone who refuses to speak to me. Furthermore, I am not here on this wobbly patch of earth to be swayed from what I perceive to be reality. To paraphrase Bertrand Russell: There's something contemptible about a man who can't face the dangers of life without the help of comfortable myths.

[*A beat.*]

What I failed to say previously in listing for you the good fortune I've had, my health, my marriage, children, grandkids, having the time to write and read what I choose . . . What I didn't tell you, what I couldn't tell you, is that there is, with aging, the oppressive burden of mortality. You can see it in the texture of your skin when you shower, you can feel it when you run your finger over the bulging blue veins on the back of your hand, you can taste it before you have breakfast in the morning. Yes, taste it. This from Montaigne, my incomparable mentor: "So I have formed the habit of having death continually present, not merely in my imagination, but in my mouth." So it is that I taste it before I have breakfast in the morning. And, finally, you can sense mortality in the uncertainty of your stride when you start off on your daily walk and you can smell the stench of mortality before you fall asleep at night.

[*Bitterly.*]

For this abomination, I fault Almighty God and the forces of evolution. They and they alone are responsible for severely limiting the lifespan of humankind. Almighty God, in a brief fit of distemper, "Dust you are and to dust you shall return," cursed Adam and Eve because Eve was eating an apple. Afterwards, he arrived at the paltry figure of 120 years. At the other end of the spectrum, evolution, without a thought in its empty head, decreed that humankind will live for an indeterminate age, hop-scotching from twenty years in medieval times, to forty-five years at the beginning of the twentieth century, to seventy-eight years at the beginning of the twenty-first century, thanks due to the revelations of medical science.

[*A note of desperation.*]

I ask you, why did God and evolution choose such paltry longevity numbers for their ostensibly preferred species? There are tortoises that live over 150 years, whales that live over 200 years, and Icelandic clams that live over 400 years! What are we, orphans, rejects, biologically inferior to the Icelandic calms? Hey, gimme a break, will you?

[*He scrounges through his pockets until he finds the piece of scrap paper he's looking for.*]

I have something here that gets into what I'm trying to . . . Listen to this.

[*Reads from scrap of paper.*]

"Over 99 percent of the species that ever walked, flew, or slithered upon this earth are now extinct. When we look at the natural world, we see extraordinary complexity, but we do not see optimal design. We see redundancy, regression, and unnecessary complications; we see bewildering inefficiencies that result in suffering and death." That's from Sam Harris's *Letters to a Christian Nation*.

[*He returns scrap paper to pocket.*]

So where does this leave us? It leaves us between a rock and a hard place, between a mute, tyrannical God and the blind, blundering force of evolution, both of whom are responsible for a failure of "optimal design" and "bewildering inefficiencies that result in suffering and death." No doubt the average lifespan for humanity will continue to increase at a snail's pace, once again, thanks due to the revelations of medical science.

[MURRAY *sits at the table, visibly distraught. He looks at each of his guests, speaks softly.*]

I have a . . . an embarrassing confession to make . . . to each of you. For the last year or so, I've been taking pills to get through the night. I find it increasingly difficult to forget that I'm eighty-two years of age, shorn of my youth, my vigor, my sexuality. My cache of good fortune seems to have petered out. More and more I find myself counting the hours left in a day, the days left in a week, the weeks left in a year. I listen with dumb fascination to the beating of my heart, the throbbing of my pulse, the scuffling of my footsteps. At times, a scream of hopelessness congeals in my throat, a burgeoning, suffocating scream.

[*In a strangled voice.*]

I can barely breathe. I stretch my mouth wide open and I try to scream . . . with all my might, with every muscle in my throat, my face, my lungs.

[*He opens his mouth as wide as he can, tilting his head upwards, but the only sound he emits is a barely audible, pitifully plaintive moan.*]

Ahhh! Ahhh! Ahhh! Ahhh!

[*Frustrated, he gives it up.*]

But there is, I discovered, no scream in me; no release; no reprieve. I gasp. My eyes see double. My body trembles. My ears ache with the piercing sound of some hellish fiend . . . howling and screaming . . . in . . . in the cave of my skull . . . and . . . and all of a sudden . . . it occurs to me . . . to pray.

[*A breath of relief.*]

To Almighty God. To pray. To ask for help. Why have I wasted all this time? How could I be so blind, so stupid? I must pray. I must ask for his forgiveness, for his absolution, for his blessings so that I may live to see the sun rising once again in the east.

[*He jumps to his feet, stands behind his chair, and prays, eyes closed, hands clasped, head bobbing back and forth, loudly, frantically.*]

"Chamois Yisroale adonoi aliena, Adonei he Chad. Baruch chem mecall melaena l'oilom voyed. Hear, oh, Israel, the Lord is my God, the Lord is one. Blessed be his glorious kingdom for ever and ever. You shall love the Lord your God with all your mind, with all your strength, with all your being. Set these words I command you this day upon your heart. Teach them faithfully to your children; speak of them in your home and on your way, when you lie down and when you rise up. Bind them as a sign upon your hand; let them be a symbol before your eyes; inscribe them on the doorposts of your house, and on your gates. Be mindful of all my mitzvot and do them: so shall you consecrate yourselves to your God. I, the Lord, am your God, who led you out of Egypt to be your God; I, the Lord, am your God.

[*In a panic,* MURRAY *interrupts the above prayer, whenever reflection supersedes impulse.*]

But then I think: What in the world am I doing? Am I going crazy? I don't believe in an Almighty God! I'm a non-believer, a secular Jew who recognizes and acknowledges that only through the genius of medical science can we look forward to living 100, 200, 400 years, like the Icelandic clam! What am I carrying on about? Nothing I do or say will change anything. I'm your run-of-the-mill naked old man, scrounging about in the dustbin of time.

[*Talking to himself.*]

The jig's up. The party's over. The days grow short when you reach September. If that's all there is, my friend, then let's keep rocking and bring down the . . .

[MURRAY *hears something in the hallway. He jerks his head to listen. Sound: The off-stage entrance door opens and slams shut.*]

[MURRAY *whispers; frightened.*]

It's Reene. She's back. She's home.

[*Glances at his wristwatch.*]

It's too early. Something must have happened. Maybe she fell, hurt herself, broke her wrist or fingers or...

[MURRAY's *three spectral guests rise and exit, downstage right. Follows them but doesn't exit, still whispering.*]

Where are you guys going? Why are you leaving? We haven't finished. We still have a lot to...

[*A beat.*]

Are you coming next Tuesday? You promised, 6:30 p.m. Don't forget. I'll be waiting for you!

[*He hurries to exit the dining area, upstage left.*]

Reene? Reene? Where are you? Why did you come back so early?

[*He searches for* REENE *throughout the apartment, his voice receding further and further away from us.*]

[MURRAY *offstage.*]

Is everything all right? Did anything happen? You didn't fall and hurt yourself, did you? Are you ill? Do you have a headache? Is your hip bothering you? Your sinuses? I'll heat up a cup of English Breakfast tea with lemon. How was dinner? Did you enjoy yourself? Was it fun? Where are you? Reene? Reene? Where did you go to? Will you answer me? Is anything wrong? Will you do me a favor and answer me?

[*Sound:* MURRAY's *voice fades out as... Lights: Simultaneously fade out.*]

• • •

acknowledgments

I would like to thank my publisher, John Cerullo of Applause Books—The Hal Leonard Group, and my agent, June Clark, for their support of this edition and my position with Applause Books.

Furthermore, I'd like thank my professional colleague Rick Pulos, my graduate assistants, Liliana Almendarez and Nicole Arvin, and the administration of LIU—Dean David Cohen, Associate Dean Kevin Lauth, and Assistant Dean Maria Vogelstein.

I'd also like to express my gratitude to all the theatres around the country and their literary managers, as well as all the playwrights whose work I read, enabling me to compile this theatre series. A very, very special thanks to Michael Messina.

I follow in the footsteps of a wonderful project—The Best American Short Plays/The Best Short Plays series published by Applause Books, and I would like to thank all the previous editors of this series: the late Stanley Richards, Ramon Delgado, Howard Stein, Mark Glubke, Glenn Young, and anyone I may have left out who came before these fine editors, who've helped make this series a success since 1937.

A quote from the 1989 edition of The Best Short Plays edited by Ramon Delgado:

> From the beginning of this series the past and present editors have sought to include a balance among three categories of playwrights: (1) established playwrights who continue to practice the art and craft of the short play, (2) emerging playwrights whose record of productions indicate both initial achievements and continuous productivity, and (3) talented new playwrights whose work may not have had much exposure but evidences promise for the future. An effort has also been made to select plays not anthologized elsewhere and, when possible, plays that are making their debut in print.... The value of these considerations is to honor the artistry of the established playwrights, encourage the emerging, acknowledge the promising, and offer a varied selection of new plays in one volume.

As the editor of this series, I plan to keep the tradition moving into the future.

—Barbara Parisi